CENTURY OF SILENT SERVICE

CENTURY OF SILENT SERVICE

GRAHAM SEAL

EXECUTIVE EDITOR
LLOYD BLAKE

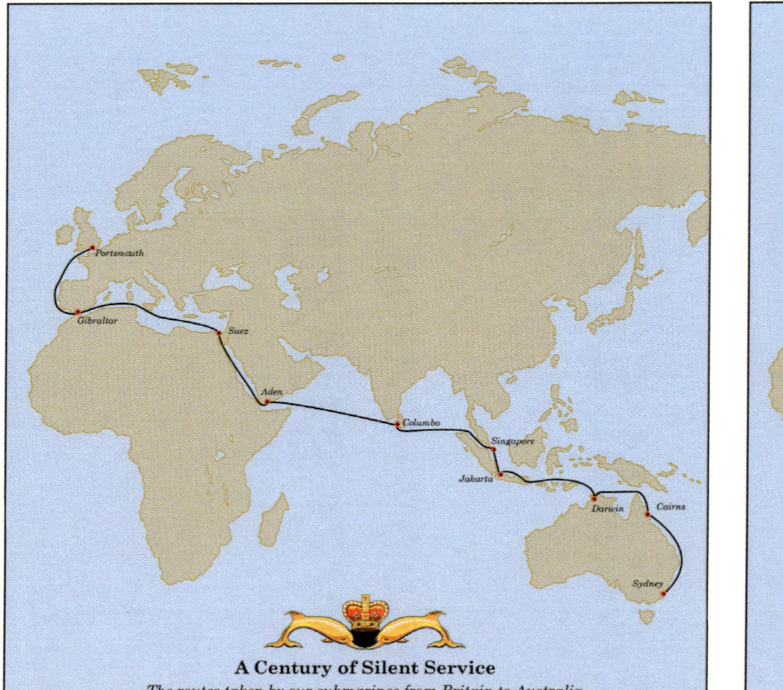

A Century of Silent Service

The routes taken by our submarines from Britain to Australia.

1. HMAS AE1 Commissioned February 1914. Arrived Sydney May 1914.
2. HMAS AE2 Commissioned February 1914. Arrived Sydney May 1914.

Ports of call: Portsmouth, Gibraltar, Suez Canal, Aden, Columbo, Singapore, Jakarta, Darwin, Cairns and Sydney.

3. J Boats 1-2-3-4-5-7 (J6 being lost). April - July 1919.

Indicated in black. Ports of call: Portsmouth, Gibraltar, Malta, Suez Canal, Aden, Columbo, Thursday Island, Moreton Bay and Sydney.

4. Oxley 1 and Otway 1. February 1928 - February 1929.

Indicated in white. Ports of call: Portsmouth, Gibraltar, Malta, Suez Canal, Jakarta, Surabaya, Thursday Island, Townsville, Brisbane and Sydney.

Artwork Michael Payne www.mipagraf.com.au

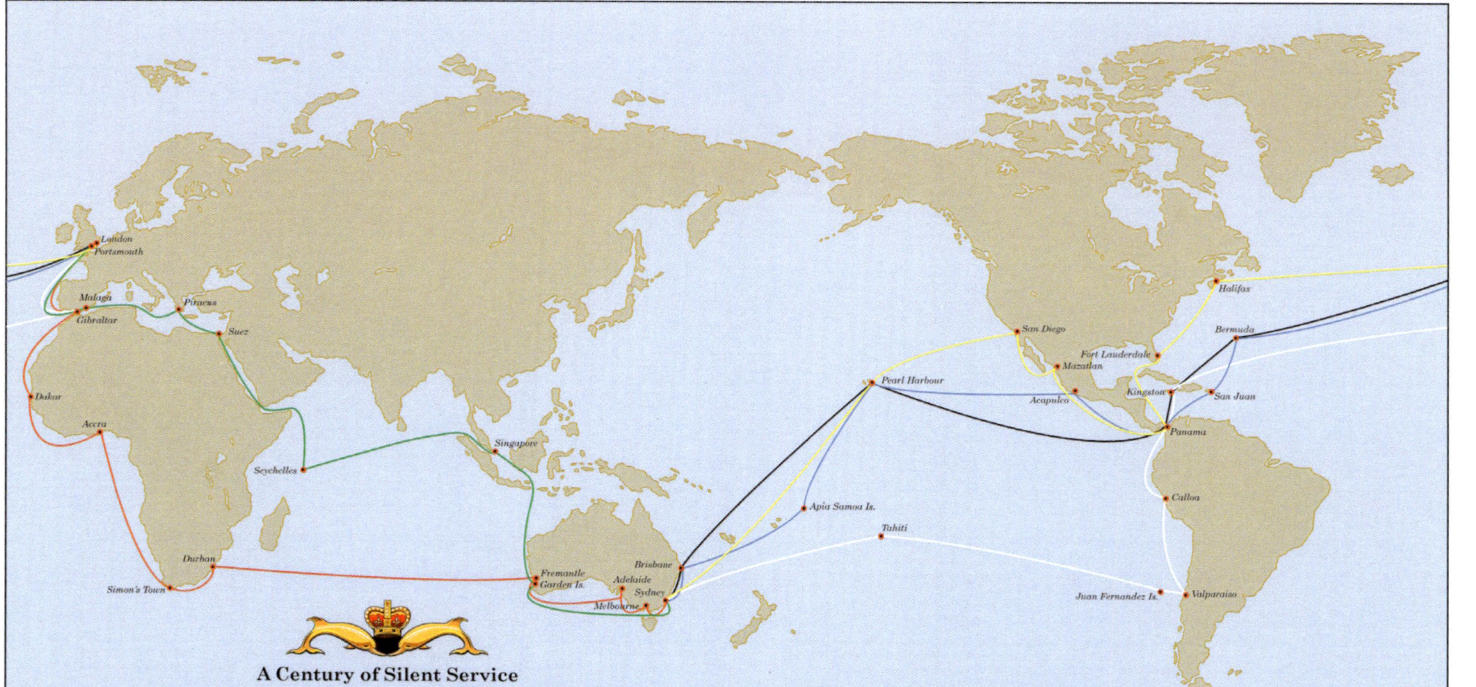

A Century of Silent Service

The routes taken by our submarines from Britain to Australia.

1. HMAS Oxley. (SSG57) Commissioned March 1967. June - August 1967.
Indicated in black. Ports of call: Portsmouth England, Hamilton Bermuda, Kingston Jamaica, Panama Canal, Panama City, Pearl Harbour Hawaii, Brisbane and Sydney.

2. HMAS Otway (SSG59) Commissioned April 1968. July - October 1968.
Indicated in red. Ports of call: Portsmouth England, Gibraltar, Dakar Senegal, Accra Ghana, Simon's Town South Africa, Durban South Africa, Fremantle, Adelaide, Melbourne and Sydney.

3. HMAS Ovens (SSG70) Commissioned April 1969. August - October 1969.
Indicated in white. Ports of call: London England, Gibraltar, Kingston Jamaica, Panama Canal, Calloa Peru, Valparaiso Chile, Juan Fernendez Island, Tahiti and Sydney.

4. HMAS Onslow (SSG60) Commissioned December 1969. April - July 1970.
Indicated in blue. Ports of call: London England, Hamilton Bermuda, San Juan Peurto Rico, Panama Canal, Acapulco Mexico, Pearl Harbour Hawaii, Apia Samoa Is., Brisbane and Sydney.

5. HMAS Orion (SSG61) Commissioned June 1977. March - July 1978.
Indicated in green. Ports of call: Portsmouth England, Malaga Spain, Piraeus Greece, Suez Canal Passage, Seychelles, Singapore, Garden Island and Sydney.

6. HMAS Otama (SSG72) Commissioned April 1978. September - December 1978.
Indicated in yellow. Ports of call: London England, Halifax Canada, Fort Lauderdale USA, Panama Canal, Panama City, Mazatlan Mexico, San Diego USA, Pearl Harbour Hawaii and Sydney.

Artwork Michael Payne www.mipagraf.com.au

First published 2013

National Library of Australia Cataloguing-in-Publication entry:

Author:	Seal, Graham, 1950- author.
Title:	Century of silent service / Graham Seal.
ISBN:	9781922109897 (paperback)
Subjects:	Australia. Royal Australian Navy--Submarine forces.
	Submarines (Ships)--Australia.
	Submarines (Ships)--Australia--History.
	Submariners--Australia.
	Submariners--Australia--History.
Dewey Number:	359.830994

Typeset in Arno Pro 12pt.

Cover Design by Michael Payne

Cartoon Artwork by Sandy Freeleagus

The cover shows a portrait of Lt. Commander Stoker, HMAS *AE2*, an *Oberon* class submarine and a submerged *Collins* class.

Published by Boolarong Press, Salisbury, Brisbane, Australia.

Printed and bound by Watson Ferguson & Company, Salisbury, Brisbane, Australia.

FOREWORD

On 24th May 1914 His Majesty's Australian Submarine *AE1* accompanied by HMAS *AE2* entered Sydney Harbour for the first time, having completed the longest ocean passage ever taken by any submarine — sailing from Barrow in Furness in the United Kingdom to Sydney in Australia.

In their very short lives they exerted significant and very long lasting influence out of proportion for their size (800 tonnes dived) and numbers in their crew (35). *AE1* and her entire crew were to be Australia's first casualty in World War I while *AE2* was the first submarine to penetrate the Dardanelles showing the way for all other Allied submarines.

AE2 successfully transited the Dardanelles as the ANZACs were landing on the other side of Gallipoli peninsular. Historians suggest that it was the success of that transit that encouraged Sir Ian Hamilton to continue the landings at Gallipoli notwithstanding the very strong recommendations to the contrary from his generals on the ground. Certainly Lieutenant Commander Stoker (Commanding Officer of *AE2*) believed that be to be the case and remarked (in 1923 in his book *Straws in the Wind*) "If I had known Hamilton would use my message" (advising that *AE2* had successfully reached the Sea of Marmara) "to make that decision, I would not have sent the signal."

Very few Australians know the stories of *AE1* and *AE2*. Even fewer know that the operations of US, British and Netherlands submarines based in Brisbane and Fremantle played a major role in the defence of Australia from 1942 to 1945. Only a handful or people know that Fremantle was the second largest submarine base in the World, and that the 160 or so submarines operating from North Wharf conducted the most successful and cost effective operation in the history of submarine warfare.

So the selection of the title for this book was very easy.

2014 marks the century of silent service to Australia by submarines and their crews.

2014 is the Submarine Centenary Year in which the known and unknown exploits of submarines on Australian service are presented to the Australian public.

Australia was a very early entrant to the business of submarine ownership. Alfred Deakin selected two submarines against the recommendations of his Chief of Naval Staff and this might be seen as a courageous act for a country of less than 6 million people. Australian Government efforts to maintain its submarine capability during the first 50 years were intermittent and difficult, but it never quite gave up.

The trend established by Deakin, where the politician has to persuade the naval officer that submarines are useful for Australia. John Gorton could see the benefit in purchasing the RAN *Oberon* class submarines while the Naval Staff of the day were not so convinced. Kim Beazley found himself in a similar situation when discussing the requirement for the submarine capability that ultimately became the *Collins* submarine.

However, because of the foresight of Gorton and Beazley, the second 50 years of Australia's submarines has been a great success.

The *Oberon* submarines quickly moved out of their "clockwork mouse" (the nickname for a submarine being used as the target to train surface ship and aircraft sonar operators) role, and developed an impressive reputation for very long range intelligence, surveillance and reconnaissance operations. The *Oberon* program also established a very clever technology capability in Australian industry.

Consistent with the silence of the submarine service, very little is known of the industrial capability that was developed in that era, and as a result, it has not been sustained as one might have hoped.

I say success in the face of the savage criticism of the *Collins* Class. There have been challenges for the *Collins* submarines, the most significant of all being that they are required to operate in the most demanding environment ever required of conventionally powered submarines. When properly supported with adequate numbers of trained personnel these submarines regularly achieve world class standards of performance.

It is timely therefore to celebrate the centenary of silent service with the preparation of the next generation of Australian submarines. The Future Submarine program will establish the submarine capability for the next 100 years. In that context I wish those who will celebrate our bicentenary of submarines all the very best. I hope that the silence surrounding the next century of Australian submarines is one of operational practice and not caused by neglect or disinterest.

It would be a grave injustice to fail to mention Lloyd Blake without whose determination and perseverance this book would not exist. Lloyd has spent many years developing the concept, searching for contributions and publishers. It is entirely due to his work that we have such a commendable volume. The submarine community owe *Joe* a great debt for his dedication and commitment to the submarine community in Australia.

This book is offered by the submariners of the past to the Australian public and Australian submariners of today and tomorrow. I hope you will truly celebrate this first century of Australian submarines and start now to make the second century even better.

Vice Admiral Ian MacDougall, AC, AFSM, RAN (Rtd)

ACKNOWLEDGEMENTS

This book is based on research undertaken in Australia, Britain and the United States since 2006, largely in partnership with the Submarine Institute of Australia (SIA). It has benefitted greatly from the generous provision of information by, and discussion with, a good many people and institutions. These include: Lloyd Blake (SIA), Peter Horobin (SIA), Peter Smith (Submarines Association Australia), Rob Willis and Olya Willis (National Library of Australia), Frank Owen (SIA), Michael White (University of Queensland), Barrie Downer (Barrow, UK), George Malcolmson and Debbie Corner (Royal Navy Submarine Museum Archive, Gosport, UK), members of *AE1* Incorporated and the *AE2* Commemorative Foundation, Tim Smith (Office of Environment and Heritage, NSW), Sue Summers (Curtin University), Dr Ian Pfennigwerth (Naval Historical Society of Australia) and many past and serving submariners. For permission to use photographs and some documentary excerpts, thanks to Jeffery Knaggs (diary of Alfred Knaggs), Andrew Mitchell (family group on *J7*), Carol Wilson (*Oxley* christening) and to the Royal Australian Navy and the Australian War Memorial for permission to reproduce many of the historical images. Sketches by Sandy Freeleagus, graphic work by Michael Payne and photography by James Lybrand; unique and freely given, are gratefully acknowledged.

CONTENTS

INTRODUCTION

The motto of the Royal Australian Navy's submarine force is 'Strength, silence, surprise.' In the one hundred years of its history to date, the submarine service has amply demonstrated these qualities in war and peace.

This book is a brief general history of that service and of those who made it, from *AE1* and *AE2* to the current *Collins* class submarines. The story is one of fortitude, perseverance and courage, not only in the face of enemies and in a rare willingness to descend to undersea depths in sometimes-unproven machines, but also in the determination of successive generations of submariners to establish an Australian submarine capability. It reveals a number of perhaps unexpected aspects, including the continual popularity of submarines with the larger Australian community and the often little-known contributions which submarines and submariners have made to the Anzac tradition.

A Century of Silent Service is not a detailed history of submarines in the defence of Australia, nor a study of any aspect of submarine technology, strategy or politics. There are a number of very fine works that pursue those aspects. Instead, it is a broad overview of the story of Australian submariners that will be accessible to the general reader as well as to the descendants and families of submariners in this country and elsewhere. One of the most powerful elements of the submariner ethos is a knowledge that each one belongs to a larger fraternity of others who have had similar experiences beneath the waves, regardless of their national affiliation and including former enemies. Once a submariner, always a submariner. The events chronicled here may also be of interest to submariners of other nations.

The book begins with a brief glimpse of submariner traditions and then traces the story of Australian submariners from 1914 to the centenary of the service in 2014. It is based on official and unofficial records, including, archived documents, memoirs, diaries, photographs, newspapers, reports and oral histories. Together, these sources produce a compelling narrative that will interest many Australians who wish to know more about the 'Silent Anzacs'.

1
TRADITIONS OF THE TRADE

'Like the destroyer, the submarine has created its own type of officer and man, with language and traditions apart from the rest of the service, and yet at the heart, unchangingly of the Service.'

Rudyard Kipling, *The Fringes of the Fleet*, 1915.

Australian submariners have a solid body of tradition that reflects their experiences and identifies them as a distinct group, even within the Royal Australian Navy, of which they are nominally a part. Many of the characteristics and concerns of Australian submariners are shared with submariners from other countries, particularly those from the United Kingdom, as Australia and Britain's submarine histories have been closely entwined through training and swapping of personnel, both in wartime and in peace.

The first serviceable submarines for military purposes were developed in the late nineteenth century using diesel-electric technology. The Royal Navy (RN) was slow to warm to submarines as a serious weapon, a situation reflected in the early Royal Australian Navy (RAN). But eventually the decision to obtain a submarine capability was taken and Australia's first two submarines, *AE1* and *AE2*, were built in Britain and arrived after a lengthy and troubled voyage in May 1914. *AE1* was lost in still unexplained circumstances off New Britain in September 1914, becoming the first Australian casualty of World War I. *AE2* was the first submarine to breach the Dardanelles passage into the Sea of Marmara to harass Turkish shipping from April 25, 1915 and so has a foundational place in the Anzac tradition.

These ill-fated but illustrious originals were followed by the troubled *J*-boats gifted to Australia by Britain in the aftermath of World War I. After these six craft were progressively decommissioned and scrapped, *Oxley* and *Otway* were commissioned and purchased by the Australian government during the late 1920s. These submarines were gifted to the Royal Navy by the Australian government in 1931. Apart from the submarine *K9*, obtained via the Dutch naval activities in Indonesia and used mainly for training purposes, Australia did not have a separate submarine presence during World War II. However, many Australians served in British miniature submarines known as *X*-craft. The *Oberon* class submarines often known generally as '*O*-boats' were commissioned from 1967 and served until superseded by the still-controversial *Collins* class submarines, constructed from 1996 to 2003. Australia's next generation of submarines is in the process of being developed, a situation in which many submariners, past and present generally maintain a keen interest and involvement.

While always closely aligned with the British Royal Navy, and more recently with the Netherlands Royal Navy, for training, Australian submariners have developed a distinctive culture. Their official existence has been terminated on three occasions due to lack of expertise, resources and finance, experiences that have further strengthened their sense of group identity. The distinctiveness of submariners can be seen in many of their traditions.

Submariners in Australia and elsewhere in the English-speaking world refer to their calling as 'the trade.' This term can be traced back to the negative views of First Sea Lord Sir Arthur Wilson VC, GCB, OM, GCVO about the fighting capabilities of early submarines. In 1910 he wrote:

> *'Submariners are nothing more than tradesmen and submarines are underhand, unfair and damned un-English. All submariners captured should be treated as pirates and hanged.'*

It is said that Wilson formed this opinion when he first set eyes upon an early submarine. Amazed at the strange shape and design of the craft, the Admiral was also affronted by the decidedly sloppy appearance of the officers and crew lined up on the casing. Instead of the smart uniforms of

Royal Navy, the submariners wore the oily work clothes, sweaters and rubber boots, necessary to operate in the cramped and messy conditions.

In the society of the period, being referred to as tradesmen was an insult. Ever since, submariners have been proud to work in 'the trade.'

The Admiral's other insult to these pioneer submariners was to refer to them as 'pirates' the Royal Navy's traditional enemy. Just as they turned the admiral's tradesman insult against him — and the establishment he represented — British and subsequently Australian submariners from that time adopted the pirate's skull and crossbones flag, the 'Jolly Roger', as their unofficial emblem. While the original Jolly Roger signified lawlessness, the submariners' use of the emblem represents stealth and cunning, the essential attributes of all submariners.

The speech of submariners is a combination of many types of language and reflects a strong sense of identity. It includes technical jargon, including acronyms for technical aspects of submarine warfare (DSEA — Davis Submerged Escape Apparatus) as well as terms derived from Royal Navy and Royal Australian Navy argot (Pusser — all things naval (RN and RAN), from the folk name of a ship's pay officer, the Pusser (from Purser). It also includes a number of unique terms, such as 'aftendy' for a sailor who lives in the rear of a submarine, 'forendy for one who lives at the other and 'snake pit' for the forward lower section of a diesel submarine's engine room. And, again in contradiction to the traditions of the Navy, submarines are not referred to as 'ships', but as 'boats.' There are established nicknames for officers. The 'bloke' is the Captain, First Lieutenant is 2nd-in-command 'Jimmy the One', usually just 'The Jimmy'. An Engineer officer is called 'E' and the Electrical officer is 'L'.

The distinctions reflected in these and other terms for officers go back to the earliest days of submarining when 'tight trousers' referred to officers and 'slack trousers' were the crew — because crew wore bell-bottoms at that time, while officers did not.

The strong 'us-and-them' character of submariner culture is also reflected in many aspects of their humour. Cartooning by submariners about their way of life is prolific and greatly appreciated. Certain individuals are noted and esteemed as producers of cartoons that, from the submariners' point of view, are able to cleverly balance the humour and the dangers of the trade. In the 1960s generation of submariners, for instance, L G Freeleagus aka 'Sandy/Hi Rob' is a celebrated exponent. His work includes humorous evocations of the submariner ethos, attitudes, interest in well-endowed young females and the occasional critical comment on perceived failures of officers and the Royal Australian Navy. Other cartoons display the same humorous treatment of the dangers of the submariner's work, including being accidentally attacked by one's own side, failure to adjust a vital item of equipment causing water to flood into the boat and trying to bring a submarine up to the required depth or being unable to stop the craft descending. These drawings 'make light' of the realities, raising a smile and relieving tensions that inevitably arise in the close quarters of even modern submarines.

The distinctive double dolphin badge of the Australian Submarine Service was introduced in 1966, against some initial RAN opposition. The Australian Submarine Service was expected to adopt the British submariner's badge, known without fondness as the 'sausage on a stick.' A group called the Submarine Project Team formed in 1964 under Commander Alan McIntosh. He was not a submariner, but is credited with designing the new badge. When a submariner has finally earned the right to wear it after extensive and intensive training, the custom is to 'drink the dolphins.' This involves the newly initiated submariner placing the badge at the bottom of a large glass of beer and sculling the liquid contents. Considerable satisfaction is expressed among Australian submariners at the Royal Navy's 1972 replacement of its 'sausage on a stick', with a badge based on the Australian design.

Australian Submarine Service Badge — 'The Dolphins'

'Drinking the dolphins' symbolises entry to the culture of submariners and this connection does not cease when a member leaves the navy for civilian life, as an ex-submariner expresses it: '... Submariners' Dolphins leave a mark on your chest, right over your heart long after the uniforms have gone. You earned them, you always *wear* them. You will always be recognised as a Submariner by the Submarine community at home and anywhere else in the world.'

Submariners engage in a busy round of memorial services and commemorations for lost boats and their crews, reunions, dinners and similar events. These extend to local, national and international conferences, as well as occasional events involving serving boats of various navies. Anzac Day is a significant day, though the emphasis here is seen to be on 'soldiers', as submariners refer to their army comrades. The Anzac legend is seen to privilege the Digger, the footsoldier, over 'sailors.' This is a point of irritation among submariners in particular as it overlooks the vital naval contributions to the Dardanelles campaign and to the Gallipoli landings of 1915, as well as those in subsequent theatres of war.

The nature of life aboard a submarine, until more recent times, meant that every crew member was able to perform all tasks required, an early example of 'multi-skilling.' This included cooking meals for all.

Consequently, food — and drink — play an especially important role in the consciousness of submariners. A few examples in use since the 1960s:

- Fray Bentos — general term for canned food, after large canning company
- Soggies — breakfast cereal
- Scran — food
- Kye, ki, ky — hot, unsweetened cocoa drink
- Duff — steamed pudding, dessert
- England water — tea
- Babies' heads — individual tinned steak and kidney puddings
- Earlier terms included 'red lead' for tinned tomatoes and 'pot mess' for corned beef stew

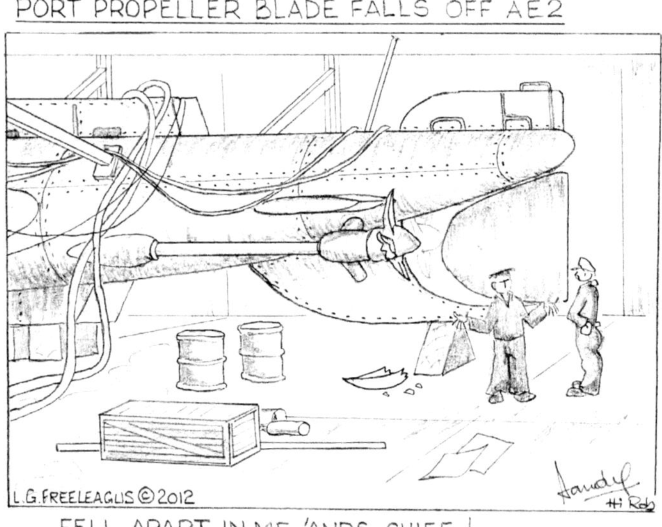

There is also in an intense interest in recipes, especially those able to be created from a very restricted range of available ingredients, much of them not fresh, particularly in the early days of submarining when refrigeration was unknown. Recipes may carry colourful folk names, such as 'Better Than Sex Cake', 'Cheese Ush', 'Elephant's Footprints' and 'Shit on a Raft', the latter depending mainly on lambs kidneys and Worcestershire Sauce and eaten for breakfast. In Australian submarines during the 1960s and 70s, a meal of mixed vegetables and mince was a 'Train Smash.'

Submariners have an intense interest in their own history, maintaining a large a number of websites, periodicals and publications of reminiscences and histories of boats, crews or generations of serving officers and men. This interest is also behind many individual research efforts undertaken in archives and libraries around the world by submariners — usually retired — who are keen to preserve and present this material. There is also an active round of national and international conferences and similar events through which submariners maintain contacts.

As with other areas of military history and tradition, the family history boom is creating a broader interest in aspects of submarine history and culture as descendants seek out service and other records of ancestors. Allied with this is the intense public interest that submarines have frequently generated, from the arrival of *AE1* and *AE2* in 1914, through the *J*-boats of the 1920s and their successors, *Oxley* and *Otway,* on to the more recent controversies over the *Collins* class submarines and their upcoming replacements. In 2014 the Australian Submarine Service will celebrate one hundred years of silent service.

2
AUSTRALIA'S FIRST SUBMARINERS

In December 1910 a nation less than one-decade old, ordered two submarines from the Vickers Maxim shipyards at Barrow-in-Furness. These were to be boats of the British E class, their national designation heralded in the prefix 'A.' There had been a strong debate in Australian and British defence circles about the value of submarines and even a report recommending against their use. But after representing Australia at the 1907 Colonial Conference in London, Prime Minister Deakin became convinced of their value and ignored the negative advice of Australian Naval Commandant Captain W R Creswell, who recommended the purchase of destroyers rather than submarines. The Commonwealth government paid just over £105,000 for each boat, taking delivery from the builders in Barrow-in-Furness in January 1914. Six weeks later *AE1* and *AE2* were commissioned into the Royal Australian Navy, their 35-man crews having joined the boats early the same month.

The *E* class submarines had been developed from earlier British designs, themselves based on the American Holland boats of the 1890s. After much technical and engineering experimentation, trial and error and some notable disasters, the submarine was just beginning to become a serviceable weapon of war, even though few people had any idea how they might best be deployed. The general seaworthiness and observational values of the two periscopes carried by the *E* class submarines, together with the navigational bridge built over the conning tower made them ideal for patrol and reconnaissance work, the role in which *AE1* was engaged when she disappeared.

At just over 54 meters, *E* boats were lengthier than most of their predecessors. They were also heavier but faster, able to achieve speeds of 15 knots on the surface and 9 knots dived. Their propulsion depended on two six-cylinder diesels and two electric motors. They were armed with four torpedo tubes, one at the bow, one at the stern and two on the beam, providing the facility to fire at right angles as well as from the bow and stern. Later *E* boats were fitted with deck guns, but *AE1* and *AE2* had none. For the first time ever, these submarines were also fitted with gyroscopes and primitive Marconi wireless equipment, the aerial mounted on a wooden frame that was folded down when diving. Wireless had not been included in the original Australian specifications for the submarines. As a communications technology for submarines it was at the experimental stage, unreliable and dependent on a cumbersome and fragile wooden aerial mast that required lowering and raising whenever the craft submerged or surfaced.

The inside of these narrow machines was around seven meters wide and crammed with pipes, levers and torpedoes. Officers and crews necessarily lived in close quarters in the cramped conditions, reading, playing cards and, on *AE1*, occasionally making music on a couple of concertinas. Even with the necessary no smoking rule, the limited air quickly becoming polluted while underwater.

In these circumstances, leadership and morale were even more important considerations than usual and the commanding officers and crews were carefully chosen. English-born Lieutenant Thomas Fleming Besant, RN, became the commander of *AE1* and Irishman Lieutenant Henry Hugh Gordon Dacre Stoker, RN, commanded *AE2*. Their crews were Royal Navy and Royal Australian Navy men, the senior sailors in particular selected for their underwater experience through a rigorous training regime and need for high physical attributes.

Besant had joined the Royal Navy as a midshipman in 1898 at the age of fifteen. He saw action in China during the Boxer Rebellion and later became deeply interested in the development of submarines. A Freemason, he was interested in horses, fishing and golf. He was described by the newspapers in Sydney as 'a clean-shaven young officer of youthful appearance.' If his other utterances were accurately reported, he was also an enthusiastic spokesman for the submariner's occupation:

> *'... it's not all beer and skittles and perhaps it is a harder life than in other branches of the service but it's the life I've chosen. Oh, yes, it's dangerous if you want to look at it like that but it's got to be done — and every man in the Navy, no matter in what branch he is in, has to be prepared to meet danger when it comes.'*

Besant was very young to be made Commander of the Australian Submarine Squadron but had a reputation as a capable and cautious officer, suggesting he would have taken no unnecessary risks with his command. Like his First Lieutenant The Honourable Leopold Scarlett and 'Third Hand' Lieutenant Charles L Moore, Besant was a single man.

The sister submarines began their pioneering voyage from England to Australia on the morning of March 7, 1914, escorted by the masted cruiser HMS *Eclipse* built in 1894. They were still largely top-secret experimental craft, with the need for constant attention to defects and non-performing machinery. *AE1* had been subjected to balancing tests before leaving England, the results of which suggested that there may have been problems. *AE2* had many mishaps. Only three days from Portsmouth a blade fell off her port propeller and the starboard propeller suffered the same problem three weeks later. Even the spare propeller was found to be faulty, with a large crack appearing, it was mostly thought, from poor manufacturing techniques. Officers and crew dealt with these problems with stoic inventiveness: 'Through a long list of mechanical difficulties and mishaps overcome by hook and crook, the miles were pushed astern, the weariness of it but lightly relieved by a few days in ports of call...', wrote Stoker Charles Suckling in his diary. These incidents caused a great deal of practical difficulty, much paperwork and considerable repairing when the submarines reached Gibraltar late on March 6.

They sailed for Malta on March 9. *AE1* broke down during the voyage and had to be towed due to one of many malfunctions of the exhaust and intake valve springs, engine clutches, toggle bolts and overheating of the motor shaft and bearings that plagued the vessel. Three days later both submarines left Malta for a rough passage to Port Said. As the small convoy passed through the Suez Canal and the Red Sea, temperatures inside the submarines sometimes reached 100 degrees Fahrenheit (almost 38 degrees Celsius). *AE1* was painted white in an effort to reduce the heat. An improvised but effective refitting of *AE2*'s starboard propeller in Aden involved placing the anchor chains of *Eclipse* across the submarine's bow then the flooding the forward ballast tanks. This forced the stern to rise high enough for divers from the submarines' crews to fit the spare propeller, itself already cracked. The ships then made a good passage to Colombo where *Eclipse* was relieved by the Town-class light cruiser HMS *Yarmouth*. Partly under tow, *AE1* and *AE2* sailed to Singapore, meeting with their Australian escort HMAS *Sydney* on April 21. Conditions had improved little for the crew, as Engine Room Artificer John Marsland, later lost in *AE1*, wrote in his diary of the voyage: 'The heat in the submarine is now almost unbearable.'

Commander and crew members of *AE2*

Unfortunately, the Royal Australian Navy had been ill prepared to host the novelty of submarines and there was no accommodation aboard Sydney for the submarine crews while in port, the men having to remain aboard their cramped and torrid craft. To make matters worse, *Sydney* coaled with poor quality fuel, her cinders and sparks blowing back onto the submarines under tow, causing discomfort and navigational difficulties. On April 25 they left for Jakarta (then still called Batavia). Here they were entertained by the Dutch authorities until their departure for Darwin on April 28.

While travelling through the treacherous currents of the Lombok Strait, *Sydney* and the submarines almost collided while *AE1* was under tow. An electrical problem aboard *AE1* jammed the rudder. The submarine began to yaw and her towrope parted, hampering *Sydney's* steering. *AE2* had luckily dropped astern of *AE1* and narrowly avoided collision with her sister submarine as *AE1* swung out of control. *AE2*'s steering then jammed, almost forcing her aground. After restoring the helm, *AE2* moved ahead of *Sydney,* only to be almost run down by the escort as she struggled to remove *AE1*'s broken tow-wire from her rudder.

With a triple disaster averted through astute seamanship aboard the submarines, they arrived safely at Darwin on May 5. After two days that included 'a very large number taking advantage of the opportunity of landing on Australian soil for the first time', they left for Cairns where they spent five days, heading for Sydney on May 18. Following delays caused by bad weather and 'angry waves', as Marsland described them, *AE1* and *AE2* sailed through Sydney Heads at 6 in the morning of Empire Day — May 24 — docking at Garden Island. The two vessels had accomplished the longest submarine voyage ever undertaken. Even though under tow for around a third of the distance, they and their crews had covered almost 21 000 kilometres, 'a significant feat of seamanship and engineering', even acknowledged by the mighty London *Times*. Marsland wrote in his diary with a justifiable note of satisfaction that they had 'completed a most wonderful journey of endurance, both for men and engines.'

Although the arrival of *AE1* and *AE2* in Sydney had been muted due to the delay and the fact that most residents were celebrating Empire Day, it was not long before the press and public became fascinated by these bizarre machines of the deep. No one was allowed aboard, as the submarines were still top-secret weapons. This simply made people more inquisitive and the crowds came and stared anyway, their interest stimulated by the press reports, which played on the secretive aspects of the craft, as well as their unusual appearance and operation, with phrases and sub-headings such as 'strange looking craft and 'the Home of Secrets.' Jules Verne's famous fantasy, *20 00 Leagues Under the Sea* had only appeared in English for the first time in 1873, so the concept of living and travelling in a self-contained capsule beneath the sea was still the stuff of science fiction for the general public.

As senior officer, Lieutenant Commander Besant was interviewed by the newspapers and seems to have become something of a minor media celebrity. Reporter for the *Sydney Morning Herald* wrote:

> *The submarines stood barely five feet above the waterline (save for the bridge and conning tower, rising some ten feet higher), and only a naval officer who has made a submarine his home and loves every bit of her, would contend that she's a lady, like 'the liner.' There are such men. You have only to talk to Lieutenant-Commander Besant, who has charge of* AE1, *for a few moments, and you discover it. It is nine years since he joined the submarine service, and he has lived a fair proportion of that time under water.*

The citizens of Sydney were greatly impressed by the arrival of these intriguing new craft in their harbour and provided their officers with a civic reception. There was patriotic applause when Besant stated that 30 of the submariners of *AE1* and *AE2* were Australian and that the submarines were important elements of Australia's naval defences. Officers and crew then enjoyed their first extended periods of shore leave, including beaches, clubs, sporting events and general socialising. Stoker, who liked to present himself as a 'philanderer', moved in more exalted social circles than did the submarine crews, or even Besant. He provides a vignette of the experience in his autobiography, *Straws in the Wind,* declaring Sydney 'the most attractive city to live in I have ever seen.'

Two months later, *AE1* and *AE2* were still being refitted from their record-breaking journey when war between Britain and Germany was declared on August 5 1914. *AE1* was to become the first allied submarine to be lost in the Great War

AE1 off Rossel Island, 9 September 1914

THE MYSTERY OF AE1

Soon after war was declared, Australian ships were tasked to attack Germany's East Asiatic Cruiser Squadron under the command of vice-Admiral Count von Spee. The recently repaired *AE1* and *AE2* with their parent ship *Upolo,* joined an Australian flotilla near Rabaul, New Britain (then the main island of what was German New Guinea) as part of the hunt for the enemy ships and the capture of Rabaul and the Bita Paka radio station. On September 14 *AE1* and *Parramatta* were patrolling together near Cape Gazelle in case von Spee's cruisers appeared. The ship and submarine — called a 'devil fish' by the indigenous people of Wirian — were exchanging visual signals until shortly before *AE1* was last seen just before 3.30pm. *Parramatta* returned to *AE1*'s last known position but did not sight the submarine. Assuming that *AE1* was returning to harbour as planned, *Parramatta* made for Herbertshohe, anchoring at 7pm.

An hour later *AE1* had still not returned and Australian Fleet Commander Rear Admiral Patey ordered a search for the missing submarine. *Encounter, Parramatta, Warego* and *Yarra* spent the next two days combing the area. *Yarra* damaged her propellers on a shoal in the poorly charted waters west of the primary Duke of York Island, further reducing the effectiveness of Patey's squadron. *AE1* was not found, nor was any wreckage and it was determined to convene a Board of Inquiry. For unknown reasons, though perhaps due to the urgency of the war situation, this was never held. Instead Lieutenant Stoker of *AE2* was asked for his expert opinions as to what might have happened. His speculations were contained in a report he made from Suva a month later. The possibility of enemy attack was dismissed, as was a breakdown leading to her being swept away. Stoker considered that the most likely causes of her disappearance were that she had either suffered a catastrophic mechanical failure while dived or had been wrecked on one of the many treacherous reefs in the area. In the absence of any further solid evidence, the speculations began and have continued ever since.

In his diary, AB Wheat aboard *AE2* recorded that 'The cause of her disappearance is still a mystery' and also speculated along the same lines as Stoker's official report. Wheat, and probably his fellow crewmen, thought that *AE1* might have been sunk by an old tug armed with a five-barrelled Nordenfeldt gun. When the burnt-out and beached wreckage of this vessel was discovered it was thought that she might have surprised *AE1*, which had no deck gun. The possibility of a mine was discounted due to diligent sweeping of the area. Wheat included the suggestion that *AE1* may have overtrimmed due to having one of her motors disabled — 'that is had not buoyancy enough with her one remaining motor to give complete control and finally she had become unmanageable and sank.' Given the troubled trimming procedures of *AE1* in England and *AE2*'s later stability problems in the Dardanelles, this is perhaps the most likely explanation for the loss of Australia's first submarine.

The failure of the search to reveal anything of *AE1*'s fate hit the officers and men of *AE2* especially hard. Wheat wrote that it 'cast a great gloom over us as we all had friends who had gone and we were the only two submarines in Southern Waters ' (original caps). The Dedication that prefaces his diary reads, in part:

> *'To the memory of our sister ship* AE1, *and her crew, Lost September 14th, 1914 in St. Georges Channel, between German New Guinea and New Ireland.*
>
> *We took the first patrol on the 13th, they took the second next day. We came back, they didn't. The path of our duty became the high-way of mystery for they never came back. They lie coffined in the deep, keeping their silent watch at Australia's North Passage, heroes all.'*

Similar speculations appeared in the Australian press. The *Sydney Morning Herald* published a not very accurate account from a 'special correspondent' in Rabaul

> *The tragedy of the* AE1 *is the first loss that the Australian Navy has sustained, and the magnitude seems all the grimmer for the atmosphere of mystery which surrounds it.*
>
> *On the afternoon of 15th September the submarine was sighted off Gazelle Point, south of Herbertshohe, heading in the direction of Rabaul. She was never seen again.*
>
> *A strange patch of oil floating on the quiet surface of the water, a nameless schooner, with a gun mounting from which the gun was missing, discovered on the coast in flames and sinking — these are the only clues we possess to the manner in which the* AE1 *came to her end, and they are by no means conclusive.*
>
> *Whether she was actually sunk by a shot from the enemy, whether an unseen pinnacle of coral ripped open her plates, or the pumps refused to do their work in bringing the vessel again to the surface after a dive, will probably remain forever unknown.*

Other press reports reveal the impact that the loss of *AE1* produced. The *Sydney Morning Herald* of September 21 contained a lengthy account, together with the official statement on the incident and the Minister's Tribute. The Prime Minister's sympathies were extended and there were sections on the crew and officers, including Artificer Lowe and Commander (as he was styled) Besant. The section of the report detailing the history of the ill-fated submarine once again focused on her top-secret nature.

Far away in Western Australia the loss was hardly less muted. *The Western Mail* carried a photograph of *AE1* titled 'The Lost Australian Submarine' and reprinted the expressions of sympathy and condolence from near and far, including those from New Zealand and from the Commanders in Chief of the East Indies and China. Also included was the official statement from the Navy Board, noting that ' ... although our men did not fall by the hand of the enemy, they fell on active service, and in defence of their Empire, and their names will be enshrined with those of heroes.'

As well as a strong popular reaction to Australia's first casualties of the war, there was considerable dismay in official circles. *AE1* and her sister submarine had arrived in Sydney to some fanfare in the press and a great deal of community interest. Not only were they the country's first submarines, they were also tantalisingly top secret and, at the time, novel fighting machines. *AE1*'s disappearance caused an outpouring of public grief and commemorative activity. There were messages of sympathy from the King and Queen and from Winston Churchill in his role of First Lord of the Admiralty. The Royal Australian Navy produced a black-edged memorial booklet and special payments and arrangements were made for the wives and families of the officers and crew.

It was a pre-radio and television age in which poetry was still an important form of public as well as private expression. A number of poems were composed in commemoration of the tragedy. These expressions of grief and remembrance echoed the public shock at the loss of *AE1*, along with the concern in official circles. But the fate of the submarine and her crew would soon be forgotten by most as the even greater tragedies of the war unfolded. The lost submarine quickly faded from the pages of the newspapers and *AE1*'s sister submarine sailed to the Mediterranean. *AE2* became the first to 'force the Dardanelles', penetrating the Narrows section of the Dardanelles and entering the Sea of Marmara. Here she engaged Turkish warships and was eventually scuttled after being forced to surface due to unexplained trimming problems. Her officers and crew spent the rest of the war as prisoners of the Turks, four of them never to emerge from captivity.

AE2 first engaged the enemy at the same moment as the original Anzacs were landing at what has since become known as Gallipoli on the other western side of the Dardanelles peninsula. The Gallipoli campaign was a failure, but culminated in a triumphant withdrawal in December, 1915. The following year the horrors of trench warfare were taken to their worst level on the Somme and in subsequent actions involving Australian troops. In the mounting body count of World War I, the relatively minor disaster of *AE1* in a colonial sideshow to the main theatres of war was quickly forgotten by the public and by the government.

THE SEARCH FOR AE1

In 1968, at the instigation of the then commander of the Australian Submarine Squadron, Commander W L 'Bill' Owen, RAN, a memorial plaque to the crew of *AE1* was presented to the War Graves Commission and located in Bita Paka War Cemetery, near Rabaul.

A few years later John Foster, a RAN Commander, now retired, began a serious search for the lost submarine. Working in Papua New Guinea as a naval officer in the 1970s, Foster first heard that a local crayfish diver thought that he had seen a submarine on the sea floor. He obtained the official RAN files on *AE2* and was astounded to find that most of them had not been opened since 1919, and then only to make administrative corrections. He managed to convince the Navy to allow him to make a side-scan sonar search from HMAS *Flinders* in 1976. A promising contact was made but was unable to be investigated. Subsequent publicity about the search resulted in a number of descendants of *AE1*'s crew contacting Foster and continuing to play a role in his quest.

In 1990 the famous undersea explorer, Jacques Cousteau conducted another search for *AE1*. Once again, this provided a tantalising contact but nothing conclusive was found due to faulty equipment. Foster was not able to put another search expedition together until 2002. Having been firmly rejected by the Australian Government, he sought financial support from a documentary film company. Following up information gleaned from local divers, Foster and a party investigated a likely site near Milia Mission Rabaul. Unfortunately, sharks prevented a thorough survey of another promising feature. The following year, Foster tried once more but was again frustrated.

He and the documentary makers then managed to convince the Australian Broadcasting Corporation to fund an investigation of the most likely area for finding *AE1*. This expedition included marine archaeologist Jeremy Green of the Western Australian Maritime Museum whose experience with the high technology of modern wreck searches was invaluable. But yet again, the hopes of Foster and his collaborators were dashed as this expedition failed to locate the submarine.

Foster held further consultation with local people, who told him that they thought he was looking in the wrong place. Oral tradition and the experience of local fishermen dragging their weighted nets across a metal object on the bottom suggested that there was a wreck a little outside the area that Foster and his expeditions had already searched. Foster provided a GPS position in deeper waters off Mioko Island that he felt should be the datum for a further search which, as recommended by Jeremy Green, should be initially conducted by an aircraft fitted with a Magnetic Anomaly Detector, followed by an ROV or diver investigation. It was also felt that an extended sonar and magnetometer search might also be fruitful.

In February 2007 HMAS *Benalla*, with Foster aboard, made a likely sonar identification of *AE1*'s last resting place. A man-made object of approximately the right size and shape was discovered at 65 metres in an undisclosed location. There was a flurry of renewed interest in *AE1* as newspapers and magazines around the world, as well as the Internet, reported the event. Foster and the Royal Australian Navy were confident that they have found a man-made object at a depth and location that fits with the known facts of *AE1*'s disappearance. A few months later, another attempt was made to identify the feature as the *AE1*. As the official press release from the Minister Assisting the Minister for Defence put it:

> *The Coastal Mine Hunter HMAS Yarra searched for four days using her mine hunting sonar, divers and the ship's camera fitted Remotely Operated Vehicle (ROV) to search a 50 square kilometer area around the position of the object identified by Benalla.*

Unfortunately, once again the search was unsuccessful:

> *The object detected by Benalla's sonar was confirmed by the ROV camera to be a submarine shaped rock formation.*

The crew of *Yarra* concluded the search with a memorial service for the men of *AE1*. In the press release the Minister Assisting reaffirmed the government's commitment to the search:

> *'The Government will continue to support the search for AE1 if credible information about its likely location comes to hand. It is important to provide some comfort to the descendants of the brave crew of the AE1, who gave their lives in the service of their nation.'*

Two further unsuccessful searches were mounted in 2009. That year, Foster was made a Member of the Order of Australia in recognition of his intense efforts to locate *AE1*. Sadly, he died in 2010. Since then, the *AE1* Incorporated body, in collaboration with those involved in the successful hunt for HMAS *Sydney* and the *Kormoran*, has continued the search. In the meantime, the fate of Australia's lost submarine and her crew remains a mystery. But when *AE1* is finally found, it seems likely that her rediscovery will have as great an impact on the public as did her loss in 1914.

Subsunk Appendix 1 Page 107.

3
THROUGH THE DARDANELLES

Greatly saddened by the loss of their sister ship and all hands, Stoker and the crew of *AE2* were soon to face dangers of their own. Back in port, Stoker convinced the Australian Naval Board and Senator Pearce, then Minister for Defence, that the remaining submarine would be best deployed in the northern hemisphere. Towed by the Transport HMAS *Berrima, AE2* joined the second contingent of the AIF that departed from Albany on December 31. Crewman AB Albert Knaggs later recorded in his diary that the submarine was 'the sole escort for 20 transports with the exception of a few which were armed with 4-inch guns.'

Originally headed for the Mediterranean, *AE2* was diverted by the Admiralty to join British *B*-class submarines patrolling the Dardanelles Straits, arriving in early February. Here, there were various unsuccessful attempts to penetrate the heavily mined area of the Straits known as 'The Narrows.' This would allow the allied fleet into the Sea of Marmara, threatening Constantinople (Istanbul) and so forcing the Turks to ease their confrontation with Russian forces on the Caucasus. This strategy was interrupted by the subsequent plan to land an invasion force on the peninsula that has since become known as Gallipoli.

Stoker was keen to have the honour of being the first to force the Dardanelles. The British submarine *E15* had been destroyed in an attempt on April 17 with the death of the captain and six crew and imprisonment of the remainder. Stoker then developed his own dangerous but potentially successful plan that was approved by Commander of the allied Dardanelles fleet, Vice Admiral Sir John de Robeck.

The first attempt on April 24 failed due to a broken hydroplane, but on the fateful morning of April 25 Stoker took his tiny metal container and her crew into the jagged narrows and minefields of the Dardanelles. They 'entered the straits at about 8 knots', as Stoker wrote in his official report, with Turkish searchlights 'sweeping the straits.' Stoker had been ordered to 'generally run amok' in the Narrows as a diversionary action to cover the landings at what was to become known as Anzac Cove. He remained surfaced as long as possible to conserve his batteries although this would make the submarine a prime target for the guns of the Turkish forts and warships. Around 4.30am *AE2* was fired on from a gun battery on the northern shore. She dived to 70 or 80 feet then proceeded through the minefield. 'During the ensuing half-hour or so the scraping of wires against the vessel's side was almost continuous, and on two occasions something caught up forward and became loose and scraped away aft.'

After escaping the mines, *AE2* came to periscope depth and was spotted by the Turks who opened fire from the forts. As he narrowly avoided being rammed by a Turkish destroyer, Stoker fired off a bow torpedo and hit and disabled a small cruiser, which was subsequently abandoned. In making her escape from the scene of this success *AE2* grounded beneath Fort Anatoli Medjidieh, fortunately too close inshore for the fort's guns to bear. AB Knaggs wrote in his diary that 'Fire was opened on us from all sides, the captain said the sea was one mass of foam caused by the shells fired at us but luckily we were not hit.' He went on to recall 'we could hear inside the boat the shrapnel dropping on us like a lot of stones.'

Stoker managed to get the boat off, only to ground again on the opposite bank beneath Fort Derinburna. Once more, Stoker was able to drag his boat off. He thought that she was now too badly damaged to fight 'but as I considered my chief duty was to prove the passage through the straits to be possible, I decided to continue on my course.' Recollecting these events AB John Wheat wrote 'Nobody knows what a terrible strain it is on the nerves to undergo anything like this.'

Pursued by Turkish warships, *AE2* settled to the bottom and waited. They narrowly escaped attempts by the Turks to detect them using two boats dragging cables slung between them on which were carried an early form of depth charge. Not until 9pm was it safe to surface, recharge the batteries and replenish the fetid air inside the submarine after sixteen nerve-wrenching hours of confinement. Stoker ordered the 23 year-old wireless telegraphist William Falconer to signal their success. This he did, but was unable to receive a reply, continuing to send the signal in the desperate hope that it would be picked up. It was, and the news that an Australian submarine had penetrated the Dardanelles and torpedoed a Turkish warship provided a much-need morale boost to the faltering Gallipoli landings when Sir Ian Hamilton received it in the grim early morning hours of April 26. Instead of agreeing with the shore commanders' recommendation that the landing forces withdraw, Hamilton informed them of *AE2*'s success and urged them 'to dig, yourselves right in and stick it out.'

Paravane Towing

After spending a rainy night on the surface, *AE2* proceeded further along the Straits. On the morning of April 26 she attempted a torpedo attack on a Turkish ship, but narrowly missed. Stoker then continued on, diving beneath a fleet of fishing boats, finally entering the Sea of Marmara. The next few days were a game of cat and mouse between *AE2* and at least six Turkish boats diverted to hunt down the submarine. Stoker raised the White Ensign as often as possible to let the enemy know that their defences had been breached. There were a number of unsuccessful attacks, mainly due to failures of the torpedoes, and *AE2* narrowly avoided being shelled and rammed. Many opportunities to attack the enemy while on the surface had to be foregone due to the frustrating lack of a deck gun.

In the evening of April 29 the crew of *AE2* were surprised to meet with *E14*. The British submarine had followed Stoker's example and also penetrated the Sea of Marmara after Falconer's message had proved that the Dardanelles could be forced. The commanders of the two submarines arranged to rendezvous at 10am the next day. *AE2* spent the night on the bottom once again. Next morning she arrived at the meeting point to find *E14* coming towards them under pursuit from a Turkish torpedo boat, *Sultanhisar,* and two gunships.

According to the diary of Able Seaman Alfred Knaggs 'E14 dived and we continued to draw the enemy on while E14 manouvered for an attack.' But the enemy got too close and *AE2* dived and waited. Half an hour later and for no apparent reason she went wildly out of control and began rising to the surface where she was easy prey for the torpedo boat's guns. Flooding a forward tank caused *AE2* to dive but she could not be controlled and sank to well below her 100-foot maximum depth where she was in danger of being crushed by the pressure. Stoker ordered full astern and *AE2* now began to rise stern first as uncontrollably as she had sunk.

Breaking the surface, *AE2* presented an unmissable target and *Sultanhisar* fired into her pressure hull and engine room. Captain Riza sent two torpedos at *AE2* but one failed and one missed. Without deck guns, *AE2* had no chance of fighting back and she was beginning to sink. Stoker reported that he:

> *... blew the main ballast and ordered all hands on deck. Assisted by Lieutenant [Geoffrey] Haggard, I then went round opening all tanks to flood the sub. Cary [Lieutenant John Cary], on the bridge, watched the rising water to give warning in time for our escape. A shout from him and we clambered up. 'Hurry, Sir, she's going down.' As I reached the bridge the water was about two feet from the top of the conning tower.*

Stoker needed to ensure a thorough scuttling that would keep the top-secret craft out of enemy hands. He was last to leave, finding the remainder of the crew who had not yet been picked up by the Turks or swum for their lives huddled on the sinking stern. All were rescued and a little before 11am '*AE2* just slid away on her last and longest dive', as Stoker later wrote in his autobiography, disappearing into 55 fathoms of water about 8 kilometers off Karaburun.

Many other allied submarines followed *AE2*'s lead into the Sea of Marmara, causing havoc with Turkish shipping and, using deck-mounted guns, on land transport. Altogether, 148 sailing vessels, 44 steamers, 11 transports, 5 gunboats as well as a destroyer and a battleship were sunk or badly damaged by submarine action against the Turks and their German allies. As the historian of Australian submarining, Michael White, observes:

> *'If AE2 had not successfully penetrated the Marmara, it has to be acknowledged that none of the others would have done so. The greatest achievement of Stoker and the crew of the AE2 was that they showed the feat was possible. Until 25 April, two submarines had fallen victim to the traps and hazards of the Narrows. By careful planning and outstanding courage and shiphandling, Stoker pioneered the route, so that those who followed had the comfort and encouragement of knowing before they set out that the feat was possible.'*

These actions, together with those of *AE2*, forced the Turks to reorganise their supply lines to their troops on the Gallipoli peninsula. Instead of using the route through the Sea of Marmara, their ammunition, reinforcements and supplies had to be taken by the much slower overland route. This provided significant relief for the hard-pressed land forces on Gallipoli.

Two Victoria Crosses and other decorations were awarded as a consequence of these activities, though *AE2*'s achievement remained largely ignored. Stoker apparently never complained about this and the nearest he came in public, at least, was in his autobiography where he drily noted that the results of the campaign in the Dardanelles for the submarine commanders ' ... was death for one; three and a half years of the living death for another; and Victoria Crosses for the other two.'

Stoker would eventually be awarded a Distinguished Service Order and promoted to Commander after the war. But the gallantry and unprecedented achievement of Stoker and his men seem to have been submerged in the desire to forget the military defeat of Gallipoli and the all-consuming events of the western front.

Stoker and his crew spent the remaining three and a half years of the war in various Turkish prisons and work camps, including Afion Kara Hissar, St Stefano and the brutal Belmedik. They were initially treated well and politely interrogated. But when the questioning failed to reveal any useful information, the submariners were subjected to bad treatment including poor and inadequate food, clothing and accommodation infested with vermin and rats. Stoker and Lieutenant Geoffrey Fitzgerald from the British submarine *E15* also suffered a long period of solitary confinement as a reprisal for alleged allied mistreatment of Turkish prisoners. They were fortunate that the American Ambassador in Turkey, Henry Morganthau, intervened with Enver Pasha on their behalf and they were finally released after thirty-two days imprisonment, twenty-five of them in solitary confinement. There were also some cases of brutality from individual guards and commandants, in particular by the notorious, Maslum Bey of Afion Kara Hissar, a camp said to have been 'a veritable hell' by late September, 1916.

AE2 crew in Turkish Prison Camp (P00371)

Numerous, mostly unsuccessful, escape attempts were made by various of *AE2*'s crew, sometimes with other captured British submariners. Stoker was involved with two of these, the first in March 1916. In company with Archibald Cochrane and Lieutenant Rice from the British *E7*, Stoker managed to reach the coast, the group having covered a distance of around 130 miles in eighteen exhausting days. But within sight of the liberating sea they were betrayed by a shepherd they believed to be assisting them. After months of imprisonment the escapees were tried by court martial, resigned to execution. The court predictably found them guilty but to the surprise and relief of the prisoners they were sentenced to only twenty-five days imprisonment. They burst into near hysterical laughter at this absurdly minimal sentence, their mirth causing the court to join in. A later escape attempt, inspired by maps sent secretly to the prisoners through the mail, ended in near farce before any of them even left the camp.

During their three-and-a-half years of captivity four crew members of *AE2* died, mainly as a result of exhaustion from overwork, poor nutrition and resultant diseases, including typhus and malaria. Charles Suckling of the scuttled *AE2* called it 'Nothing but a sorry existence and went on to write in his prison diary: 'I don't think, if we had known what was ahead of us, that one of us would have left the boat.'

The survivors were repatriated mostly to Britain at the war's end, though Stoker Petty Officer Kinder travelled back to Australia direct. After his recovery, Henry Stoker briefly continued his submarine career but after serving in them since 1906 'I was tired of them', he wrote, and took to the stage, a talent for acting having surfaced during amateur theatricals while a prisoner of war. He retired from the Royal Navy in October, 1920 and went on to become a noted character actor, producer, director and writer. Stoker served again in the Royal Navy during World War II and died in 1966 on his eighty-first birthday. Sooner or later after the end of the war, most of the surviving *AE2* crew returned home to Australia or emigrated.

Their gallant submarine remained lost beneath the Sea of Marmara until the determined research of Turkish maritime historian Selçuk Kolay OAM discovered her in 1998. The Silent Anzac was lying upright in the mud, encrusted with more than 80 years of weed, shellfish and discarded fishing nets. Her hatch was still open, as Stoker had left it, a large eel having taken up residence inside. Discussions about appropriate procedures for the protection and preservation of *AE2* have been in progress since then and in 2007 the Commonwealth government provided funds for a feasibility study into appropriate preservation measures. The Submarine Institute of Australia has established 'The Silent Anzac' project 'to ensure the protection, preservation and promotion of *AE2,* to contribute to an informed debate on her future and ensure that *AE2*'s contribution to the Gallipoli campaign is duly recognised ....'

In his autobiography, *Straws in the Wind,* Henry Stoker summarised the accomplishments of *AE2,* a record in which the ill-fated *AE1* and her crew also had a share:

> *AE2 was in commission as a unit of His Majesty's Australian Fleet for exactly fourteen months. During that time she traversed 35,000 miles, of which the greater portion was under war conditions. The first submarine to travel half-way round the world, she all but completed the return journey. The first submarine to pass the Dardanelles, to her fell the honour of proving this aforethought impossibility possible.*

AE 2

THE DIARY OF ABLE SEAMAN 7893 ALBERT EDWARD KNAGGS R.A.N. OF AE2

Kept from his capture in 1915 until his death in 1916 (excerpt)

- July 12th Started work on the road as before sunrise to sunset. Here we were short of food for a couple of days so we refused to work.
- July 19th 19th inst sent back to Kara Hissar leaving camp at 7am arriving there at 3pm and found we all had to be inoculated which was done three Sundays following a Russian had contracted Typhoid and died. All rooms were washed and disinfected also clothes were fumigated.
- August 3rd Beds of hay were made for us.
- August 4th The 4th, 5th and 6th the rooms were limewashed and disinfected again, shelves put up, tables and stores made. We were equalled out to 16 men in a room where 32 were previously. Very cheap civilian suits were issued.
- August 7th 1919 The American Ambassador visited us from Istanboul bringing us provisions, soap, pipes, tobacco, underclothes, a quantity of insect powder and each man received 1 Turkish Pound 18 Shillings and all complaints were given to him. He told the Turkish officers the place was not fit to live in etc.
- August 20th Started work again on the road and was promised payment but never received any so asked for better food but nothing doing.
- August 24th 24th inst stopped work on account of Russian contracting Typhoid fever. More whitewashing and disinfecting, being placed under quarrantine for 14 days.
- October 4th Received 2 boxes of cigarettes.
- October 5th 39 British prisoners entrained for Angora at 2pm but did not leave until 6pm. All this time were shut up in a horse van in which was not room to sit down comfortable in this condition we remained until 10pm the next night.
- October 6th 6th inst we arrived at Angora, and after walking about 3 miles we arrived at the prison. Here we joined up with E7s crew and other French and British prisoners.

- October 14th 274 British and French left Angora at 11.30am to march to fresh Quaters at Kangkeri 4 days march, a distance of about 80 miles arriving at villages for the night where we would be distributed in different barns in different barns to sleep. Many of the prisoners were suffering from wounds, not having been long out of hospital and the march being on bread and water. Many of the best amongst us fell out with some of them to help along the way.
- October 17th 17th inst at 7pm arrived at Kangheri. Here we found beds and Quilts to lay on, which was very acceptable, but the place was full of vermin, lice etc as usual. The barracks here appear to be an old training establishment which was very cold and draughty. One water tap in the yard for all hands to wash, no soap being provided and no working clothes.
- November 16th 33 more prisoners arrived from Angora. Also some clothing etc from the American Embassy. Received 1 box of cigarettes.
- November 26th Had a heavy fall of snow.
- November 30th 30th inst £5.10.0 per man arrived from the Red Cross Society for AE2s crew of which we received one from the commandant.
- December 4th 1915 Received £2 from Commandant.
- December 17th Survivors of Submarine E20s crew arrived from Angora.
- December 18th Received £1 from commandant.
- December 22nd Representative of Red Crescent Society visited us to find out what clothes were needed and to hear all complaints. Snapshots were taken of prisoners.
- December 25th Xmas day was made as bright as possible by our Turkish officers who gave us permission to play football outside in a field. We played a match Navy versus Army in which Army won 4 goals to 1. A concert was held amongst ourselves in the evening.
- December 26th Boxing day another football match took place AE2s versus E7s ended in a drawn game.
- January 1st 1916 New Years Day the commandant visited us and wished us a happy new year and hoped we would soon be home with our families. This day the Australians played Rugby against the Scottish Borderers, Australians won 6 points to 3. In the evening another concert was held.

HMAS AE1 & AE2 MEMORIALS

AE1

Garden Island Heritage Centre, Sydney NSW

Chapel HMAS Watson NSW

HMAS Cerberus Victoria (between the two chapels)

Bita Pala War Cemetery, near Rabaul PNG

AE2

Garden Island Heritage Centre, Sydney NSW

Maritime Museum Fremantle WA

Peace Park, Albany WA

Naval Museum Instanbul, Turkey

AE1 & AE2 JOINT MEMORIAL

Garden Island Chapel, Sydney NSW

Barrow-in-Furness, England

4
THE PEACE BOATS

In January 1915 eight *J*-class submarines were ordered under the United Kingdom War Emergency Program. Only six were constructed. These submarines were able to reach surface speeds of nineteen knots, attained through a triple propeller system powered by three eight cylinder Vickers Diesel engines. This allowed the submarines to operate with the main battle fleet, trapping slow enemy craft between surface vessels and very fast submarines, a technique that led to them being known collectively as 'The Reapers.' They were around 100 feet longer than the *E*-class submarines, of which Australia had two during the war, and were also equipped with long-range wireless. Together with their speed, this enabled them to operate effectively as reconnaissance vessels, with a safe diving depth of 300 feet. As part of the 11th Submarine Flotilla, the *J*-class boats were to play an effective role in North Sea Naval operations.

Life on board a *J*-boat was a cramped and dangerous affair. Leading Torpedo-man Tom, or 'Taff', Jones had been among the landing boat crews at Gallipoli aboard HMS *London*. Inspired by the well-reported Dardanelles exploits of VC-winnner Lieutenant Norman Douglas Holbrook in British submarine *B11*, he joined the submarine service. Jones subsequently served aboard *J2* and in 1935 published a rare account of the *J*-boat experience in his *Watchdogs of the Deep*.

According to Jones, after some brief but intense training in HMS *Thames* at Sheerness, including just one practice dive, he was posted to *J2* under Lt-Commander Cooper, DSO. *J2* was crewed by five officers and forty men.

Jones described the inside of *J2* and the living and working conditions as they were in 1916:

> *'... it is divided into eight compartments separated by means of strong bulkheads with watertight doors. The first compartment, as we come from the bows, is the torpedo room, or 'Fort End', as we call it. In it are four torpedo-tubes, each containing a torpedo; and on each side of us there are two more spare torpedoes, in all eight 'tin fish.' All round us are dozens of pipes and valves, polished to perfection. The valves are for flooding the tubes and the hundred and one controls for operating the torpedo-tubes. At the back of the tubes are four tanks containing the air-charge for firing the 'fish.' Leaving Fort End we step through a bulkhead door to the ward-room. The captain and officers feed and sleep in the ward-room. Here again, we find all valves and pipes polished. On one side are the officers' bunks; on the other the wireless cabinet. At the after end of this compartment is a tiny officers' pantry.*

Jones goes on to describe the operating hub of the control room, crammed with pipes, levers and gauges. 'Just abaft the control room are two beam or broadside torpedo-tubes, with two spare fish on top ready for loading.' He describes the fore engine room with wing Diesels on each side, the main motor room and the after engine-room, with another Diesel making a 'terrific din' and air compression equipment equally as noisy.

The final compartment was the crew space 'where we ate, slept and played patience.' Half the crew would eat their meals here at any one time, 'otherwise the other half would have had to stand on their eyebrows as we termed it.' On deck was a three-inch recessing gun and a telescopic wireless mast. The *J*-boats were notorious for rolling and pitching, with sea-sickness afflicting even the hardiest submariners, including Jones. It was not considered good form to show that you were seasick and so Jones, like many others, suffered silently.

In these confined quarters, the submariners worked, ate, slept and socialised as best they could. Some played cards, some read, some talked about their girlfriends or wives. 'The air seems thick, even in the morning', Jones wrote. 'After a very long day of diving, about eighteen hours, breathing becomes very hard, and a sort of mist can be seen over the deck-boards, indicating that the fresh air is diminishing fast.' Smoking was officially banned but officers and men smoked pipes and cigarettes surreptitiously, no doubt contributing to the breathing difficulties. Jones says that the only air supplies on board were used for the operation of the submarine, though he did see engineers occasionally open the airlines to 'put a little kick in the stale air.' Apart from this occasional assistance, the only pleasure was the daily ration of rum in the tradition of the British navy.

Despite the dangers of enemy craft, Jones wrote 'I think I voice the opinion of most submarine men when I say that the British Navy was our biggest enemy.' The British warships were frequently so nervous of *U*-boats that they attacked their own submarines, even after they had given correct recognition signals. The submarines would have to dive rapidly in sixty seconds to escape. Referring to the openly expressed warning by the British destroyers that the submarines must keep out of the way or risk being attacked, Jones wrote: 'I don't think I am giving away secrets when I state that a very large number of British submarines never returned through these circumstances.' Jones and his fellow submariners appear to have accepted this situation due to the seriousness of the *U*-boat menace.

As well as contending with such friendly fire, the *J*-boats were not very maneuverable. Commander Norman Shaw served recollected many years later that 'Their diving qualities were not the best, it being asserted by one experienced submarine captain that if you could drive a *J*-boat you could drive a bath.' The very flat upper deck and casing of the *J*-boats operated like one large hydroplane if the boat attained an angle of more than 5 degrees.

But it was on the surface that *J*-boats seem to have had the most trouble. Jones relates one event that took place as *J2* was returning to Blyth Harbour with one engine and a desultory tugboat. It was late at night but the submarine showed no navigation lights as the tug and the single engine maneuvered her around a notoriously sharp corner. A large Norwegian freighter suddenly loomed out of the darkness. The tug let go the towrope and sped away, leaving the helpless submarine to be hit behind her bows, damaging the after hydroplane and holing the hull. The freighter then dropped her very large anchor, narrowly missing the submarine. Fortunately, *J2* was still seaworthy, though she bore the scars of the encounter in the form of a large patch for the rest of her career.

It was near the end of the war that the first major disaster befell the *J*-boats, proving the hazards of World War I submarining mentioned by Jones. *J6* became the victim of a mistaken attack by a Royal Navy decoy ship, *Cymric*. She was sunk with the loss of sixteen crew on October 15, 1917. A replacement was immediately ordered. Built on an existing *K*-class hull, the new *J7* had her bridge and control room set further back than the others of the class. She was completed in February 1918.

After the loss of Australia's first submarines, *AE1* and *AE2*, the government and the Navy still wanted to have a submarine capability. There were considerable exertions in Australia and in Britain to determine what sort of capability it should be and also to develop facilities within Australia for the maintenance and possibly even the building of submarines. While these investigations and deliberations were wending their way through the government and military, the war itself came close to its end. Prime Minister W M Hughes and Sir Joseph Cook, Minister for the Navy, were both in Britain for the 1918 Imperial War Conference and the peace talks at Versailles. While they were there, engaged in high level talks with the British government and defence forces, they were told that it was possible that the British government might present a number of submarines to Australia.

In January, 1919, it was agreed between the two governments that six submarines and six destroyers would be given to the Royal Australian Navy, a gift valued then at around one-and-half million pounds. *J1, J2, J3, J4, J5* and *J7* were commissioned into the Royal Australian Navy in March, 1919. Lieutenant Commander O H Halifax of *J7* was the senior officer of the flotilla that assembled for the first time at Portsmouth in early April, together with the cruiser *Sydney* and supply ship *Platypus*.

Preparations began to ready and crew the *J*-boats for their long journey to Australia. There were shortages of men in both the Royal Navy and the Royal Australian Navy, though crews for the six submarines were relatively quickly assembled from volunteers from both navies and serving submariners, including some of the crew of *AE2*, now recovered from their lengthy captivity in Turkish POW camps. The plan was for the *J*-boats to voyage to Australia in time for the Peace Day celebrations scheduled for July 1919.

Even before the *J*-boats began their voyage to Australia they were plagued with defects. It was not until April 9, 1919, that the six submarines were able to leave Portsmouth, escorted by *Sydney* and *Platypus*. They were followed by three more support craft, an oiler *Kurumba* and the *Australia* and *Brisbane*. As with the earlier voyage of *AE1* and *AE2* from Britain to Australia, the *J*-class boats suffered problems, breakdowns and other disasters. In poor visibility *J5* collided with a French sailing ship, which later sank as a result. Further problems were experienced with the intermediate shafts and the submarines were frequently under tow as they proceeded from Gibraltar, to Malta. One of *J2*'s engines failed as soon as she had left Gibraltar and the submarine had to be taken in tow by *Sydney*. But in the evening the tow wire parted. The next day it broke again but they managed to make another engine operable and made a slow passage to Malta, arriving on the 20th.

Commander Norman Shaw

All the other submarines also suffered engine problems on this stage of the voyage and *J7*, at least, was towed for some days by *Australia* between Aden and Colombo. Aboard *Australia* was a young Australian Midshipman, Norman Shaw. With the rank of sub-Lieutenant and after submarine training in England, he would later be briefly appointed to *J7* in Australia in February 1920. He was one of the second group of Cadet Midshipmen at the Royal Australian Navy College at Osborne House, Geelong, a location destined to play an important role in the Australian history of the *J*-boats. Together with Frank Getting, who had been in the first Royal Australian Navy College intake, he was the first Australian submarine officer to complete the 'Perisher' training course in Britain. In his recollections, Shaw notes that as well as himself and Getting there were another five Australian sub-Lieutenants in the submarines, Calder, Larkins, Sadleir, Showers and Watkins.

The flotilla passed through the Suez Canal and on to Colombo by May 16. The heat and cramped conditions caused the crews great distress and there was a much needed few days rest, including leave. From there, the submarines sailed at various times for Singapore, 'Another very welcome port', as torpedo-man Jones recalled. Again they were able to rest and obtain much-needed fresh food. From Singapore the submarines had all departed by June 18 for Thursday Island.

During this final stage of the voyage tragedy again struck the *J*-boats. Due to the oppressive heat of the tropics, the crews had taken to sleeping on the casing. But on the morning of June 20, the men of *J2* discovered the empty blankets of Sub-Lieutenant Larkins. All the submarines immediately conducted a search until late in the afternoon, but without success. *J2*'s captain held a burial service with all the crew mustered — 'They were a band of downcast men who stood there bareheaded', Jones wrote.

On reaching Thursday Island on June 28, the luck of the *J*-boats did not improve. There was dissatisfaction among the crews about the quality and quantity of the food supplied by the 'tin pot', as they called the poorly suited and prepared *Platypus*. Rations were no better at Thursday Island — 'a few tins of corn dog and a few old biscuits' — and the crews then confronted the pandemic scourging the post-war world, destined to kill more people than the war itself. All the submarines were quarantined, but the influenza claimed Stoker Henry Haggis of *J7* who was buried there.

The flotilla sailed for Moreton Bay on July 5 where they rested for three days. However, they could not go ashore, even though they had 'tons of spondulix' and *J2*'s crew 'voiced our protest by staging a mild mutiny.' Their officers talked the crew around, however, holding up a vision of the tumultuous welcome they would receive when they reached Sydney. 'This made us quite a band of good boys again', wrote Jones.

Most of the submarines finally arrived in Sydney on July 15, 1919. *J5*, still under tow by *Brisbane*, had arrived already arrived in June. They were welcomed by the Governor-General and, as Jones remembered the scene 'We received a great welcome: hundreds of boats met us; the ferry steamers cock-a-doodle-dood themselves hoarse.'

The Peace Day celebrations had been planned as a large-scale day of national thanksgiving to mark the end of hostilities. In the event, the day turned out to be a more muted event than envisaged. The influenza pandemic, the seaman's strike and the threats of the dockers to join, together with haggling over the peace terms with Germany took most of the general public's attention. As well, large numbers of troops were now returning and it was becoming difficult to repeat the initial enthusiasm each time a new boatload arrived. And people wanted to get on with their peacetime lives after more than four years of war and loss.

On July 19 the event duly took place, featuring a march through Sydney streets by the companies of a number of warships in the harbour, as well as the crews of the *J*-boats. The *Sydney Morning Herald* covered the march only briefly and made no mention of the submarines. But regardless of the indifference of the Sydney press, the men of the *J*-boats were happy to be home and to take part in the march, though they were understandably more interested in the after-march festivities. Jones passes over this event with barely a sentence: 'After the impressive march, we returned to our ship, where we 'spliced the main brace.'

But after the celebrations, troubles continued for the *J*-boats. They had not been refitted in England and were in need of serious repair and refurbishment after war service and the gruelling voyage to Australia. The program began at Garden Island from July 30. Unfortunately, there was a lack of expertise in submarine maintenance at Garden and Cockatoo Islands, nor was the Royal Australian Navy well prepared for the specialised needs of submarines. These difficulties were compounded by the unavailability of necessary spare parts and the long delivery times for their eventual arrival from Britain. As the historian of Australian submarines, Michael White drily observes 'The refit of the submarines was not noted for its vigour.' Jones called it 'a half-hearted refit.'

From February 16 1920, the *J*-boats were gradually moved to the new submarine base being established for them at Osborne House, Geelong. This had been built as a family residence by a wealthy landowner in 1858 and had been, from 1913 the first Royal Australian Navy College, and subsequently a military hospital and nurses' convalescent quarters. Despite its heritage value, Osborne House was not very suitable as a submarine base. It lacked many of the storage facilities necessary for maintaining submarines, as well as a suitable deep water pier for the vessels and their tenders.

Nevertheless, under Commander E C Boyle VC, the submarines and their crews trained hard to reach and maintain the high level of efficiency required for war duty. The submarines also took part in the ceremonies of greeting for the visit of the Prince of Wales in mid-June, 1920. Following this they successfully conducted what would now be called war games against the battle cruiser HMAS *Australia* and four destroyers.

While these enjoyable peacetime activities were being carried out, darker influences were coalescing in official circles. The Navy was being subjected to major cost cutting in the post-war climate and also experiencing difficulty obtaining and retaining personnel, especially trained men. These influences would gradually come to determine the fate of the *J*-boats over the next few years.

Albert Mainstone and family aboard *J7* c. 1920

The high point of the *J*-boats' chequered career was probably the voyage of *J1, J2, J4* and *J5* to Tasmania to take part in the summer training cruise and, fortuitously, the Hobart Regatta of 1921. Though even here they were to be dogged by bad luck and poor seamanship. Accompanied by 'our faithful old mother ship' HMAS *Platypus* and MTB *Swordsman, J1, J2, J4* and *J5* moored at Prince's wharf on January 16, 1921. The submarines were objects of intense curiosity to the local community, as a reporter for the Hobart *Mercury* wrote: 'Interest in the submarines, novel to the Hobart populace, is widespread and many people made their way to the wharf yesterday and indulged in respectful and fascinated inspection from the wharfside.' Tasmanians had to wait a few more days before they were able to get aboard a submarine. On January 23rd 'a very large number of people availed themselves of the opportunity to see the vessels.'

A few days later, in Storm Bay, *J2* and *J4* conducted a 'sham attack' on HMAS *Sydney* carrying the Governor-General, Lady Forster and their staff to dock in preparation for the Hobart Regatta. Using dummy torpedoes, *J4* scored a hit beneath *Sydney's* bridge, while *J2* registered another between A and B funnels. On the 30th large numbers again flocked to inspect the submarines, twenty at a time, and were titivated with the exciting news that *J2* would perform a demonstration dive during the next day's Regatta program. This proved to be the highlight of the regatta, enthused the *Mercury's* reporter: 'It is not too much to say that this event alone was the biggest draw of the regatta.' The article also acknowledged that 'The wonderful work performed by this kind of vessel during the great war is now a matter of history.'

Yet even this triumph was to turn to disaster for the *J* boats. As *J4* left for her daily practice run up the river on February 18 she unaccountably rammed the stern of a wooden schooner loading timber for New Zealand. When the vessels were parted the damage to the schooner, *Omega*, was a large hole, fortunately above the waterline. *J2* broke her flagpole and put a slight dent in her bow. Repairs to the damaged schooner were estimated at ten pounds.

Other peacetime activities turned out better. The Governor of Tasmania and Lady Allardyce were dived for forty minutes in Sandy Bay, as were the Bishop and Dean of Tasmania at another time. The *J2's* crew also had the satisfaction of beating *Sydney's* cutter in a two-mile race during the 83rd Annual Regatta. As Jones writes: 'Three weeks later our visit to Hobart terminated. All had enjoyed their stay and it was with reluctance that we left.'

The submarines sailed for Geelong on February 24. Their stay in Tasmania had been lengthy, eventful and, especially for the crews, enjoyable. They had the leisure to see the sights, climb Mt Wellington, play cricket and generally enjoy the festive atmosphere of the Hobart Regatta, even as they attended to their routines and duties. But things were not to remain so rosy for very long.

In April an inquiry into the costs of the submarines revealed the lack of preparedness for submarines within the Royal Australian Navy. As well, there was the usual need to cut costs and the cost of the submarines compared with their strategic value was considered by the Australian Naval Board to be too great and would preclude keeping the light cruisers Melbourne, Brisbane and Sydney in commission. As a result, three *J*-boats were placed in Reserve and their crews paid off from Oct 4, 1921. Again, bad luck followed the remaining submarines. The following February, *J1* collided with the River class torpedo boat destroyer HMAS *Huon* during routine exercises off Hobart. There was no damage to the submarine, but *Huon* was holed below the waterline and kept afloat through temporary repairs until her scheduled visit to Sydney the following month.

By this time it was only possible to fully crew two of the submarines, with an almost complete reserve crew. In November 1922 a naval conference concluded that the *J*-boats were too obsolete, too worn out and too expensive to be retained. From that time they were progressively scrapped.

J3 was the first scheduled to go, but had a brief reprieve. In December 1922 the submarine was moored near Swan Island so that she could be used as an auxiliary power generator for the Mine Depot. In February the following year, the Australian Naval Board gave permission for the hull to be sunk though this was apparently not carried out until 1926. In January that year *J3* was sunk near the northeastern tip of Swan Island to do further peacetime duty as a pier and breakwater.

Between May and June 1926 *J1* was sunk, along with *J2, J4* and *J5*, off Port Phillip Bay. *J1* was the only one of the class to have a winged lookout on its conning tower and is also thought to have been the only submarine ever to have attacked another using depth charges, for which she was uniquely fitted out. *J2* was stripped and left on the mud banks near the Flinders Naval Depot pier, then towed to sea and sunk together with *J1, J4* and *J5* off Port Phillip Bay. The day that Torpedoman Jones's beloved *J2* was towed to the mud banks he went sick. *J5* was sunk with *J1, J2* and *J4* off Port Phillip Bay. Prior to sinking *J5* was used for aerial bombing practice, but the bombs fell short and her seacocks were opened to sink her.

J3 at Cowes

J7 was the only one of the submarines in operational condition by 1923 after a thorough and expensive refit. She was used as a power supply for the Flinders Naval Depot and at one point was under consideration to be retained in service. After various reprieves and continued use as a source of cheap electricity, *J7* was stripped, sold for further stripping then finally sold to the Melbourne Ports and Harbours SPG Department for sinking at Hampton as a breakwater near the Sandringham Yacht Club in August 1930.

Even after their scrapping, misfortune haunted the *J*-boats. *J4* had been sold to the Melbourne Salvage Syndicate but was still in the possession and care of the Commonwealth while items of value were stripped from her as she lay along the outer west berth of Dock Pier, Williamstown. Around 4.30 in the afternoon on July 10, 1924, she mysteriously sank. The inquiry and report into the incident were unable to find a cause for the sinking. The possibilities canvassed were rough weather, damage to a sea connection during stripping and the possibility of a prank by a party of schoolboys shown over the submarine earlier in the afternoon. None of these explanations was thought to be very likely and the exact cause of *J4*'s sinking remained a mystery. She proved difficult to raise, though efforts were finally successful on December 6, 1926. The Harbour Trust then made her seaworthy again at a cost of over 2500 pounds, though this sparked a legal battle between the Trust and the Commonwealth over who was to pay this bill. This was eventually settled and SS *Minah* towed *J4*'s hull outside Port Phillip Heads, where she was sunk on April 28, 1927.

J1 and *J5* also had further troubles. After they were stripped they were moored at Williamstown Pier, along with the *Cerberus*. Here they were considered a nuisance, as the space they occupied was required for more important matters. On March 22 1926 *J1* and *J5* both broke their mooring ropes during bad weather and had to be re-moored to prevent them drifting dangerously into the harbour.

After his sick leave, Torpedoman Jones, along with many other of the *J*-boats' crew members transferred to *Platypus* which had been re-designated as a depot ship for destroyers. The routine and discipline aboard the ship were in sharp contrast to that of the submariners and Jones was not happy until the second-in-command of *J2*, Lieutenant Lowther, came aboard as First Lieutenant. 'From then on the crew were a happy crowd. Our new 'Jimmy the One' understood us.'

In 1923 Jones's time with the Royal Australian Navy ended and he returned to England by liner, planning to take leave and then rejoin the British Submarine Service. But, 'during my holidays I felt a keen desire to return to Australia.' This he did and became quartermaster of the depot at Flinders Naval Base until joining the *S*-class destroyer HMAS *Tasmania*. He served aboard her until February 1926 when he was discharged to try and fit himself into civilian life after what he called 'a fair amount of experience' as a sailor, including training in a wooden ship, serving on a battleship, in submarines and finally in destroyers, together with 'a fair amount of land fighting.' Jones then worked in Sydney as a painter. After a serious fall in

1929 he spent several years in recuperation but at the time of writing his undersea classic published in 1935 felt 'as fit as ever.'

By the end of World War I, the exploits of Australia's first submarines *AE1* and *AE2,* together with the activities of British and German submarines had convinced the Australian government and navy that submarines had a role to play in naval strategy. What that role might be was much less clear. As the urgencies of war receded and the days of peace continued to heal a badly shattered nation, matters of naval offence and defence received less and less priority. The difficulty and expense of maintaining the *J*-boats as their once up-to-date technology became inevitably obsolete were increasingly apparent to a cash-strapped Royal Australian Navy. But even while the *J*-boats were being consigned to oblivion over the period 1923-24, funds were provided for their replacement by the *O* class *Oxley* and *Otway*. Thanks largely to the presence of the *J*-boats, the Royal Australian Navy had sufficient numbers of qualified officers and crews to continue a Submarine Service.

Another dimension of the story involves the Australian public. Ever since the arrival of *AE1* and *AE2* in May 1914, the national community had demonstrated a strong fascination with submarines. The officers and crews of *AE1* and *AE2* were lauded in the press and feted in Sydney. The inexplicable and still unexplained loss of *AE1* was deeply mourned throughout the country in 1914. When the *J*-boats finally arrived in Sydney they were considered by many to be the main attractions of the Peace Day March and associated celebrations. They were certainly a hit at the Hobart Regatta and in their various ceremonial peacetime duties. This interest would continue in relation to the *J*-boats' successors, *Oxley* and *Otway* and is apparent today in the intense media and general interest in the search for *AE1* and the rediscovery and possible raising of *AE2*. While such popularity does not figure in the strategic and tactical considerations involved in naval warfare it certainly has an impact upon the elected politicians who control the defence budget. It is also an indication of the importance that many in the community attach to the country's maritime and naval heritage.

More metaphorically, the story of the *J*-boats in many ways parallels the experience of large numbers of Australians. Figuratively 'born' in Britain, they subsequently 'migrated' across half the world's oceans along the most common route of migrant ships, 'crossing the line', and experiencing the discomforts of tropical passages, poor food and disease. They received a less-than-perfect reception and early experience of Australia when they arrived and were only gradually being incorporated into the naval community at the time of their scrapping. Brief though their Australian 'lives' were to be, the *J*-boats and their crews enjoyed a period of participation in many aspects of Australian society, including the Peace Day celebrations and the Hobart Regatta. When they finally 'died', victims of cost-cutting and an absence of will, their remains were broken up in various ways and distributed around Victoria in practical and visual forms — breakwaters, power generators, dive wrecks — to become part of the largely taken-for-granted fabric of the community's material culture.

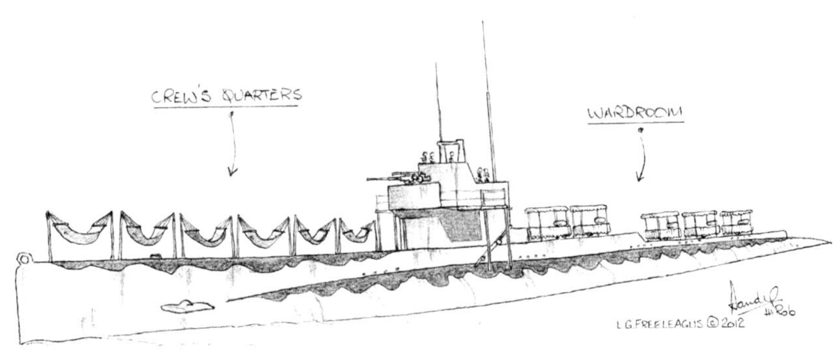

'J' CLASS. OPPRESSIVE HEAT IN TROPICS – CREW SLEEPS ON CASING.

Through this process, the remnants of the *J*-boats became unacknowledged artefacts of the fundamental Australian experiences of war and migration. Forgotten by the Navy and most of the community, a few individuals and organizations have been the unofficial curators of the *J*-boats. Naval historians and scuba divers have discovered, or re-discovered, these rusting relics, carefully recording their last resting places in the vast outdoor museum of the nation. Finding and using these remains compels people to investigate their histories and attempt to understand something of their significance during their days of glory, and after.

Troubled though they were, the *J*-boats of peace played an important role in the history of the Australian submarine service.

And they continue to do so. In 2007, these wrecks were again put to good use. Preparations for a survey of *AE2*, lying still at the bottom of the Sea of Marmara, included training dives on the *J*-boats as the only World War I submarines still able to be accessed.

The fondly remembered tender, or 'mother ship' of the *J*-boats, *Platypus*, saw service in World War II, including the bombing of Darwin. She did not go out of service until the 1950s. The Sydney submarine base is named after her.

LIFE ABOARD A WORLD WAR I SUBMARINE

On these patrols we never washed, shaved, or took off our clothes and after a couple of days at sea were hardly on speaking terms with each other. We lived in a strange and weird dream world, just doing our watches, maintaining the boat, facing unsavoury meals, attending to diving or action stations and then sleeping as much as possible. This was particularly so in my case, because there were only two 'Sparkers' so we were on watch and watch about. The remainder of the crew were in three watches, so they did one on and had two off. As there were only six bunks available for the seamen and stokers, crew members just lay on the decks, wherever they fancied and fell asleep. We all became terribly constipated and many had bad sores from the arsenic in the oil fuel. However, after returning from a trip, we longed to be out on patrol again, always hoping to bag something.

G. Hawthorne, J-boat submarine

TECHNICAL SPECIFICATIONS OF J-BOATS

1210 tons surface, 1820 tons submerged;

"*J7*" 1760 tons submerged;

Length 275 feet; beam 22 feet; draught 14 feet;

Machinery: diesel engines, triple screws:

Speed 19 knots, submerged 9-15 knots:

Complement 44;

Range 4,000 miles at 12 knots

Armament: six 18 inch torpedo tubes and one 4 inch gun.

NB: During R.A.N. service "*J7*" differed in appearance from the other vessels in that her conning tower was placed further aft and the 4-inch gun mounted in a lower position.

THE FORGOTTEN SUBMARINE BASE

In 1911, retired Admiral Sir Reginald Henderson was asked to conduct a strategic overview of the Royal Australian Navy's disposition and support facilities. As part of his report to the Commonwealth government, Henderson recommend that Port Stephens (NSW) would make an excellent base for submarines *AE1* and *AE2* and, indeed, for Australia's future submarine needs. It was not until World War I that construction began of a floating dock, oil tanks, magazines, workshops and associated facilities, construction wound on until 1922.

While the facility never served Australian submarines, the activity on the site attracted the attention of real estate developers and even the architect of Canberra, Walter Burley Griffin, who was keen on what was called *Port Stephens City*, expected to become the *New York of Australia*. There were other real estate developments in the area, but all that remains of these almost equally grandiose plans are the layouts of a number of streets in Nelson Bay.

Though Henderson's vision for a submarine base at Port Stephen did not eventuate, he showed considerable foresight in also suggesting that Australia should base submarines on the west coast, at Cockburn Sound. Responding to these suggestions the Commonwealth government resumed land near Cockburn Sound for the proposed base. In recognition of the Admiral's work, this area is now known as the suburb of Henderson.

5
OXLEY AND OTWAY

The history of Australian and British submarining has been closely connected since Australia's first submarines, *AE1* and *AE2*, were launched in 1914. These craft were followed by the *J*-boats during the 1920s, which were themselves superseded by two Odin or O-class submarines, *Oxley* and *Otway*. These boats were destined to serve both in the Royal Navy and the Royal Australian Navy at opposite ends of the world. Their oscillating careers were a consequence of changing official policies and deepening gloom as the declining economic situation caused governments to cut defence budgets. The story of these two submarines reflects the rapidly changing defence and economic circumstances of the 1920s and 30s as the world lurched through the Great Depression and towards World War II.

Despite these realities, the chance survival of a newspaper produced aboard the *Otway* as it voyaged back from Australia provides us with some insight into life aboard an O-class submarine. The means and methods employed by officers and crew to deal with the technical failings of their craft as well as the difficulties of such a long journey are tellingly displayed in these rough and ready typewritten pages of sometimes-forced humour and comment. The *Oxley Outlook*, as the periodical was named, was a direct peacetime continuation of the newspapers and magazines produced by soldiers and sailors during World War I. As far as is known, the paper is a unique survival of its time and place and is of considerable historical interest and value, revealing as it does the activities, attitudes and occasional irritations aboard a submarine voyaging from one end of the globe to the other. It also suggests that, as in wartime, the existence of such publications might have an important positive effect on morale.

Even while Australia's post-war gift submarines from the British government, the six *J*-class boats, were being progressively decommissioned, their replacements were under consideration. The strategic thinking of the Australian government and Australian Naval Board was that the *J*-boats were obsolete and expensive to maintain. The funds made available for the Royal Australian Navy in 1923-24 were needed to avoid cutting the light cruiser contingent from four to three. Nevertheless, it was agreed by the Naval Board and government that Australia should have a submarine capability. As early as November 1923 it was likely that the number would be two.

The details of type (ocean-going), tender (HMAS *Platypus*) and basing (Geelong) were finalised at the 1923 Imperial Conference in London. Quotations for construction of the submarines were called in October 1924, it having been earlier decided that Australia lacked the capability to build submarines of her own. Vickers of Barrow-in-Furness won the tender for what were to be known as *O*-class submarines. These were to be powered by an unproven engine, the cause of later problems. Each boat cost £439 942 to construct, store and arm.

After some construction delays due to design modifications and industrial action *Oxley* and *Otway* were launched and sea — trialled between June 1926 and mid-1927, both being taken over from the builders in September 1927. The submarines travelled to Chatham for military fit out, then to Fort Blockhouse at Gosport, with a voyage to Portland taking them to the end of 1927. This period was taken up with testing and trialling of the vessels and allowing the crews to learn how to operate the submarines.

Problems began early. As Norman Shaw, who served on *Oxley* and *Otway*, recounted in his memoirs:

> *While Otway was at Portland we developed a serious steering defect — after clearing the breakwater one morning she would not answer her helm and started turning circles. Examination showed that the rudder crosshead had fractured, and as the rudder was "overbalanced" it would only remain in hard over position while making way through the water.*
>
> *We were taken back to harbour by tugs and after the rudder had been clamped to the tail fin in an amidships position we left for Portsmouth,*

steering with our engines and with a tug as escort. Eventually a team from Vickers arrived to fit a new and modified crosshead.

Oxley and *Otway* were powered by two sets of Vickers Diesel engines (3000BHP) and two sets of electric motors (1350HP), with twin screws. They were just over 278 foot in length and 27 foot six inches beam, with a mean draught of 13 foot 3 inches. The Odin class had a surface speed of over 15 knots, with 9 knots submerged. Armaments consisted of six 21-inch bow and two stern torpedoes, a 4-inch Mk4 gun and two machine guns. While these specifications were theoretically advanced and made the first *O*-boats into the cutting edge of submarine technology, the reality was rather different. Many of the design features were valuable, but some of them were so new that techniques for their construction did not exist and had to be invented from scratch. This was to be the root cause of ongoing technical problems, as Norman Shaw would later note, and the source of much humour among the boats' crews.

Oxley and *Otway*

Oxley and *Otway* were designed for optimum crews of four officers and forty-eight sailors, though numbers varied from time to time. Crews and officers were to be obtained from the Royal Navy and the Royal Australian Navy, the first two Australian commanders being Frank Getting and Norman Shaw who undertook the 'Perisher' course at Devonport from March 1926 and joined their submarines in February 1927. By February 1928 the boats were ready for the voyage to Australia.

OXLEY & OTWAY 1929

The band played 'Waltzing Matilda' as they departed Fort Blockhouse shortly after noon on February 8. Commander H R Marrack DSC RN commanded *Oxley* and *Otway* was commanded by Lieutenant-Commander G J D Tweedy RN. The submarines reached Gibraltar five days later and started for Malta the following day. Two days into this leg of the voyage the engine problems that would plague *Oxley* and *Otway* for the rest of their careers began. Numerous fractures appeared in the engine columns of both boats. Effective running repairs were made by engine room officers and crews aboard both boats, and these were later the subject of official commendation. But it was clear that there were structural faults in the engines of all the *O*-boats due to untested casting methods being used in the construction of the untried engines. The submarines were detained in Malta for six months while new engines were built, transported and fitted. Trials were carried out and the new engines accepted, enabling the boats to proceed to Australia on November 15.

The new engines proved unsatisfactory in terms of fuel consumption, efficiency and exhaust and by the time the boats reached Batavia on January 2, 1929, the oil and water pump armatures on both vessels had burned out. These were replaced with the help of the Dutch Navy and both boats sailed for Timor on January 11. A week after landing a sick rating from *Oxley* at Surabaya, *Otway's* second oil and water pump armature burned out. This was replaced when the boats reached Thursday Island where depot ship *Platypus* met them on January 23, 1929. *Platypus* and the two submarines arrived at Townsville on January 31 and, via Brisbane, tied up at Garden Island on February 14.

The voyage had not been a happy one. A considerable number of men were left behind at various ports due to sickness or misbehaviour. As Michael White points out in his *Australian Submarines: A history* 'The high number of men left behind and the number of disciplinary incidents indicate that *Oxley* and *Otway* had a significant problem with morale during this voyage.' This situation was not apparently repeated when the submarines returned to Britain two years later.

And the problems did not cease with the submarines' eventual arrival in Australia. There was an outcry in the press and among the public about the costs and mechanical problems. These issues were also causing concern within the RAN and the government, especially as the Great Depression loomed. After considerable debate in official circles, the fact that the originally envisioned six boats for the Australian submarine flotilla would not now be a possibility, together with Britain's need to make up the number of her own submarines, would lead to the decision to return *Oxley* and *Otway* to Britain. While discussions and arguments raged through the press and within and between Cabinet and the Australian Naval Board, *Oxley* and *Otway* went into training and working up mode.

Officers and crews were without recent attack experience and needed to conduct diving exercises. Crews were partly inexperienced, with over 30% having changed since the submarines' initial working up in England. Both boats went to Jervis Bay in June, 1929, and practiced attack methods. *Oxley* and *Otway* took part in exercises with the Australian squadron through August to October and carried out some minor gunnery exercises into the start of 1930. But on May 10 that year the submarines were placed in reserve. Lieutenant Commander Shaw was put in command of the depot ship *Platypus,* now renamed *Penguin,* his remit including the two submarines, each with reduced crews.

Over the next eleven months, officers and crews were gradually dispersed and *Oxley* and *Otway* were handed back to the Royal Navy on April 9,

1931. After considerable deliberation and argumentation it had been decided to return the boats at no further cost to either the Australian or British governments and to concentrate the decreasing funding available on the building of a new cruiser for the Royal Australian Navy. A secret government document of the time stated that 'Money is not available to keep the submarines in commission.'

The reasons for this situation were various. They included the cost of the submarines and the view that they were insufficient in number to be effective in wartime (the original plan had been for a flotilla of six). There was also an argument that the boats were more effectively deployed as part of the flotilla in Britain, strengthening the Empire defence capability overall. Finally, return of the submarines would allow Britain to maintain its allotted Empire tonnage under the London Naval treaty without the need to build further ships. This fatal combination and the decision stemming from it meant, as Michael White notes: that 'Australia's third attempt to establish a submarine arm was brought to an end.'

Oxley and *Otway* were placed in reserve and the next year paid off from the Royal Australian Navy on April 9, 1931 and were recommissioned the following day into the Royal Navy. On April 29 1931 they sailed back to Malta to join the British submarine flotilla stationed there. Ironically, the arguments used to justify their disposal were the same as those used to dispose of their *J*-boat predecessors only a few years before. In his reminiscences, Norman Shaw expressed an opinion that was probably an accurate assessment of the decision to purchase the first O-boats:

> *'It is my opinion that (a) it would have been wiser for Australia to have waited until the "O" class had been proved before ordering Oxley and Otway, for they were in fact the guinea pigs of the class, and (b) had it not been the financial depression we would have had a fair prospect of establishing successfully, on the third attempt an Australian Submarine Flotilla.'*

THE OXLEY OUTLOOK

Brief and troubled though their careers as Australian submarines proved to be, and though they are long gone, *Otway* and *Oxley* did leave an until-recently unknown and rare archival legacy. With the exception of occasional diaries and memoirs, there is little material available to tell us a great deal about daily life aboard a submarine in the interwar years. While personal records of this type are valuable, they are the views and experiences of individuals rather than of a whole company. In the case of *Oxley* we now have an opportunity to see something of the communal aspects of submarine life and submariner humour through the fortunate preservation of the *Oxley Outlook* in the submarine museum archives at Gosport.

On Monday May 25 1931, the *Oxley Outlook* announced its existence to the crew of RN submarine, *Oxley*. The initial editorial stated that there were eight weeks of voyaging ahead before they tied up alongside Store Wharf in Malta. 'Much may happen during this time', the editorial continued with reference to the ongoing mechanical problems, 'the *Oxley* herself might conk out, one never knows.' The staff of the submarine's own newspaper said they were 'hopeful of producing at least one laugh a day.' They finished by noting that, should their attempt to raise a regular laugh be successful the staff lived in 'The Torpedo Arms, Fore Ends', and informed any potentially grateful reader that 'They drink. Anything.'

Subsequent editions contained satirical advertisements, hoax radio broadcasts, a 'Things We Would Like to Know' column and many humour cartoons and spoofs. Many of these were complaints about the food and conditions aboard the submarine.

By issue number 12, the *Outlook* aspired to literary achievement, previewing a new serial due to begin in the following day's edition. It was to be an 'amazing human drama of love amid untold dangers.' It's principle characters were to be the passionate Parisienne heroine, Norma la Spudnet, her dashing dare-devil lover, Lionel Limers and the dastardly villain, 'the man who invented murder', Murgatroyd Messtrap. The serial duly began, grinding on through subsequent editions, avoiding resolution and rationality in equal measure. So lugubrious was this story that the wife-beating cad and villain, Murgatroyd Messtrap, was only just being introduced by issue number 15.

Despite the continual complaints in the *Outlook*, there is other evidence that things were perhaps not as bad as they might seem, at least from the perspective of the officers. *Oxley* and *Otway* were later remembered by

Norman Shaw as being 'very good diving craft and most manageable. For their time, they were comfortable to live in.'

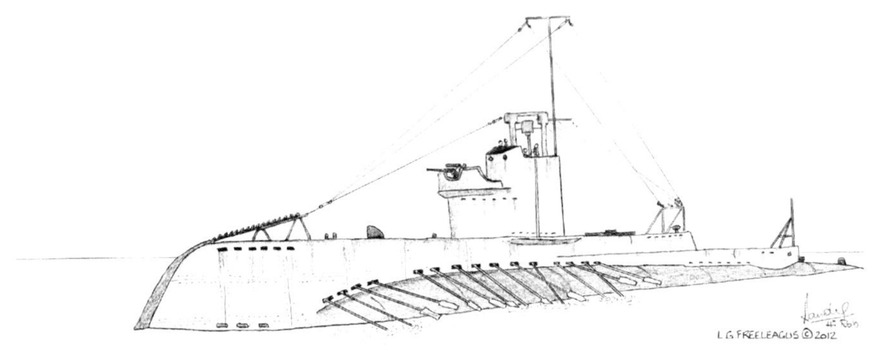

OXLEY & OTWAY MKI: ENGINE PROBLEMS FOR ALL OF THEIR CAREERS

The final issue of the *Outlook* appeared on Tuesday July 21. It was number 40. 'If we have, at any time, injured anyones [sic] feelings with our little tilts, we trust they will accept our sincere apologies', wrote the editor. And although the voyage was over, the *Outlook* was still at work announcing 'Another Great Competition.' This one was called 'pear-woffling' and involved teams from each mess competing to see who would most speedily open and down the contents of a tin of pears. The 'Rules' were 'go as you please.'

While we can never know, it is worth speculating that the existence of the *Oxley Outlook* may well have prevented a repeat of the unhappy voyage out to Australia. The opportunity to poke fun, comment on conditions and personalities and to generally let off steam within the sanctioned, if limited, constraints of the magazine must have contributed to the maintenance of morale and a generally good-natured living and working atmosphere. Cartooning and other forms of humour are a notably strong and continual element of submariner culture. As the editors modestly wrote in the final edition: 'It has been a pleasure to the Staff to try to raise 'a smile a day' and has been an added pleasure to know that the 'Outlook' was appreciated.'

Oxley and *Otway* went on to play their parts in the naval operations of World War II. *Oxley's* role was brief. On September 14 1939 she became the first naval casualty of World War II. *Oxley* was mistakenly torpedoed by her sister submarine, *Triton,* while both boats were on the surface off Norway. Only the commanding officer and lookout survived. *Otway* continued in service throughout the war and was scrapped in 1945.

6
AUSTRALIAN SUBMARINERS OF WORLD WAR II

Although Australia did not have a submarine service during World War II (1939-1945), a number of Australians served with distinction in other navies. Many of these men were involved in the top-secret miniature submarines known as *X* craft, introduced by the Royal Navy as covert attack vessels. Others served in Royal Navy submarines and Royal Australian Navy surface ships. The actions of these submariners, British and Australian, were highly awarded with four Victoria Crosses, four Distinguished Service Orders, seven Distinguished Service Crosses, one Conspicuous Gallantry Medal, two Distinguished Service Medals, one Bronze Star (USA) and eleven mentions in dispatches. Their mostly little-known stories provide a new World War II dimension to Australian submarine history.

X-CRAFT

In 1942-3 the Royal Navy developed a special class of miniature submarines known as *X*-craft. With a four-man crew, these vessels were designed to attack enemy shipping in port. The *X*-craft were just 48 feet in length and weighed 30 tons. They had a theoretical capability of 6.5 knots surfaced and five knots submerged and were designed to be towed — on the surface or submerged — to their targets. Lacking torpedoes, they were instead armed with detachable clockwork mines that could be released from inside the vessel or placed beneath enemy ships by a diver, allowing plenty of opportunity for the submarines and crew to escape before the blast. In practice, this all proved to be very difficult and dangerous, a situation worsened by the often unreliable operations of the craft, as well as their sometimes fatal buoyancy problems. Nine submariners were lost in these extremely hazardous operations, many of them in non-combat accidents.

The *X*-craft first went to combat in Operation Source, an attempt to sink the German battleship *Tirpitz* at her Norwegian base at Kaafjord in September, 1943. Submarines *X5* – *X10* were deployed, towed dived and surfacing every six hours to change crews. The tow of *X9* parted on the way to the target and two men were lost with the vessel. *X8* was also lost on the way to the attack. On September 22, the three remaining miniature submarines, *X5, X6* and *X7* did attack *Tirpitz,* causing substantial damage that delayed her deployment for some vital months, though all three submarines were lost during the action or afterwards. Over the next two years, the *X*-craft carried out other operations in Bergen harbor, off the French coast in preparation for the D-Day landings, and in the Pacific. Australian submariners were prominent in all these operations.

Lt Kenneth Robert Hudspeth RANVR had been a Hobart schoolteacher before the war and joined the RANVR in July 1940. He was in command of *X10* (known as *Excalibur*) during Operation Source, penetrating Alten Fjord and coming within four miles of the *Tirpitz* on September 22, 1943. Unfortunately the submarine developed mechanical troubles and could not be repaired, despite the efforts of her crew. Hudspeth was forced to withdraw but received the Distinguished Service Cross (DSC) for this exploit.

In January 1944 Hudspeth was in command of *X20* conducting reconnaissance off the French coast, for which he won a second DSC. The citation read, in part:

> *For outstanding courage and devotion to duty whilst commanding HM submarine X20 in a hazardous operation. He showed great coolness, grasp and ability in manoeuvring his X craft submerged in shallow water close*

under enemy defences during the first experimental beach reconnaissance from X craft in January 1944 ...

In a similar location later the same year, he received a third DSC 'for gallantry, skill, determination and undaunted devotion to duty....' As one writer described this event:

'More than 2500 Australians took part in the D-Day operation, in the air, on land, or at sea. Although no Royal Australian Navy (RAN) ships were present, Australian naval personnel, mainly members of the RAN Volunteer Reserve (RANVR), did serve in or command landing craft, coastal craft and warships of the naval force. One notable individual was Lieutenant Ken Hudspeth, RANVR, who commanded the X-Craft (midget submarine) X20. Prior to the planned departure of the invasion force X20 crossed the Channel to take up a submerged position off Juno Beach. On the night of 4 June X20 surfaced to pick up a BBC broadcast, which contained a coded message that the invasion was postponed. This meant another 18 hours in the cramped, smelly, humid submersible.

On the night of 5 June the coded message indicated the invasion was to proceed. Hudspeth and his crew mounted and checked their equipment. As the pre-invasion bombardment began they turned on their radar beacon and shone a light to seaward to allow the assault craft to navigate to the correct beaches.

For his part in the invasion Lieutenant Hudspeth was awarded a third Distinguished Service Cross. He had received the first award for his part in the attack on the Tirpitz in 1943 and the second in January 1944 for beach reconnaissance operations in preparation for the D-Day landings.'

Hudspeth is thought to have been the most highly decorated member of the Royal Australian Navy Volunteer Reserve.

Born in Melbourne in 1919, Ian Stewart McIntosh spent much of his childhood in the Western District. He was educated at Melbourne Grammar and Geelong Grammar. By all accounts he was not considered by his family or teachers to be a prospect for the navy but in 1937 he passed the entrance examination for the Royal Navy and travelled to England to attend Royal Naval College at Dartmouth. In 1940 he graduated first and qualified as a submariner.

McIntosh's first exploits were on the water rather than below it. At twenty-one years of age, he was aboard the converted troopship *Britannia,* torpedoed by the German raider *Thor* in early 1941. In a badly damaged lifeboat carrying eighty other survivors, McIntosh and the third officer of the *Britannia,* Bill McVicar, managed a harrowing twenty-three day survival voyage across almost 2500 kilometres of the Pacific Ocean. McIntosh's knowledge of Captain William Bligh's epic voyage of survival and a deep knowledge of navigation allowed him and McVicar take charge of the situation and to guide the lifeboat to Sao Luis in Brazil with almost perfect precision. Thirty-six people survived the ordeal. It is unlikely that any would have lived without McIntosh's skill and knowledge. He was awarded the MBE for his leading role in this 23-day epic of maritime survival.

After recuperation, McIntosh served in submarine *Porpoise* bringing supplies to the island of Malta and the following year joined *Thrasher* as First Lieutenant. After four patrols in *Thrasher* he was awarded the DSC. He commanded *H44* in 1942 and the following year took command of *Sceptre,* one of the submarines that towed the *X*-craft to Norway to attack the *Tirpitz.* McIntosh later towed Max Shean and the crew of *X24* to Bergen where a German merchant ship was sunk. *Sceptre* subsequently took *X24* south, where she sank the blockade-runner *Baldur* off the Spanish coast. While McIntosh was in command, *Sceptre* destroyed almost 15 000 tonnes of enemy shipping. He was twice mentioned in dispatches and in 1944 was awarded the DSO.

Macintosh's post-war career was a steady upward trajectory powered by his many talents, beginning with an involvement in the use of radar in submarines. The first to be fitted with the then-new device was *Alderney,* which McIntosh commanded before returning to Australia in 1948. As Lieutenant Commander he was loaned to the RAN and based near his home in Geelong. Congenial though this was, Australia's lack of a submarine capability caused his return to the UK in 1950 where he commanded *Aeneas* and subsequently was appointed 'teacher' for the 'Perisher' course. He went on to be, at various times, second in command of the carrier HMS *Ark Royal,* Deputy Director of Naval Equipment and, from 1961-63, commanded the 2nd Submarine Squadron. From 1963-1966 he was at the Admiralty where he eventually became Director of Naval Warfare.

He returned again to Australia in 1967 as commander of the carrier HMS *Victorious* and became Rear Admiral in 1968. In 1970 he was appointed CB and three years later became Vice-Admiral, being knighted in the same year. He finished this illustrious career in the role of Deputy Chief of Defence (operational requirements), retiring to a long period as a consultant, patron of naval charities and related activities. In one of these roles, a patron of the National Submarine History Task Force, McIntosh played a role in securing HMAS *Ovens,* now displayed at the Western Australian Maritime Museum in Fremantle.

Vice-admiral Sir Ian McIntosh died in 2003. He was eighty-three years old and had given seventy of those years to outstanding naval service in Britain and Australia.

A number of other Australians also served in *X*-craft in the European theatre.

Brian Mahoney 'Digger' McFarlane, a 'happy, short, fair man' was born in Cremorne, NSW, but apparently presented himself as a Victorian. He began his naval service as a Cadet Midshipman PNF in 1933. McFarlane was 'loaned' to the Royal Navy in 1937-1939, during which time he served on HMS *Hood* as well as a number of other British ships. By 1940 he had worked his way up to Lieutenant. He was one of the original *X*-craft trainees, among whom he was generally known as 'Mac', and was in command of *X8* which had to be scuttled in 1943 after her charges accidentally detonated. On February 7, 1944 McFarlane was in command of *X22* when she was being towed into Pentland Firth by *Syrtis*. In rough and stormy weather, *Syrtis* collided with *X24* and the submarine was lost with all hands.

Max Shean described Lieutenant Jack Marsden RANVR as 'a burly man of the world from South Australia', though he was born in Kalgoorlie on 10 July 1917. He was a sub-Lieutenant and subsequently Lieutenant in 1943. He served on HMS *Dolphin,* the Royal Navy training base at Gosport, and on HMS *Varbel,* the naval base on the Island of Bute in the Firth of Clyde where the *X* craft men had their initial training. Marsden was lost when *Syrtis* collided with *X24*.

Dr David Clements Jackson RANVR AM DSC was born in Brisbane in 1912 and was working as a trainee paediatrician in Birmingham at the outbreak of war. He joined the RANVR and then enlisted as a Medical

Officer in the Royal Navy in 1941. He was awarded the DSC for his medical service under difficult combat conditions in the engagement between HMS *Worcester* and several enemy ships in 1942. His citation reads:

> *"For daring and resolution in daylight attacks at close range and against odds on the German battle cruisers Scharnhorst and Gneisenau and the cruiser Prinz Eugen".*

As Medical Officer on HMS *Dolphin* from 1942-1944, he was involved with the *X* craft. David Jackson wrote two published books about his experiences, *The Six Horseshoes: Memoirs of a personal and professional life* (1987) and *One ship, one company*. (1996). He died in 2006.

Max Shean

Born in Perth in 1918, Max Shean joined the Royal Australian Navy Volunteer Reserve (RANVR) at the outbreak of war. He was then studying engineering at the University of Western Australia but in 1940 was called up for training, firstly at HMAS *Cerberus* and then at HMAS *Rushcutter,* where he was introduced to anti-submarine warfare techniques. From 1941 he served in the Royal Navy corvette *Bluebell,* mainly escorting Atlantic convoys. After fourteen months of this dangerous work, he volunteered for 'hazardous service'. This turned out to be serving in the highly experimental *X*-craft.

Max was involved in the attack on the *Tirpitz* in 1943 and was in command of *X24* in another raid on German shipping in Norwegian waters in April 1944. Known as 'Operation Guidance', the mission was to sink a floating dock in Bergen harbour. Due to poor intelligence and inaccurate charts, *X24* laid her charges on a large German merchantman, *Barenfels*. The ship was sunk and Max Shean was awarded a Distinguished Service Order (DSO).

In 1945 six *XE* craft, refinements of the earlier versions, were sent to Pearl Harbour to take part in the Pacific war. Admiral Nimitz of the Unites States Navy observed that they were 'suicide craft' and the Americans were reluctant to put them into operational roles until they discovered that the *X*-craft had a longer range than they assumed. The *XE* submarines went into training off the Queensland coast to prepare attacks on Japanese warships and on underwater telegraph cables. This would eventually be known as 'Operation Sabre', designed to cut the cables linking Tokyo with Singapore, Saigon and Hong Kong, an important communication channel for the Japanese high command. Special tools and techniques had to be developed for this unprecedented operation. After training in Hervey Bay, during which period two divers, David Carey and Bruce Enzers were lost in accidents. Max Shean was in command of *XE4* when the undersea cable was cut off the coast of French Indo-China (Vietnam) on July 31, 1945. Three days later the *X*-craft made it back to their depot ship *Bonaventure,* waiting for them at Brunei Bay. Max added a bar to his DSO and the United States of America awarded him a Bronze Star for severing the Japanese undersea communications. The other members of the crew were also decorated.

After the war Max completed his studies and worked in Western Australia as an engineer and remained in the RANVR until 1956. A keen sailor, he won the Open division of the Parmelia race from Plymouth to Fremantle in 1978, sailing his yacht, *Bluebell* single-handed, having already voyaged from Fremantle to reach the start. He wrote about his life and exploits in *Corvette and Submarine* (1992) and was a celebrated member of the submariner community until his death in June 2009.

Kenneth '(A)cid' Briggs was born in Glen Innes (NSW) in 1923. He enlisted in the RANVR in 1941 and saw service in Gibraltar and Operation Torch against Rommel, a precursor to the D-Day invasion. He received officer training and volunteered for submarine duty, which turned out to be in *X*-craft.

SLT Kenneth Briggs

Ken Briggs was aboard *XE4* on July 31, 1945, together with Max Shean, ERA V 'Ginger' Coles, Sub-Lt Ben Kelly RNVR and Sub-Lt Adam 'Jock' Bergius. Ken Briggs and Adam Bergius were the divers for the mission, which allowed divers to be out of the submarine at the expected operating depth for only very short periods. This brought the complement of the submarine from the usual four to a very cramped five. On that day, *XE4* and her crew were submerged off the mouths of the Mekong River in what was then French Indo-China, now Vietnam. They were dragging a grapnel across the seabed in an attempt to locate the vital telegraph cables. After several futile runs, described in Max Shean's book *Corvette and Submarine*, they finally located the southbound cable beneath sand and silt at a depth of fifty feet. At 1229 Ken Briggs left *XE4*, found the cable, cut it with the hydraulic cutters specially developed for the task and was back aboard by

1242, carrying a length of cable as evidence of his success. Adam Bergius RNVR then left the submarine at 1402 and, after several attempts, managed to sever the northbound cable and return by 1452. Ken Briggs and Adam Bergius both received the Distinguished Service Cross for their work. The citation for Ken Briggs' medal read:

> *For gallantry, perseverance and outstanding skill as a diver in HM submarine XE4, in successfully cutting the Singapore to Saigon cable, off St Jacques, French Indo-China on 31 July 1945. The operation was performed in water much deeper than expected and hampered by tide and rough weather (18 December 1945).*

The cutting of the undersea cable forced the Japanese to use radio for their communications. The Americans had already cracked the Japanese radio codes and so were now able to access information that had been unavailable when transmitted beneath the sea. *XE4*'s action that day provided information that was reportedly a factor in the decision to use nuclear bombs on Nagasaki and Hiroshima.

After the war, Ken married, started a family and lived in Perth for some years, working for the British United Shoe Machinery Company, which had supplied components for naval use during the war. Later he lived in Queensland and now lives in retirement in Brisbane.

A considerable number of other Australians also served in British submarines between 1939 and 1945.

Lieutenant Commander Don Wilson joined the RAN in May, 1940 after serving for three years in the Citizen Military Forces, or Militia. He underwent anti-submarine training, was commissioned as a Sub-Lieutenant and then seconded to the Royal Navy. He had the unusual experience of sailing to Britain aboard the same ship that had taken his father, a 13th Battalion Gallipoli veteran, to war in 1915. After serving in trawlers and the destroyer HMS *Whitshed,* Don transferred to submarines in January 1942. He completed an officer's submariner course and was given charge of ferrying the British-built submarine *Murat Rhys* to its Turkish owners. He served on HMS/M *P31,* based in Malta, where enemy bombing of the port was so intense they often had to submerge to carry out repairs.

After a bout of pneumonia, Don Wilson became second-in-command of HMS/M *Untiring.* On 14 December 1943, *Untiring* torpedoed a German minelayer in Monaco harbour. The explosion was said to have broken every window in Monaco and, as Don later joked: 'We were the man who broke the bank in Monte Carlo!'

Early in 1944 *Untiring* torpedoed a ship in Toulon harbour. *Untiring* was attacked and badly damaged from over three hundred depth charge explosions but was able to escape destruction through a thermal layer. Don Wilson's role in this action won him the Distinguished Service Cross for his 'courage, skill and devotion to duty'. In mid-1945 he was promoted to Lieutenant and given command of HMS/M *Voracious,* bound for the Pacific Fleet. The war ended shortly after and he commanded *Voracious* on a tour of Hobart, Melbourne and Brisbane. Donald Wilson was discharged in March 1946. He died in 2009, aged 92.

Lieutenant Commander Geoffrey Gellie was born in Euroa (VIC) on 22 September 1915. He enlisted in the RANVR in July 1939 as a Sub-Lt. He served in Royal Navy submarines during the war and was also in command of HMAS *Melbourne*. He commanded HM Submarine *Varangian* from May 1944 to August 1944 and also commanded the British World War I *H33* in 1944. He was the first RANVR officer to be given effective command of a submarine. Gellie retired in 1958 with the rank of Lt Commander.

Born in Ivanhoe (VIC) in 1920, Lieutenant Commander William Littlejohn was educated at Scotch College and Melbourne University, joining the RANVR as a Sub-Lt in (probably) 1940. He trained in anti-submarine roles then served in Royal Navy submarine depot ships and submarines from 1941, including *Tuna, Thrasher, Trusty* and *Shakespeare,* of which he briefly had acting command in 1944. He had command of HMS/M *Vox* in 1945 and became a Lt Commander in 1950, retiring in 1972. He was Honorary ADC to the Governor of Victoria from 1950 to 1968 and died in 1994 aged 74. He is buried in the Launceston Garden of Remembrance.

Lieutenant Dick Saunders was born in London in 1919, the son of Albert Frank and Laura Alice Saunders, of Cremorne, New South Wales, Australia. He was husband of Mary Howard Saunders, of Ascot, Berkshire, England. He joined the RANVR in 1939 and served in the Services Reconnaissance Department (SRD), a branch of the Special Operations Executive, also known in some contexts as 'Z Special Unit.' The SRD was established to carry out surveillance and missions in Japanese-occupied territory. Saunders commanded motor torpedo boats from 1942 and commanded HMAS *Nyanie* in 1945. He was awarded the DSC in 1942 for an attack on battle cruisers. Dick Saunders was killed in an unspecified action on December 13 1945 and is buried in Ambon War Cemetery.

Lieutenant C E Taylor joined the RANVR in December 1940 and by 1945 had served as First Lt in two Royal Navy submarines in the Aegean and Java seas. On 19 June 1944 he was Mentioned-in-Dispatches for skill and devotion to duty while First Lieutenant of HMS/M *Vivid* through 5 patrols in the Aegean and sinking four enemy ships.

Lieutenant Phillip Evatt was born in North Sydney in 1922 and joined the RANVR in 1940. In 1944 Lt Evatt was in command of HMS/M *Tapir* when she sank the German submarine *U-486* off Fejersen Fiord, Norway. Evatt won the DSC in 1945, the citation reading:

> *For exceptional skill, audacity and judgment while serving in HMS Tapir. He trimmed the submarine during a successful attack on a German U-boat in rough and difficult weather in which U-486 was destroyed by a salvo of torpedoes off Fejerson Fjord on the 12th April 1945 and for efficiency of a very high order in training the crew and for a generally high standard as an officer during 13 war patrols.*

He left the service in 1946 and went on to an illustrious career in law and public service, including heading the Royal Commission into the Use of Chemical Agents in Vietnam from 1983. Justice Evatt died in 2010.

Sub-Lieutenant John Ryder RANVR was born in Brisbane in 1920. He was educated at the Church of England Grammar School, Brisbane and took medicine at the University of Queensland. Ryder joined the RANVR in 1941 and served on HMAS *Rushcutter*, HMAS *Cerberus* and then in the Royal Navy. He was at Blyth submarine base in 1943 and in the same year aboard HMS/M *Trooper* as T/S/Lt when she was lost in the Aegean Sea, presumably to German mines around the Dodecanese islands on October 17.

Although not born in Australia, Captain George Hunt made Australia his home and was adopted by Australian submariners after a glittering career in the Royal Navy. He served in eleven British, Dutch and Polish submarines. He commanded HMS/M *Ultor* from late 1942 until October 1944 for seventeen patrols. In a total of 32 patrols *Ultor* sank 28 enemy ships. Hunt then commanded the *T* class submarine *Taku* and was promoted to A/ Lieutenant Commander submarine for a German *U*-boat and a later attempted ramming by the Italian ship *Sagitario* in 1942. Although the Italian damaged Hunt's submarine, *Proteus*, it did not sink her. In 2006, George recollected the aftermath of this incident with some satisfaction:

> *"After the Italians surrendered I tracked down the Sagitario sitting with a number of other Italian ships in Algiers.*
>
> *"I ordered a boat and went across to her. The ship's chief engineer pointed to a piece of our fin ... a souvenir on the bulkhead and said, 'we sank that submarine'.*
>
> *"I was able to tell him, 'oh no you didn't' ".*

George Hunt's World War II submarine exploits resulted in him being awarded DSO and Bar, DSC and Bar, and he was twice Mentioned-in-Dispatches. After the war his adventures continued both in surface ships and submarines. He commanded HMS *Ambush* when she went beneath the Arctic ice in 1947 and was Commander of the submarine Commanding Officers' Qualifying Course. He later served on aircraft carriers and an anti-submarine frigate and was honorary Commodore and Senior Naval Officer West Indies until 1958. He then became Chief of Staff to Flag Officer Submarines (FOSM) in 1959, retiring from the Royal Navy in 1963 as Director of Naval Equipment. He and his family migrated to Australia and settled in Brisbane, where he went on the RAN Emergency List. George Hunt was Patron of the Submarines Association Australia, Queensland branch and was made a life member in 1997. He died in 2011, aged 95.

These men, as well as a still uncertain number of other Australian submariners played significant roles in the 1939-45 conflict. While there were no Australian submarines in which to serve — other than the briefly Australian *K-9* (see box) — their experience and example provided an ongoing link between the earlier submarines and those of a new generation of craft.

K-9

Australia did, briefly, have a submarine during World War II. The Royal Netherlands Navy's *K-IX was launched in 1923* stationed in what is now Indonesia, escaped the Japanese advance in March 1942 and sailed to Fremantle. The Netherlands government gifted her to Australia as an anti-submarine warfare training vessel and in June 1943 she was commissioned into the Royal Australia Navy as HMAS *K9* commanded by Lt. F.M. Piggott RNR. Other officers and crew who subsequently served on *K*-9 were a composite of volunteers from the US Navy and the Royal Australian Navy, including Commodore Bryan Cleary RAN and Harry Churchill RAN. The submarine had already been damaged during the Japanese miniature-torpedo raid on Sydney Harbour earlier that month and her subsequent career was marked by accidents and unavailability of spares. She was decommissioned in March 1944 and again became a Dutch vessel, storing oil until she was washed ashore near Seal Rocks (NSW) when her line to the Dutch minesweeper towing her to Darwin parted in June 1945. The wreck and cargo of oil was subsequently sold for scrap. The wreck is something of a local feature and the beach where she lies has been renamed 'Submarine Beach'. The wreckage is intermittently revealed by tidal movements and was documented by marine archaeologist Tim Smith and a team from the New South Wales Heritage Office in 1999. The last time *K-IX* was uncovered seems to have been in winter 2001. Earlier that year a commemorative plaque was placed some kilometers north of the wreck site.

7
COLD WAR WARRIORS

After the end of World War II in 1945 the world quickly moved into the era known as 'the Cold War.' Tensions between the Soviet bloc and the western countries were fought out through land combat in Vietnam and Cambodia, while the need for undersea deterrence and intelligence gathering provided the motivation for the next generation of Australian submarines — the *Oberon* class. Australia would eventually have six '*Oberons*', as they were usually called — *Oxley, Otway, Ovens, Onslow, Orion* and *Otama*. These steel warriors of the cold war were to make vital contributions — some still classified — to strategic warfare in the region and beyond.

Built in Scotland by Scotts of Greenock, the *Oberons* were introduced from 1967. They replaced the Royal Navy's 4th Submarine flotilla operating in Australia between 1949 and 1969. The Royal Navy had decided to reduce its presence 'East of Suez' and would not replace those submarines when its 'T' class submarines retired. This caused the Commonwealth government to search for suitable vessels for Australian needs. The submarines eventually selected were advanced diesel-electric versions of the Porpoise class and designed for silent operations, abilities that were enhanced by extensive refitting programs throughout more than 30 years of service.

HMAS *Oxley* was the first submarine built for the Royal Australian Navy in almost forty years. She was commissioned in March 1967 by Lieutenant Commander D.H. Lorrimer RAN and arrived at HMAS *Platypus* in Neutral Bay, Sydney in August 1967. *Otway* was commissioned in April 1968 by

Lieutenant-Commander G.R. Dalrymple RAN and berthed in Sydney in October that year. *Ovens* and *Onslow* were both commissioned in 1969, *Ovens* under the command of Lieutenant-Commander B. Nobes RAN and *Onslow* under that of Lieutenant-Commander C. Nixon-Eckersall RN. They both arrived in 1970. Two further *Oberons* were ordered in the mid-1970s. *Orion* was commissioned in June 1977 under the command of Lieutenant Commander R.J.H. Woolrych RAN, arriving in July the following year. *Otama* was commissioned under the command of Lieutenant Commander F.V.R. Wolfe RAN in April 1978 and reached Sydney in December. The fourth attempt to establish an ongoing Australian submarine service had succeeded, with a squadron of six powerful and silent boats based at HMAS *Platypus* under the command of Captain Bill Owen. Subsequently, Lieutenant Commander Ian MacDougall would become the first Australian born commander of the Australian Submarine Squadron and also the first RAN submarine officer to achieve flag rank, Vice Admiral; Appointed Chief of Navy in 1991.

The *Oberons* were theoretically able to circumnavigate the world without refueling. Like the *AE1* and *AE2*, the *J*-boats and the first *O*-boats, they were sailed the great distances from Britain to Australia. Each had a surface speed of 15 knots and up to 19 knots submerged. They could dive to a safe depth of 180 meters and fire up to 22 torpedoes and, later in their careers, Sub-Harpoon missiles. At almost 90 meters long, the *Oberons* had a beam of just over 8 meters and a draught of just less than six meters. The submarines were fitted with a snorkel system — known as a 'snort' — that allowed their batteries to be recharged while submerged. This enabled them to remain underwater for extended periods. In combination with their various other technological innovations, this made the *Oberons* the best conventional submarines of their era, able to operate almost undetectably when beneath the water.

THE OBERONS

On New Year's Day 1969 the British Submarine Squadron officially changed its name to the First Australian Submarine Squadron. The six submarines that would come to make up the squadron were to have eventful careers over 35 years, as would their officers and crews. All the *Oberons* participated in trials, exercises and patrolling, punctuated by often-lengthy periods of maintenance and refitting. The first year of the squadron's operations would see a number of milestone events, as would the decades that followed.

In June 1969, Lieutenant Commander I D Roberts RAN took *Oxley* to sea, becoming the first Australian-born officer to command an *Oberon*. This was the start of a series of 'firsts' for the boat and her crews throughout *Oxley's* long career. Between 1977 and 1980, *Oxley* became the first *Oberon* to undertake the SWUP program in which the main attack sonar was replaced, a new passive ranging sonar fitted, and a digital fire control system installed capable of controlling Mark 48 torpedoes. In 1981 she was the first non-United States submarine to be certified proficient in the deployment of Mark 48 torpedoes. *Oxley* had a third major refit from 1985-1987 and was officially re-dedicated in June 1987. She was the first *Oberon* at the new HMAS *Stirling* submarine base in Western Australia, formally received there in 1987 though only permanently relocated there in 1988 as part of the Two Ocean Navy policy. *Oxley* won the Squadron Fighting Efficiency Shield in recognition of superior performance in 1987. For the 75th anniversary of the Gallipoli landings, the submarine attended at Anzac Cove and took part in the Dawn Service at Ari Burnu. *Oxley* then led the French, Turkish and British ships attending the event through the Dardanelles to the Sea of Marmora for a memorial service above the last-known location of *AE2*. That year, while docked in Taranto, Italy, the crew and Commanding Officer, Lt Commander Peter Earlam were invited to a private audience with His Holiness, Pope John Paul 11.

Oxley also took part in 49th anniversary commemorations for the Battle of Crete the same year, marking a little-known Australian submarine connection with the Crete campaign. At Prevelly in south-west Western Australia stands a Greek Orthodox church known as St John the Theologian chapel, built and opened in 1979 by Geoffrey Edwards as a grateful memorial to the Cretan priests and people. As a Corporal in the 2/11 Battalion, Geoffrey Edwards had been caught in the rapid German occupation of Crete in May 1941. Like many other soldiers he managed to escape and was cared for by the Cretan people and the monks of the Preveli monastery of St John the Theologian, a centre of resistance to the Nazi occupation of the island. Edwards and others were rescued by the Royal Navy submarine *Thresher* in August 1941. *Thresher* was under the command of Australian Ian McIntosh, a highly decorated sailor who became a Vice Admiral in the Royal Navy and was also knighted for his service.

After several more years of maintenance, trials, exercises and patrols mainly in south-east Asian waters, *Oxley* returned to HMAS *Stirling* for the last time in 1992, where she was decommissioned on February 13 after a quarter-century of service, travelling over 403 000 nautical miles and logging almost 55 000 hours underway. Her 18-tonne fin now stands near the Submarine Training Systems Centre at HMAS *Stirling*.

From her launching in 1966 to her decommissioning, *Otway* was in service for twenty-eight years. Like the other *Oberons,* she experienced a busy life of exercises and patrols, as well as participating in the major refitting programs that were an intermittent feature of the *Oberons'* experience. North of Middleton Reef in 1972, the boat was commanded by Lieutenant Commander T A A Roach. He and his crew rescued the crew of a ketch named *One and All.* This operation earned Chief Radio Supervisor Brian Coultas the British Empire Medal, while the Captain, the Executive Officer and an Able Seaman received Naval Board Commendations.

After decommissioning, the town of Holbrook received the submarine's fin. Holbrook's connection with submarines stems fro the First World War when a Royal Navy Lieutenant N D Holbrook commanding *B11* torpedoed and sank a Turkish battleship in December 1914. Holbrook won the first naval Victoria Cross for this action. In a moment of patriotic enthusiasm, the citizens of the town, then named Germanton, changed it to Holbrook in honour of the deed. A 1/5 scale model of B11 was placed in the town's park. Commander Holbrook died in 1976 and six years later his widow, Mrs Gundulu Holbrook, gifted his medals to the town. In 1995 the Royal Australian Navy gave *Otway's* fin to the town. A fund-raising campaign with a generous donation of $100.000 from Norman Holbrook's widow, then allowed the town to purchase a 90-meter section of *Otway*, which is now also on display in the town, forming an eye-catching memorial to all submariners.

Beginning in April 1970 when she joined a host of other vessels in Sydney to commemorate the 200th anniversary of Captain James Cook's landing on the east coast, *Ovens* had a busy life of multinational exercises. Five years after her launching, she became the first RAN submarine to contribute to the Five Power Defence Arrangements (FPDA) when she served with ANZUK forces in 1972. Her commanders included Lieutenant Commander (later Captain and Commander of the First Australian Submarine Squadron) B Nobes RAN and Lieutenant Commander I D G MacDougall. In 1969 Second Officer Jan Pickering joined Ovens, becoming the first woman to serve in an Australian submarine.

Ovens had the first of three major refits between 1973 and 1975, becoming the first *Oberon* to carry the long-range passive sonar system. This was followed by another updating of weapons and intelligence systems from 1980 to 1982 in which year she gained her Mark 48 torpedo certification. In 1985 she became the first *Oberon,* and so the first conventional submarine, to fire a sub-surface Harpoon missile near Hawaii, scoring a direct hit on a target over the horizon at the US Navy's Pacific Missile Range Facility. From 1987 to 1990, Ovens underwent a final major refit. The boat was awarded the Submarine Fighting Efficiency Shield in 1993 and, for the third time, the Mk48 Firing Proficiency Shield. *Ovens* was decommissioned at HMAS *Stirling* in 1995. Her operations in three oceans had taken her well over 410 000 nautical miles. *Ovens* is now the most popular attraction at the Western Australian Maritime Museum.

Named after the Western Australian town, *Onslow* performed thirty years of good service in the Australian Submarine Squadron. Her first commander was Lieutenant Commander C Nixon-Eckersall and his boat was well suited to intelligence work, mine laying, anti-submarine and surface warfare. *Onslow* 'sank' the largest US nuclear aircraft carrier during an exercise in 1978. It was recorded that 'The Americans were not amused.' During Exercise Kangaroo in 1980, *Onslow* successfully attacked seven surface ships without herself being 'sunk.' On returning to port, she flew the traditional submariners' 'Jolly Roger.' The following year saw an accident in which many of the crew suffered carbon monoxide poisoning, leading to the death of Able Seaman Christopher Passlow.

From 1982 to 1984 *Onslow* took part in the SWUP refits and had sonar, data processing and fire control capabilities upgraded. She visited the west coast of America in 1985. During the 1998 RIMPAC exercise, *Onslow* located and 'sank' the super carrier USS *Carl Vinson*. During her long career, Onslow won the 'Best Fighting Submarine' award six times. She is now on display at the National Maritime Museum in Sydney's Darling Harbour.

Under Lieutenant Commander R H Woolrych RAN, *Orion* was commissioned in 1977. She gave thirty-one years busy service as part of the First Australian Submarine Squadron. In 1987, *Orion* was the first submarine to be presented with the Gloucester Cup, an award for the most efficient RAN vessel over the previous year. Her commander between 1992 and 1994, Rick Shalders received the Conspicuous Service Cross.

After being docked for twelve years, *Orion* was environmentally decommissioned and broken for scrap in 2006. Interviewed for *Navy* magazine in relation to the decommissioning, Commander Shalders and WO Len Carr recalled their boat with affection. Len Carr voiced the feelings of all submariners on seeing their craft go out of service: 'Orion's last voyage under tow was a day of mixed emotions for those who served on her, because it was like watching a close friend being laid to rest.' After an extensive environmental cleanup and an unsuccessful plan to turn her into a museum or dive wreck, she was broken up and sold to China for scrap. Her port propeller was given to the Western Australian Maritime Museum and her fin to the Rockingham Naval Memorial Park.

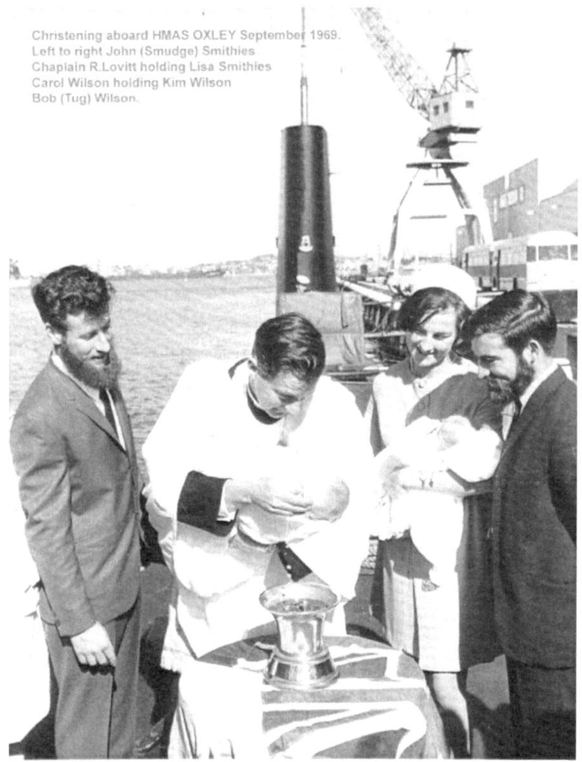
Christening aboard HMAS OXLEY September 1969.
Left to right John (Smudge) Smithies
Chaplain R.Lovitt holding Lisa Smithies
Carol Wilson holding Kim Wilson
Bob (Tug) Wilson.

Otama, the last *Oberon* to be launched was named after a North Queensland Aboriginal word for 'dolphin.' From the time she joined the Australian Submarine Squadron in 1978 to her final decommissioning in 2000, ,followed a similar busy schedule to the other *Oberons.* She was part of the Australia Squadron involved in a 5-vessel flag-showing exercise in the Indian Ocean in late 1980. This activity, including HMA Ships *Melbourne, Perth, Derwent, Stalwart,* and *Supply,* was said to have been the largest deployment of Australian naval craft since Word War 2. Known colloquially among *Oberon* submariners as 'the Gucci boat' due to the very high standard of internal fittings and design, *Otama* was the last *Oberon* to be upgraded through the SWUP process, completed in 1985. In August 1987, two of *Otama's* crew, Able Seamen Damien Humphries and Hugh Markrow, were lost in a tragic accident in heavy weather while securing a new hydrophone array for sea. *Otama*'s decommissioning had been planned for the late 1990s but was delayed due to teething problems with the new *Collins* class. Her subsequent career involved being sold to a Victorian community group hoping to use the submarine as a tourist draw card. The group was unable to gain the necessary council approvals for this activity and the submarine had the probably unique distinction of being offered for sale on E-bay. *Otama* was not sold and is now located in Victoria's Westernport Bay.

THE OBERON EXPERIENCE

Oberons rapidly demonstrated their suitability for the kind of strategic operations demanded by the cold war. Their stealth characteristics, continually enhanced during their lives, made them ideal for sophisticated intelligence gathering. At the same time, their advanced weapons systems gave them a deadly capacity should that be required. *Oberons* generally undertook six to eight week patrols. For much of this time they might remain submerged. Crew members were not encouraged to know the nature or location of their missions and the chart table in the control room was sometimes curtained off from casual inspection.

From the early *A*-class boats, submarines have always been at the forefront of technological innovation. As technical and strategic demands have become ever more sophisticated, so submarine design and maintenance has quickly adapted. While the *Oberons* — themselves a development of the earlier Porpoise class — were of an innovative design and fit-out, they fairly quickly came to need updating of their communications and weapons. In the early 1970s an upgrading program was designed and initiated by the RAN under the title 'Submarine Weapons Update Program' (SWUP). This involved a new digital fire control system, upgraded weapons, including Harpoon missiles, and a passive/active attack sonar system. All the *Oberons* were refitted along these lines from 1972 to 1981. For all the high-tech nature of the *Oberons*' gadgetry, much of this was done in the early days on an almost *ad hoc*, improvisatory basis. With assistance and equipment from the Royal Navy, *Orion* was fitted for its intelligence-gathering role before it left the United Kingdom.

All these enhancements were designed to improve the ability of the *Oberons* to undertake what became their main cold war tasks. In particular, the specially equipped *Otama* and *Orion* were known colloquially as the 'mystery boats', though the term has also been applied to all the *Oberons*. Their intelligence gathering operations up to 1992, when they were controversially suspended by the Australian government, have been — and still are — the subject of considerable speculation in the media and elsewhere. In an effort to contain what was then a powerful Soviet Pacific Fleet, *Oberons* conducted sensitive missions around the coasts of China, India, Vietnam and Indonesia — though remaining always outside territorial waters. The maneuvers performed during these operations involved recording soviet vessels on film and audio equipment in some extremely tense close-quarter undetected encounters known as an 'underwater look.' The information gathered in these exercises is assumed to have been required for any targeting of Soviet craft. *Oberons* also shadowed soviet submarines out of Vladivostok using a route through Australian waters that took them — undetected, they believed — to the Arabian Gulf.

While the details of political and strategic relationships between Australia, New Zealand, Britain and the USA remain unclear today, it is fair to say that the *Oberons* and their high-risk activities allowed Australia to be a vital element of the global strategic efforts of the time. The boats, their officers and crews also proved the viability and value of an Australian submarine service.

Oberon crews could exceed 70 submariners, five of them officers. They were crowded and uncomfortable craft, always smelling of diesel fumes. Work operated on six-hour shifts in two action-ready watches. It was sometimes necessary for the crew to share berths, with the same bunk being more or less continually occupied as men went on and off watch, a system known as 'hot-bunking.' Once on patrol there were no opportunities for contact with family or friends. In a 1978 media article a journalist was allowed aboard *Onslow* for two days. He reported on the cramped conditions, narrow bunks, large serves of food, as well as the self-discipline necessary within the crew. The journalist was given the experience of 'silent running.' All mechanical devices, including the air conditioning, were turned off to deaden any sound, together with matting laid on the floors. Snorting exercises were also carried out. While the snorkel sucked in air from above everyone's eardrums would pop from the change in pressure. The commander pointed out that it was important to take these exercises —

or 'evolutions' — seriously: 'After all', he said, 'there are only two types of ships — targets and submarines.'

In these circumstances, health was an important issue. In the early 1990s an investigation into the microbiological conditions on the *Oberons* was commissioned. The report, published in 1994, found that while there was a risk of atmospheric contamination by fungal spores and other 'pathogens, allergens and toxin producers to multiply' a satisfactory atmospheric quality could be achieved and maintained. The report also pointed to the level of chlorine gas due to the burning of oxygen candles being of 'concern.' Recommendations included thorough cleaning of fans and filters in galleys, regular cleaning of mattress covers and of the air conditioning units.

As *Oberon* submariners became due for pensions and other recognitions of their service they were dismayed to find that the Australian government did not consider their roles to have been in 'operational service.' Because they were classified as 'Special operations', *Oberon* personnel were effectively denied the acknowledgment of the nation they had served. After years of lobbying by many individuals and groups such as the Submariner's Association, the RSL and the SIA, the Veterans' Entitlements Act of 1986 was amended to state that 'A member of the Defence Force is taken to have been rendering operational service during any period of continuous full-time service…' if serving on submarine special operations between 1978 and 1992. Submariners meeting these criteria are also entitled to the Australian Service Medal with Clasp 'SPECIAL OPS.'

In his memoir recording the history of the *Oberons* up to 1988, the first Commander of the Australian Submarine Squadron Bill Owen wrote:

> *'These submarines are now, de facto, the navy's long range offensive strike force. This function may not have been formally assigned to them, but the mantle fell on them, with very little publicity, in 1983 — when the Navy's only aircraft carrier, HMAS Melbourne, was taken out of service without replacement.*
>
> *Given their remarkably low acquisition cost and the powerful deterrent value of a mix of 18 Harpoons and Mark-48s on board each submarine, Our Oberons must be seen as the most cost-effective assets in the nation's Defence inventory.*
>
> *They are the navy's quiet achievers.*

Owen argued that due to their original design and construction, together with the SWUP refits, the *Oberons* had an effective life of thirty years, taking the youngest, *Otama*, potentially up to 2008. A little over ten years later, all the *Oberons* had been scrapped as the new *Collins* class submarines came slowly into service.

8
THE COLLINS CLASS

Designed to replace the *Oberon* boats, the *Collins* class of submarines were to be the most advanced conventional long-range submarines ever built. Like the *Oberons* they would be diesel-electric. With greater stealth characteristics than nuclear powered vessels they were to continue the extended covert operations pioneered by the *Oberons* and have an offensive capacity. To achieve these aims, it was decided early that the weapons system would be specified by the Navy and developed in a separate but related suite of projects. This was a new approach, as was the decision to build the submarines in Australia.

Evolved from a Swedish design, the *Collins* class was a radical computerised design departure from previous vessels and their construction in Adelaide was an epic story of surmounting technical, logistic and other hurdles, again a feature of Australian submarine history. Although the submarines were delivered behind schedule, the average 26-month delay was relatively short by the standards of military hardware. Despite the complexity of their technology and the issues encountered in their building, the submarines were delivered at close to their original budget.

The first of the class to be built was HMAS *Collins*. Sir John Collins KBE, CBE, was a highly decorated World War II Captain of HMAS *Sydney* (II) and later Commander of HMAS *Australia* (II). He was among the earliest graduates of the Royal Australian Naval College to achieve a flag rank, that of Rear Admiral in 1947. Collins had a distinguished subsequent career, retiring in 1955 as Chief of Naval Staff. The submarine named for him was launched in August 1993 and commissioned into the RAN in 1996. She was approved for operational deployment in 2000. Unlike the other boats in the class, *Collins* was partially constructed in Sweden, but has the same operational capabilities as the other five boats, able to mount patrols for as long as 70 days and with a range of up to 20 000 kilometers. *Collins* was involved in successful testing of her capabilities with the United States Navy in 2000 and was also the first of the class to launch a Harpoon missile.

The second *Collins* class vessel was laid down in 1991 at the Australian Submarine Corporation's facilities in Adelaide and was the first submarine to be constructed wholly in Australia. She was launched as HMAS *Farncomb* four years later and commissioned in January 1998. The name was in honour of Harold Farncomb CB, DSO, MVO who commanded HMAS *Canberra* (1) in a number of significant engagements during World War II. Farncomb later became a Rear Admiral.

Despite some ongoing generator problems, *Farncomb* succeeded in sinking the decommissioned HMAS *Torrens* with a Mark 48 Mod 4 torpedo in 1999. Eight years later the submarine was engaged in a mission in Asian waters when her propeller became entangled in fishing lines, forcing her to surface. Five crew were washed into the sea in bad weather while trying to clear the obstruction, all eventually rescued by three other crew members. This incident was not widely-known outside the submariner community until 2009 when the rescuers were nominated for bravery awards. A link with the World War II generation of submariners was made in 2007. Max Shean of the *X*-boats fame was invited aboard for a day on a modern submarine. It was the first time he had been in a submarine since 1945.

Laid down in 1992, HMAS *Waller* was commissioned in 1999, having been launched two years earlier. The submarine was named for Captain Hector Waller, DSO and Bar, commander of the cruiser HMAS *Perth* (1) in 1942 when she was sunk in action against a Japanese convoy in what is often known as the Battle of Sunda Strait. *Waller* has been extensively involved with United States Navy war games and has performed with credit, both in attack and defence roles. Like the other boats in the class, *Waller's* armaments include Mk 48 Mod 7 CBASS torpedoes, sub-Harpoon anti-ship missiles and she also has the capability to lay Stonefish Mark III mines.

In 2008, *Waller* took part in the RIMPAC exercise in Hawaii, becoming the first to fire the Mk48 CBASS. The return journey was 'The Long Way Round' and the 'Long Way Down' passing through Kota Kinabula, Guam and Singapore. These visits provided opportunities to meet with submariners of other nations. By the time the submarine returned to Fleet Base West she had been away for 197 days. *Waller* berthed on November 29, being greeted by many friends and family — 'It was an emotional reunion for many', Lt Adam Masters reported in *The Trade*.

Captain Emile Dechaineaux, a Tasmanian, was in command of HMAS *Australia* (II) in October 1944 as part of the allied landings at Leyte, Central Philippines. A Japanese dive-bomber crashed into the ship and Dechaineaux died of wounds received from the ensuing fire. He was awarded the United States government's Legion of Merit (Degree of Officer). He gave his name to HMAS *Dechaineaux*, the fourth of the *Collins* class to be laid down. She was launched in 1998 and commissioned in 2001. A burst seawater hose brought the submarine close to a dangerous level in February 2003, leading to a reduction of the safe diving depth of all the *Collins* boats. *Dechaineaux* underwent a four-year refurbishment and returned to service in 2010 equipped with a new heavyweight torpedo developed in conjunction with the United States Navy.

The only Australian naval vessel to be named after a sailor, HMAS *Sheean* was laid down in 1994 and commissioned in 2001. Ordinary Seaman Teddy Sheean strapped himself to the aft anti-aircraft gun of HMAS *Armidale* (1) during an engagement near Timor in December 1942. As the *Armidale* sank from an aerial torpedo attack he continued firing at attacking Japanese aircraft, going down with the ship. *Sheean's* performance in exercises such as RIMPAC 02 showed that the *Collins* boats were effective in attack and defence roles, even against larger and more powerful craft. The RAN award for efficiency, the Duke of Gloucester Cup, was presented to *Sheean* in 2006. The boat went into maintenance cycle in 2008.

Lt Commander Robert 'Oscar' Rankin commanded the sloop HMAS *Yarra* (II) during convoy escort duties through the northern Indian Ocean early in 1942. A much superior Japanese force attacked and Rankin sailed the *Yarra* between them and the convoy. He was killed by enemy artillery. The last *Collins* submarine was named in his honour.

Laid down in 1995, HMAS *Rankin* was commissioned in 2003. *Rankin's* construction was delayed by the need to 'fast track' the building of *Dechaineaux* and *Sheean* and because parts were needed for other *Collins* submarines. Nevertheless, *Rankin* performed well in multinational exercises in 2003 and in 2005 was presented with the RAN efficiency award, the Gloucester Cup. The then Governor-General, the Duke of Gloucester established this award in 1947. It acknowledges excellence in operational efficiency, seamanship, supply and administration, officer and sailor training, maintenance and resourcefulness. Every Australian naval ship is evaluated for the award. *Rankin* was the first of the *Collins* class to win this recognition and the only submarine to win it since *Orion* in 1987. *Rankin* won the award again in 2008. The boat was the subject of an extensive SBS documentary screened in 2005, the patrol undertaken at that time being the then longest for a *Collins* submarine — 37 000 kilometers. This voyage took 126 days, during which *Rankin* was submerged for over 100 days. *Rankin* entered a prolonged period of maintenance in 2008.

The exact details of *Collins* class submarine deployments are mostly secret. Their range, extended underwater abilities and even their maneuvers indicate that their primary missions are surveillance of the vast waters around and beyond Australia. Their basing at HMAS *Stirling* in Western Australia is a result of the 'Two Oceans' defence policy. As Commander J

J Cupples said in a television interview with an ABC journalist aboard *Dechaineaux* in 2011 'The whole capability, the submarine capability is a covert one. That's how we do our business. And we've done a lot of great things over the years which you won't necessarily read about in the paper.' Just how far beneath the surface the *Collins* submarines can dive is classified but according to one commander they can go 'very deep.' A feature of the *Collins* boats has been the deployment of mixed-sex crews. The pioneer Australian female submariner had been in the *Oberons,* but in 1997 *Collins* and *Farncomb* each received six female submariners to test the viability of mixed-sex crews. The success of the trial led to the training of a female officer and eleven female crew the following year. Mixed-sex crews presented a challenge to the previously all-male culture of submariners, as well as practical issues in the cramped quarters aboard submarines. These challenges have been met and female submariners are now an accepted component of modern crews. It is also notable that Australia is one of the few submarine operating nations with mixed messing at all rank levels.

Interviewed aboard *Waller* in 2000 for *Navy News,* two of the three women among the crew said that they were happy to be aboard and that, as submariners, they had far more responsibility than they would have been given on a surface ship, or 'skimmer.' One woman said that she did not 'join the navy to be a male. I have never been harassed and I give as good as I get', though she did note that there was one disadvantage to working on a submarine — you could not ring in sick. Although mixed messing among first officers in mixed sex crews began around 2006-7, separate male and female accommodation arrangements were made available on every boat in 2011. By this time 44 of the Royal Australian Navy's 560 submariners were female.

Maintaining crew levels has been an ongoing challenge for the *Collins* class boats, as it often has been for Australian submarines throughout their history. In the current climate of economic boom, crewing has become especially difficult. The Navy has instituted an intensive recruiting and retention program as part of the New Generation Navy initiative. *Collins* crews are necessarily more specialised than previous generations of submariners, though it is still necessary for all crew members to know at least something of each other's jobs. Life aboard even a modern submarine is cramped, with low ceilings, narrow passageways and small sleeping areas. There are extended periods underwater and six-hour work cycles, a limited number of toilets and one shower a week.

These realities present an occupational and lifestyle challenge that few are prepared to meet. One commander reported spending only six weeks ashore during one twelve-month period. Despite these factors, the traditional bonding of submariners is still an important factor in retaining crews. In 2011 a journalist from the *Adelaide Advertiser* spent a day aboard *Dechaineaux*. He interviewed members of the crew and was told by Able Seaman Zack Pasterfield that 'Nothing compares with this job. I'm a fan of camaraderie — these guys are my family.'

In March 2010, then-Chief of the Defence Force, Air Chief Marshal Angus Houston told the Senate's Joint Standing Committee on Foreign Affairs, Defence and Trade that there were 468 people in the submarine force and he expected this to increase to 500 by the end of the year, allowing the establishment of a fourth crew.

Over the course of the *Collins*' life there have been numerous reports and inquiries. In 1999 an investigation for the Minister of Defence by Malcolm K McIntosh and John B Prescott addressed the identified issues with the submarines. As well as the technical and resourcing matters, the report noted that 'All major projects, both civil and military, of the scale and complexity of the submarines have design defects and other problems, sometimes on a comparable scale.' The report went on to note that '... the Submarine Project has been subject to leaks and public vilification on an unprecedented scale.' The report was concerned that sensitive details of the *Collins* class noise profiles were 'the subject of widespread public speculation ...'

A number of Parliamentary Research Library papers were produced on different aspects of the *Collins* controversy in 2001-2002. The Australian National Audit Office has conducted a detailed review of the financial aspects involved and in 2009 a Defence White paper was issued outlining the current state of Australia's military capacities and plans for future developments. Submarines were an integral element of these plans, including the building of the next generation of submarines to replace the *Collins* class:

> *The Government is determined to respond decisively to deficiencies in the current availability of operationally ready submarines. The Navy will embark on a major reform program to improve the availability of the Collins class fleet, and will also ensure that a solid foundation is laid for the expanded future submarine force. These reforms will change how we attract, remunerate, train and manage the submarine workforce, and improve the deployment and maintenance of the submarines.*

The white paper also noted that:

> *The Government has also agreed to further incremental upgrades to the Collins class submarines throughout the next decade, including new sonars, to ensure they remain highly effective through to their retirement.*

The controversies around the current *Collins* class submarines are in many ways an echo of the history of all Australian submarines from *AE1* and *AE2*. The Australian public has always been interested in submarines, an interest reflected in extensive media coverage and speculation. The technical aspects of design, construction and operation have usually been widely debated, not only within the Navy and the government of the day but also in the broader community. The necessity for secrecy about many aspects of submarine design, weaponry and operations has also been continual. In the case of the *Collins* class, these debates and speculations have often involved negative media depictions of the *Collins* boats. Difficulties with crewing have also been a frequent element of Australian submarine history.

While these debates have raged, a number of more dispassionate reports and other publications have shown that among submariners there is a very different appreciation of the situation, based on a deep understanding and experience of the issues involved. In August 2011, the then-Minister for Defence ordered a review of the *Collins* class submarines. Headed by John Coles, the review produced an interim report in November 2011 that highlighted the complexities and difficulties of the situation. These included issues of human resources and available technical expertise.

While few would argue that the *Collins* boats have been without technical, operational, financial and political difficulties, the story of their conception, execution and deployment from 1978 is one of unique achievement in Australian — and arguably world — submarine history. The lessons learned from the experience will provide a solid foundation for the next generation of Australian submarines already in development.

COLLINS CLASS – WASHING DAY

9
SUBMARINE FUTURE

The next generation of Australia's undersea force does not yet have a class name. Known officially as 'Future Submarines', there will be twelve of them — possibly more if required. They will be, according to the 2009 Defence White Paper, 'assembled' in South Australia in 'a major design and construction program spanning three decades' — 'Australia's largest ever single defense project.' They will be sophisticated technologies of construction, capability and endurance 'to be able to undertake prolonged covert patrols over the full distance of our strategic approaches and in operational areas.' They are expected to have a life cycle well into the 2050s and, in all likelihood, beyond. The job that they are expected to do is outlined in the White Paper:

> *In the case of the submarine force, the Government takes the view that our future strategic circumstances necessitate a substantially expanded submarine fleet of 12 boats in order to sustain a force at sea large enough in a crisis or conflict to be able to defend our approaches (including at considerable distance from Australia, if necessary), protect and support other ADF assets, and undertake certain strategic missions where the stealth and other operating characteristics of highly-capable advanced submarines would be crucial. Moreover, a larger submarine force would significantly increase the military planning challenges faced by any adversaries, and increase the size and capabilities of the force they would have to be prepared to commit to attack us directly, or coerce, intimidate or otherwise employ military power against us.*

The White Paper recognises that there will be a need to develop and extend partnerships with other nations, in particular the United States 'to continue the very close level of Australia-US collaboration in undersea warfare capability.' The *Collins* class vessels and their crews have already had extensive training and other contacts with the United States Navy. In 2007, six American naval personnel were stationed aboard *Waller, Rankin* and *Collins* as part of the joint USN and RAN Armaments Cooperative Program for development of the Mk 48 CBASS torpedo and the installation of new fire control systems aboard the *Collins* boats. An Australian submariner was stationed with the American Pacific Fleet Submarine Force. These connections are set to continue through the 'Two Oceans' defence policy and the orientation of strategic and economic resources in the Indian as well as the Pacific Ocean. These alliances represent a change in the traditional linkages between the United Kingdom and Australian submarines and submariners. Australian submariners will continue to crew conventional vessels, while the USA and UK run only nuclear submarines. Diesel-electric powered submarines are capable of more covert operation than nuclear vessels. For this reason, Australian submarines are likely to be deployed in these roles, in conjunction with the United States and other allies, for the foreseeable future.

Who will sail the future submarines of Australia? In his address to the Submarine Institute of Australia Conference in 2008, Captain Peter Scott noted that 'In a warfighting sense, the submariners are the submarine. Well equipped, well trained and well led, they are capable of anything ....' This observation reflected the recognition that submarines are operated by people and that, regardless of their technological complexity and military attributes, they are machines. They cannot do their work without trained and committed men and women to officer and crew them. The situation was the same when Australia commissioned *AE1* and *AE2*, as it was with the *J*-boats, with *Oxley* and *Otway* and with the *Oberon* and *Collins* classes. As it always has, the unique demands of the submariners' duty require individuals with rare temperaments. The ever-evolving technological complexity of submarines means that submariners need ever-more specialised skills. The main challenge for the future of Australian submarines is not the technologies and resources to design and build them, but finding the people to run them. The reform strategies already embarked upon by the Navy in relation to submarines 'will change how we attract, remunerate, train and manage the submarine workforce.'

Submariners are a group with an extremely strong sense of identity that goes well beyond occupational comradeship or even the *esprit de corps* of military life whether in peace or war. The unique skills, attitudes, values and demands of the work they do and of the environment in which they do it have forged camaraderie probably unparalleled, except perhaps by astronauts. It is a camaraderie that extends beyond nationality and embraces the submariners of every other country, past, present and future. None but other submariners can know the experience of diving deep beneath the waves in tubes of steel, fibreglass and technology, each one totally dependent upon the other for a safe return to the surface. The ethos of the submariner is based upon these factors and remains strong even when they leave the sea and take up other occupations. Different though the future submarines will be in terms of sophistication and technology, the necessary characteristics of submariners evolved over the previous generations will remain much the same.

As the Australian submarine service celebrates its centenary, the Australian Defence Force is preparing the next generation of submarines. Even by the high technological standards of the *Collins* class, these vessels will be sophisticated and complex machines requiring many advanced skills to sail them. It is envisaged that they will be built and maintained in Australia, creating an unprecedented civil and military industrial capability that should keep Australia at the forefront of submarine warfare for many decades. Their design, construction and operation will be challenging. But Australian submariners are well equipped and prepared to meet those challenges, just as they have met and surmounted so many others over a century of silent service.

SUBMARINES ASSOCIATION OF AUSTRALIA (SAA)

This body was formed in 1937 on the model of the Submarine Old Comrades Association in the United Kingdom. The association is a national body with branches in all states and territories with the exception of the Northern territory. It assists with the welfare of submariners, runs social events, a publication 'Up Periscope, and holds an annual reunion at the Submarines Association Australia Conference, or SUBCON. It is the second oldest submarine association in the world.

10
THE NEXT CENTURY OF AUSTRALIAN SUBMARINES

Submarines have played a significant albeit silent part in Australia's history over the last 100 years. They have grown to occupy a position of strategic importance in response to Australia's need to become more self-reliant as it matures as a country.

Over the century, submarines have exercised significant influence at critical turning points in our national journey. That this influence is not widely known rests on the nature of submarine business in peace or war, which is usually unable to be reported until some considerable time after the event (at least 30 years in some cases, and never in some others).

SUBMARINE FORCE IN THE SOUTH WEST PACIFIC – A BENCHMARK IN AUSTRALIA'S MARITIME DEFENCE

From 1942 to 1945, Fremantle and Brisbane hosted a substantial number of United States, Netherlands, and later British submarines while those boats conducted the most successful submarine operation in history. Fremantle became the second largest (Pearl Harbor was the largest) submarine base in the world. These submarines accounted for some 70% of Japanese naval and merchant shipping during the Second World War.

The operations of the Allied submarines have become a benchmark for the Maritime defence of Australia. The primary effect of the submarines was to cut the Japanese supply lines so that the Japanese forces found it impossible to fight and hold the ground they had gained so quickly in 1942.

LESSONS FROM SOWESPAC

Several lessons were learnt in these operations that continue to be relevant today:

- Fremantle, and Brisbane are strategically more important bases for Australian submarine operations, and if the centre of gravity of the action is north or west of Papua New Guinea, then Fremantle is the optimum base. This is why the Australian submarine base is in Garden Island in Western Australia.
- The USN submarines were larger (2400 tonnes dived, four diesel engines, air conditioning and a crew of 70-85), than the British and Netherlands submarines (1500-1000 tonnes dived, two diesel engines, built for the North Atlantic, no air conditioning and a crew of 30 to 45). The USN submarines enjoyed much greater freedom of action and were able to operate in all areas in the region.The British and Netherlands submarines on the other hand were unable to operate very much further north than Singapore, and found themselves in much more disadvantageous patrol areas.
- The larger boats enjoyed other advantages. Four engines allowed redundancy for maintenance. Air conditioning meant that the crews got reasonable rest when off watch. Larger crews allowed more flexibility and less fatigue. Less fatigue made for safer and more alert submarine practice.
- The Indonesian Archipelago, the Philippines, Malaysia, Singapore, Papua New Guinea, and the Islands of the South Pacific provide a barrier through which our trade must pass, and through which Australia wishes

to exercise influence. To be effective that influence needs to be exerted at a point on the side of the barrier opposite to the Australian side — on the northern side of the barrier. If one allows the opposing influence to penetrate the barrier the Australian problem is infinitely greater. In WWII Allied submarine patrols in the barrier were expensive and difficult. No patrols were attempted south of the barrier as none of the submarines had the speed to catch up with the target. The most effective patrols were north of the barrier.

LESSONS FROM THE O-BOATS

The RAN *O*-boat era extended from 1968 to 1998. Among the successes of this period were the Submarine Weapons Update Program for the *Oberon* submarines, the strengthening of the Intelligence, Surveillance and Reconnaissance (ISR) capability and development of an operations and maintenance regime that sustained quite high availability against a back ground of reducing support from the *Oberon*'s "parent navy".

It was in this period of its life that the Submarine Force learnt that it had to be self-reliant.

LESSONS LEARNED FROM COLLINS

Construction in Australia of the *Collins* class from the late 1980s marked a very significant and progressive step in the Australian submarine capability. Australia knew that it would be continuing to operate diesel electric submarines at very long range in a very demanding environment.

There have been some harsh and very helpful lessons from the *Collins* program.

- Engines that might have survived in the short-range environment of the North Atlantic are no match for the very demanding conditions of Australian submarine operations.
- The experiment to operate the boats on a minimum manning standard failed — as it should have. The submarine operations in the South West

Pacific demonstrated the imprudence of that idea. Fatigue is the most insidious of challenges faced by a submarine crew, and in the period 1995 – 2005 submariners voted with their feet.

- There is always a lot Australia can learn from European, British and US submarine operators and designers. In the last 50 years, however, it has been Australian submariners and Australian industry that have maintained the effectiveness of Australian submarines. Australia should not discount its own very significant depth of knowledge in this field.
- Sovereignty is an important part of the submarine capability. If there is not an enthusiasm at the highest level in Government to "own" and use the submarine capability, the capability loses its effectiveness and value.
- The *Collins* program stimulated the creation of some highly capable Australian companies and it caused other companies to "lift their game" in order to enter the submarine support market.

THE NEXT 100 YEARS

Australia is in a unique position in time and in geography. It is enjoying economic growth at a time when many nations are experiencing recession. This growth is largely attached to the growth of the new superpowers, China and India.

Australia's trade and therefore its income are almost totally reliant upon safe sea lines of communication. The lessons of the past 100 years have taught Australians that submarines make a unique and powerful contribution to their country's capacity to protect its sea lines of communication and to influence events in its region.

The Royal Australian Navy has learnt a lot about submarines. In the past fifty years the complexity and effect of its submarine operations place it comfortably among the top five submarine operators in the World. No other nation operates sophisticated diesel electric submarines continuously at such long range from their base.

As a consequence the RAN can be very confident that it has established some fundamental and enduring principles in relation to submarines as follows:

- A single submarine can have a vastly disproportionate effect on the strategic environment, demanding enormous effort from its opponents.
- Submarines operating in Australia's interests are most effective employed at very long range from their home base.
- The nature of their operations is amongst the most demanding of any submarine operation in the World.
- Complex and demanding submarine operations conducted at very long-range place very heavy demands on the material capability of the submarine (especially the propulsion train) and the stamina and skill of its crew.
- On the occasions that submarines have been required to act in Australia's interest they have been devastatingly effective, and required very few people for that effect.
- While the sea remains opaque submarines will enjoy the advantage of surprise.
- No other country builds the submarines that meet Australia's requirements and therefore Australian industry is a fundamental input and element of this capability.
- The experience and knowledge gained by Australian submariners and their supporting industry in the last 100 years is unique and very important.

The last 100 years of history inform Australians that their submarines will be their primary vehicles of strategic influence for the next 100 years.

Peter Horobin MBE RAN (Rtd)

APPENDIX 1

SUBSUNK

HMAS AE1
14TH SEPTEMBER 1914

TABLE OF CONTENTS

Executive Summary

1. This document summarises the collective work of a number of volunteers who have worked cooperatively to assess the range of possible scenarios that could have led to the loss of HMAS *AE1*, with a view to identifying primary, secondary and tertiary search areas. [2.1]

2. *AE1* was one of the first batches of E class submarines built 1911 to 1913. Her predecessors, the D class, were the first submarines designed by the Admiralty with saddle tanks containing external main ballast tanks. The E class were significantly larger at 800 tons displacement dived, fitted with two eight cylinder diesel engines for power on the surface and to charge the two battery banks; the batteries powered two electric motors when dived. Vickers Ltd, now BAE Systems, built *AE1* and *AE2* at Barrow in Furness, UK during 1913. [3.3]

3. The design was robust, with good sea keeping qualities, reserve of buoyancy and stability. [3.1] This was the infancy of the submarine as a weapon system, so the E class contained a number of firsts for British submarines; the first to be fitted with Wireless Telegraphy (WT) sets for transmitting and receiving messages on the surface [3.6], gyrocompasses [3.4], (a great improvement on the magnetic compasses fitted to earlier classes) and the first (and last) fitted with broadside torpedo tubes firing on either beam. [3.2.7] Some things however, remained unchanged — there were minimal creature comforts for *AE1*'s crew of 3 officers and 32 men.

4. The surfaced passage to Australia in early 1914 was a world record for submarines at the time. It was particularly arduous and very demanding on the crew who made frequent repairs to the main engines; engine clutches, and in *AE2*'s case, changed two propellers en route. They were under their own power for more than two thirds of the 12,000 nautical miles from Portsmouth to Sydney.

5. After a docking in Sydney in June, the submarine refit and crew rest were truncated by the onset of war in August 1914. *AE1* and *AE2* sailed from Sydney in late August to join the Australian Fleet dispatched to take over German New Guinea. The colony was centred on the town of modern day Rabaul. [5.1]

6. Following a successful Fleet entry into Rabaul on 11th September and the surrounding anchorages, naval landing parties and troops were landed to take over the colony and disable the WT station being used to support the activities of the German Pacific Squadron. [5.7] The principal heavy ships — the armoured cruisers SCHARNHORST and GNEISENAU, remained unlocated. *AE1* and *AE2* were ordered to patrol the southern approaches to Rabaul to guard against these ships attacking the Australian Fleet's anchorages.

7. *AE2* and HMAS YARRA undertook the first patrol on Sunday, 13th September 1914. Contrary to orders *AE2* to did not arrive back until after dark, (sunset was at 1750) and received a public rebuke from the Admiral for their tardiness. [5.4] It was during this patrol that late in the afternoon YARRA sighted an unidentified steamer off the

south coast of Duke of York Island. The Commanding Officer's declared intention to investigate was countermanded by RADM Patey, possibly because of the need to have YARRA available for other duties.

8. *AE1* was directed to undertake the second patrol on Monday 14th September in company with HMAS PARRAMATTA. [5.5] *AE1* had a significant defect on the starboard shaft. [3.5] We assess that this defect arose from a defective starboard main engine clutch – *AE1* had experienced numerous failings of this clutch on the passage to Australia. Whilst her technical staff was familiar with dismantling and fixing the clutch, they would have required external workshop support to manufacture replacement toggle bolts to refit the clutch. On the delivery trip from Singapore, HMAS SYDNEY had twice manufactured these. From an exchange of signals between SYDNEY and the engineering staff supporting *AE1* from the depot ship SS UPOLU, we assess that SYDNEY once again carried out this task and transferred the bolts to UPOLU during the course of 14th September. [3.5.3]

9. Full power was available on the surface from both diesels; however, the starboard shaft would be unavailable for going astern on the surface and completely unavailable when dived. This was a significant defect and we find it extraordinary that *AE1* undertook a potentially hazardous war patrol in this condition, particularly as *AE2* was available and serviceable. [3.5.4]

10. *AE1* sailed at 0700 in the morning of the 14th and received a reminder from the Admiral to be back by dark. We assess this instruction so directly given would have been a significant factor in *AE1*'s decision-making later in the day. [5.5.4]

11. After rendezvousing with her consort and a brief exchange of signals about orders for the day, *AE1* and PARRAMATTA parted company; PARRAMATTA headed south to the ordered patrol line off Cape Gazelle. *AE1* was the senior officer of the two, and apparently without further explanation, headed off to the northeast, contact was soon lost. [5.5.4]

12. Later in the day, PARRAMATTA turned northwards from her patrol line off Cape Gazelle in an endeavour to relocate *AE1*. She reported that at 1430 she was 'close to the submarine' in a position two miles to the east of Duke of York Island. Visibility was reported at five nautical miles in an afternoon haze, common in this part of the world. [5.5.2]

13. It is not apparent how PARRAMATTA was able to relocate *AE1*. In one report, Rear Admiral Patey indicates that they were exchanging signals by WT. This probably would have required *AE1* to have rigged her WT mast on top of the conning tower and strung up the aerials. This was not only a time-consuming and difficult task for the small crew, but most significantly, would also have prevented *AE1* from diving – not a suitable arrangement for an encounter with the enemy. None of the signals reported by PARRAMATTA to have been passed between the two ships was recorded in any other vessel in the Fleet, tending to suggest that instead of WT, flashing light, or megaphone were used. Use of WT communications by *AE1* remains one of many unknowns, but we consider it unlikely.

14. PARRAMATTA moved away, turning back at 1520 after losing sight of the submarine and *AE1* was not seen again. PARRAMATTA assumed that she had headed for Rabaul (Simpson Harbour) and herself turned north, circumnavigating Duke of York Island before anchoring off Kokopo (Herbertshohe) on the southern side of Blanche Bay, several miles south of Rabaul for the evening. [5.5.2]

15. *AE2* was awaiting the return of her sister ship; arrangements had been made to repair the defect on the starboard shaft that evening. At 2015 Lieutenant Stoker, the Commanding Officer of *AE2*, raised the alarm.

'**8:15 pm** *HMAS AE2 to HMAS AUSTRALIA Submit had AE1 a destroyer scouting with her today. She has not yet returned to harbour'* (HMAS AUSTRALIA signal log 14th September 1914).

16. After checking with PARRAMATTA and conferring with Lieutenant Stoker, the Admiral ordered a search. [5.6]

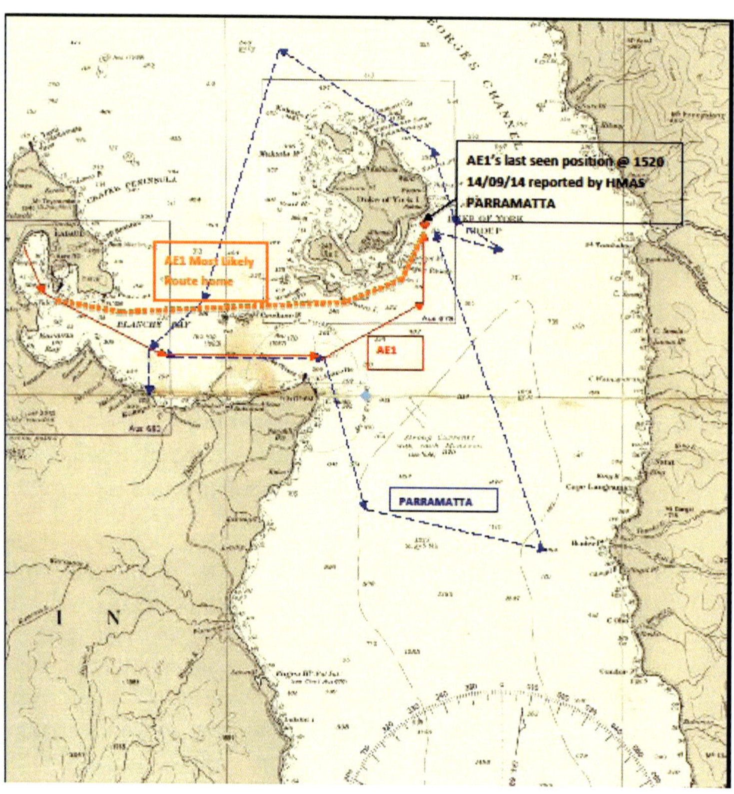

Figure 1 – *AE1* & HMAS PARRAMATTA's estimated tracks during the patrol on 14th September 1914.

17. PARRAMATTA sailed at 2320 and was joined by YARRA. Together, these ships, using searchlights and flares retraced *AE1*'s potential course back to Rabaul, passing to the east of Duke of York Islands anticlockwise, with PARRAMATTA then searching out to the north-west for some 30 miles and YARRA to the west coast of New Ireland, in the hope of finding *AE1* floating disabled on the surface. They were joined by HMAS ENCOUNTER at first light on the 15th, (circumnavigating Duke of York Islands S and E about) until 1045 when she returned to anchor in her role in support of landings ashore. ENCOUNTER reported an oil slick but no other sightings. The oil slick subsequently dispersed and was believed at the time to have come from one of the passing ships, no precise location for the slick was recorded. HMAS WARREGO also joined the search for a brief period on the 15th. YARRA entered Mioko harbour at 1300 to search and ran aground on an uncharted rock while leaving via the NW passage. Motorboats were used to search the shoreline of Duke of York Island and the coastline of New Ireland nearby. [5.6]

18. In a brief period of several hours, AE 1 had vanished, without leaving any trace, debris, bodies, distress message, or persistent oil slick. The local people have a handed down story of a 'monster' (a submarine?) that approached their location in a cave on the southern side of Mioko Island, the western entrance to Mioko Harbour, situated on the southern side of Duke of York Island. The 'monster' approached the reef stopped and then moved away to the north-east before disappearing. It is time stamped and bracketed by two stories; one recalling ENCOUNTER's bombardment of German shore positions on the morning of the 14th and an 'evil spirit' that rose like a small ball of fire out of the sea — one of the flares fired by the searching ships on the evening of the 14/15th September?

19. We have endeavoured to assess a range of scenarios explaining *AE1*'s disappearance against these largely negative clues. [6.6] What follows is knowledgeable supposition, weighing the balance of probabilities, not certainty or fact. We simply do not know.

20. The St George Channel/Blanche Bay area was under the influence of the southeast monsoon that blows regularly at this time of the year. As a result, there is strong current flowing through St George's Channel towards the northwest at speeds of up to three knots. This very large body of water is channelled upwards from the very deep waters of St George's Channel by the rapidly shoaling waters in the approaches to Duke of York Island and hits the near vertical faces of the surrounding reefs near Mioko Island. First-hand accounts describe the water boiling in a maelstrom as it endeavours to make its way around the obstruction. The current separates into two main streams, flowing NNE then NNW along the eastern shore of Duke of York Island and the second to the W/NW between Credner and Kabakon Islands. Some flows through the narrow entrance between the reefs into Mioko Harbour (in combination with the tidal stream), exiting from the NW entrance. [6.5.1]

21. We assess that on the balance of probabilities, *AE1* deviated from her orders on the 14th in order to investigate YARRA's sighting made the evening before, of a steamer near Duke of York Island, believing it to be a German vessel. We think it is most likely that *AE1* departed from the last seen position given by PARRAMATTA to return to Rabaul

at about 1530; the trip would have taken two hours and 25 min, giving her a little time to spare before arriving at sunset at 1750. En route she may have been tempted to approach the entrance to Mioko Harbour to check for any sign of the steamer. [6.6.2]

22. This would be a dangerous course of action for *AE1*; the sun, setting low in the west would be reflected off the water, making off-lying reefs and outcrops difficult, if not impossible for observers on *AE1*'s low bridge to see. The current and south-easterly wind combining to push *AE1* towards the danger of the reefs, the several minutes taken to stop the diesels, declutch the port diesel, engage the port electric motor (the starboard motor was not available, believed to be due to the faulty main engine clutch), to obtain astern power and time then taken to stop the submarine compounded the hazard. [6.5.1]

23. *AE1*'s command team were inexperienced in independent operations and in operating in tropical reef areas. By today's standards, they had had minimal operational training as a command team, such training did not exist – submarines were in their infancy and a war was on the way! It therefore seems likely that they may well have unwittingly placed themselves in a position of danger by approaching too close to the reefs of Mioko Island.[5.1]

24. In this situation it is easy to imagine them being set by the current beam on to a reef outcrop in a sliding impact due to the headway still on the submarine, an impact that cut through the thinner plating on the external ballast tanks situated in the saddle tank on one side of the submarine. These tanks would then partially fill with water, causing the submarine to list heavily, making it difficult for the crew to retain their positions and manoeuvre the submarine clear of the ongoing danger. The flooded tanks would also reduce *AE1*'s reserve of buoyancy and stability. With the dangerous reefs still in close proximity, reduced astern power and manoeuvrability (because of the defect on the starboard shaft) and difficult conditions for the crew, the submarine was then very vulnerable to any further factors that reduced stability or reserve of buoyancy. [6.6.3.9]

25. We assess it is most likely that a further such factor intervened; perhaps a breach in the pressure hull at the bulkhead encasing the annulus in the pressure hull that accommodated the broadside tubes that may well have absorbed much of the force of the grounding(s), perhaps a jammed helm, perhaps a further impact with a reef outcrop, pinned there by the current, perhaps a failure to restore full buoyancy following a trim dive earlier in the day. We don't know, but we assess that a further combination of factors sufficed to cause a loss of buoyancy and/or stability, sending *AE1* to the bottom. It is possible that the crew managed to shut the conning tower hatch; although this would have been difficult given the list and rapidly developing situation. [7.1]

26. We considered a range of other scenarios; bow on grounding, dived grounding, run down by a surface ship or sunk in action with an armed German steamer. All of them are possibilities but none fitted the limited facts as well, none passes the 'sanity check' as highly. [6.6] All scenarios are discussed in the body of the report.

27. Our conclusion is the same as Commander John Foster RAN Rtd, whose dogged research and dedication precedes our efforts and stands as an example to us all. We are

of the view that *AE1* was likely lost due to grounding on a navigational hazard in the Mioko Harbour region.

28. From this analysis, we are able to recommend a search area that takes account of the likely grounding area, direction of drift as the submarine settled on the bottom and impact of the bottom topography on the final position. [7.2] The primary area is about 5 Sq NM of which 15-20% is deeper than 300 metres. The secondary area is approximately 62 Sq NM of which about 87% is deeper than 300m. The tertiary area is approximately 40 Sq NM of which about 78% is deeper than 300m.

29. We note that, irrespective of whether the loss of *AE1* was due to a navigational error as we conclude, or by enemy action – sunk by the KOLONIALGESELLSCHAFT, as we discount — there would be considerable overlap of the likely location of the loss, which adds weight to the recommended search areas.

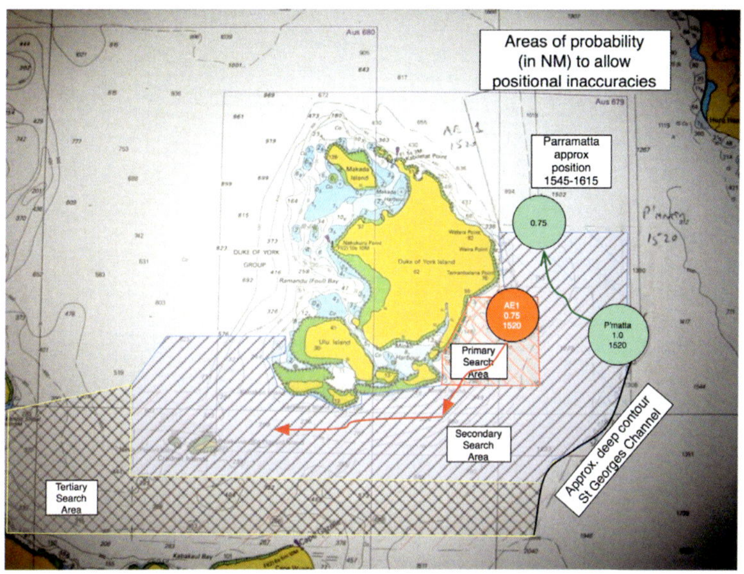

Figure 2 – Recommended Search Area.

30. Finding the submarine may be the only way to solve the puzzle. We have searched diligently through the records and reminiscences, we assess that there are no undiscovered sources of truth as to what happened on that day — that all died with the crew of *AE1*.

31. These recommendations will provide a firm foundation to develop a Search Plan using modern technology for a comprehensive search. A separate Report will be made on a Search Plan which will enable soundly based costs to be estimated with confidence for inclusion in a Proposal to the Australian Government to find *AE1*.

32. It is time to marshal the technology and find *AE1*. Given the resources and this technology, we are confident that *AE1* will be found in our search area.

(End of Executive Summary)

AE1 Inc Search Area Committee Report

Figure 3 – HMAS *AE1* at Portsmouth UK 17th February 1914. AWM P01075.041.

Section 1 — Purpose

1.1 This Report has been prepared in order to provide a summary of the research work of the *AE1* Search Committee with a view to better directing future searches for *AE1*.

Rear Admiral Peter D Briggs AO CSC RAN Rtd. Principal Writer

Commodore Terence Roach AM RAN Rtd Editor

Section 2 — Background

2.1 Acknowledgements

The Search Committee acknowledges the dedicated and invaluable work undertaken by a number of researchers. These efforts have been freely and unselfishly made available and have significantly eased the task of trying to reconstruct the events surrounding the loss of HMAS *AE1*.

2.1.1 Darren Brown

Darren Brown's extensive work in UK and Australian archives has uncovered many of the original ship logs, signal and wireless telegraphy (WT) logs and other documents that have contributed to his construction of a timeline (Annex B). This compendium of research and the time line produced from it has proved an invaluable foundation for the work we have undertaken.

2.1.2 Peter Richardson

Peter Richardson's research, particularly the work he has funded by professional researchers in the German archives has added a significant and important dimension to our understanding of the German context of this puzzle.

2.1.3 Gus Mellon

Gus Mellon's work as a long-term member of *AE1* Inc has provided continuity, a reconstruction of events, an invaluable summary of the earlier searches and an excellent basis for further research. The environmental data that he has identified will be important as we move to undertake searches.

2.1.4 Tim Smith

Tim Smith's experience as a maritime archaeologist, professional researcher, familiarity with maritime sources and role as the leading maritime archaeologist on *AE2* CF's team has been invaluable in uncovering some hitherto un-researched data.

2.1.5 Richard Arundel

Richard Arundel's specialist knowledge of naval communications and historical research into the WT capability of *AE1* has been most useful in understanding this aspect of the situation surrounding the loss of *AE1*.

2.1.6 David Nicholls

David's skills as a specialist navigator and experience as a submarine Commanding Officer underpin the construction of the geographical plot at Annex C that provides the foundation for much of this analysis.

2.1.7 Ian Noble

Ian Noble has been indefatigable as a tireless reader at the Australian War Memorial and National Australian Archives in Canberra.

2.1.8 John Foster

John Foster's extensive research and search efforts have set the precedent for our efforts. His book, 'Entombed but Not Forgotten', published in Sydney in 2006 contains a huge amount of research that underpins his efforts to locate the wreck. Whilst we may differ with some of his conclusions and take issue with some of the technical aspects, we are indebted for his dedication and recognise his role as the forefather of our work. After a long journey, we have essentially reached the same conclusion.

Further details about these contributors are set out in Annex A.

2.2 Sources of Information and Relevant Issues

2.2.1 Lack of Comprehensive Documentation.

There are significant gaps in the availability of original documentation. Much of the original German colonial documentation appears to have been destroyed, or not surprisingly, never made it back to Germany. Given the gaps in the official records, we have directed significant effort to obtain informal records of events, such as those in original diaries and letters from descendants.

2.2.2 Ship's Logs

These documents are the formal record of events affecting the ship. Whilst underway they were maintained on the bridge by the officer of the watch and provide a summary of movements, positions, and interaction with other units. Whilst at anchor, the ship's log was normally maintained by gangway staff under the supervision of the officer of the day. Once completed the logs were forwarded to higher authority for assessment, archiving, and storage. A poorly written or dirty log was considered a poor reflection on the ship. Given its importance as an historical document and scrutiny by higher authority, many ships chose to rewrite it, producing what is called a 'fair' version of the 'working' log. The difference between a 'fair' and 'working' log can generally be quickly detected in the quality and uniformity of the writing and absence of stains. The potential for details to be amended or omitted in transcribing from the working to the fair log must be borne in mind in evaluating the contents of a fair log.

2.2.3 Reports of Proceedings (ROP)

In today's Navy, these are formal, monthly reports of activities undertaken by the ship, rendered by commanding officers to their higher authority. They are routinely scrutinised and are another measure used to assess the performance of the ship and her commanding officer. The reports are then archived. Accordingly, significant attention is paid to the drafting in order to reflect well on the ship; in some circumstances they may be incomplete or biased in the way they present information and should be interpreted accordingly. In 1914 only the Fleet Commander, RADM Patey submitted an ROP. It appears that the smaller ships and submarines did not submit regular monthly ROPs. PARRAMATTA wrote a specific report covering the loss of *AE1* and ENCOUNTER wrote a report covering the few days in charge during HMAS AUSTRALIA's absence.

2.2.4 Signal Logs

These logs record the receipt and transmission of messages to and from a ship. At any one time there could be several signal logs in use; on the bridge and its associated signal deck;

they recorded messages received and sent by flashing light, flag signals, and semaphore. This distinguishes them from the WT office logs; these were maintained for each circuit of messages received and sent by wireless and are discussed further below. Where an admiral was embarked, it is likely that his staff maintained their own dedicated signal logs of messages to and from the admiral.

2.2.5 Flashing Light Signalling

Two methods were used to pass messages between ships by flashing light using Morse code; an omni directional light or signal projectors. The omni directional light was mounted high on the ship's mast and used for passing messages to a group of ships in close proximity, such as an anchorage. The signalling lanterns or projectors were directional, reasonably discrete and generally, only the intended recipient would read and log the message. The effective range for both methods was limited and varied depending on the size of the light/lantern and visibility conditions at the time. Messages sent and received by flashing light would be recorded in the bridge signal log.

2.2.6 Megaphone (Voice Trumpet)

The use of megaphones between ships in close company was not unusual. This would quite often be CO to CO and it is quite possible that these conversations were either inaccurately recorded or not recorded at all.

2.2.7 WT Signal Logs

WT logs were maintained for a particular WT circuit. Messages were passed by Morse code. Since the sets operated at medium/high frequencies, friend and foe alike could intercept these messages. Cipher or code could be used where the subject matter warranted. It appears that the RAN ships were operating only one WT circuit for conducting operations, most messages were passed unencoded and were sometimes recorded in more than one ship's WT log. There could be multiple addressees, messages were addressed to one or more 'action addressees' and also passed 'for information' to other ships. It does not appear that the RAN had introduced date time groups or the precedence used in contemporary naval signals.

2.2.8 Diaries

2.2.8.1 Aubrey Hodgson MBE

Aubrey Wilfred Donald Hodgson (Chief Petty Officer) MBE was a naval signalman loaned to the merchant ship AORANGI, his AWM records, including his diary is at:

http://cas.awm.gov.au/item/3DRL/6032

Australian War Memorial — 3DRL/6032 — Hodgson, Aubrey Wilfred

Further details are discussed at para 4.4.1 below.

2.2.8.2 Dr Fred Hamilton

Dr Fred Hamilton was the medical officer of the UPOLU, the depot ship to *AE1* and *AE2*. His diary was presented to the Mitchell Library, State Library of NSW in 1964 by Fred Hamilton-Kenny. Tim Smith transcribed the relevant sections on 19 April 2011.

2.2.8.3 SBLT Henry Hastings McWilliam

McWilliam transferred to ENCOUNTER on 15th September 1914 before AUSTRALIA left for Sydney, and re-joined AUSTRALIA on 20th September, after she unexpectedly returned to Rabaul. His diary is available in the AWM at 1DRL/0467.

2.2.8.4 LCDR Cyril John Percy Hill

LCDR Cyril John Percy Hill HMAS PARRAMATTA, diary and private papers available at http://cas.awm.gov.au/item/1DRL/0350

Australian War Memorial 1DRL/0350 (Private Papers collection) Hill, Cyril John Percy (Lieutenant Commander, RN).

2.2.8.5 LCDR Gerald Ashby Hill

LCDR Gerald Ashby Hill's papers contain a copy of HMAS YARRA's log book and observations by HILL. These are available at AWM 1DRL/0351.

2.2.8.6 Engine Room Artificer Class (ERA) II Petty Officer Henry James Elly Kinder

Kinder was a member of *AE2*'s crew and wrote an excellent account of his experiences undergoing submarine training in the UK, *AE2*'s passage to Australia and in the Dardanelles. He survived imprisonment, returned to Australia very ill and died in 1964. A typescript copy of the diary is held in the AWM at PRO1466. Fred and Elizabeth Brenchley[1] 1 record that his grandson, Mr Ross Kinder, of Nundah, QLD, holds the original.

2.2.8.7 Chief ERA J Marsland

Marsland appears to have been one of the passage crew on *AE1*; his diary describes the voyage to Australia only. A copy was published in the Naval Historical Review, December 1974.

2.2.9 Charts & Hydrographic Reference Books

The charts and hydrographic publications in use by RAN ships in 1914 have been provided by the Australian Hydrographic Service and used as the basis for the geographical reconstruction at Annex C. The assistance of the Hydrographic Service is gratefully acknowledged.

1 Brenchley, Fred & Elizabeth, *Stoker's Submarine*, Sydney 2003, p268.

Section 3 — Relevant Technical Description of AE1 and Material State

3.1 Principles of Submarine Stability & Control Relevant to Our Inquiries

3.1.1 First Principles

A submarine must be neutrally buoyant when submerged; it floats like an airship underwater, displacing its weight in water. It must also be balanced fore and aft.

- The control surfaces (hydroplanes) can then provide effective control when underway dived.
- Internal compensating tanks provide the capacity to adjust the bodily weight and trim tanks forward and aft adjust the longitudinal balance whilst dived.
- Ballast tanks (internal and external) provide buoyancy whilst on the surface; these would normally be full of water when dived.
- The amount of water in various internal compensating/trim tanks depends on the density of the seawater, quantity/weight of stores, fuel, oil, water and personnel carried and their disposition in the boat.
- Regular adjustments, called 'trimming', must be made using these compensating tanks whilst dived to maintain neutral buoyancy and fore and aft balance.
- There must be a sufficient capacity in these tanks to cope with a range of loaded conditions – e.g. fully stored, armed, and fuelled at the start of a patrol to no weapons, little fuel/stores/water at the end of a patrol.
- And a range of water densities.
- This is part of the challenge for the designer.
- Each boat is marginally different, depending on variances in the construction.
- Fixed lead ballast is added to the keel to adjust for these variances, to adjust for different water densities and provide some reserve for growth in weight during the life of the SM — e.g. adding a gun.

3.1.2 Trimming

Following a period in harbour when the submarine embarked fuel or stores, adjustments were made to the compensating tanks to offset the changes in weight; this is called 'putting on the trim' and could only be an approximation. This uncertainty is resolved as soon as possible after leaving harbour, when a submarine would normally conduct a 'trim dive' to ensure that it had a good trim.

3.1.3 Stability Data

According to in the Royal Navy's Book of Reference (BR) 3043 Chapter 4, the first batch of E boats (*AE1* and *AE2* were part of this group) displaced 796 tons submerged and 665 tons surfaced. The reserve of buoyancy was 21.5% (143 tons), with a surfaced transverse metacentric height (GM) of 20" (508 mm) and dived righting arm (BG) of 10" (254 mm). These terms are explained at http://en.wikipedia.org/wiki/Metacentric_height. Compared with contemporary single hulled submarines these are quite respectable figures, giving a good sea keeping capability and relatively good (for a submarine) capacity to absorb damage.

3.1.4 Dimensions

AE1 was 178 ft (54.2m) long, maximum beam of the pressure hull 15 1" (4.6m) (increased to accommodate the broadside tubes), a maximum beam at the 'saddle tanks of 22' 6.5" (7.1m), a draught of 12' 6" (3.9m). The freeboard from the surfaced waterline to the superstructure (the casing in current parlance) was 6 ft (1.82m) and the bridge deck (top of the fin) was 12 ft (3.65m). The distance from the top of the raised periscope to the keel was 36-37 ft (10.9m), resulting in a practical periscope depth of ~ 32 ft keel depth. These figures conflict with diary accounts of periscope depth of 22 ft – this depth may have possibly have been measured from the surfaced waterline, rather than the keel?

3.2 Structure, Fuel Tanks, and General Arrangements

3.2.1 Sources

Michael W D White, *Australian Submarines — A History,* Appendix I, page 217[2] — the Technical Detail of The E Class Submarine, the Specification for construction of *AE1*[3] and BR 3043 – The development of HM Submarines from Holland No.1 (1901) to PORPOISE (1930)[4] are the primary sources for this summary. Michael Rikard-Bell, a practicing naval architect and experienced submarine mechanical engineer has assisted with interpretation of the General Arrangement drawings and Specification for construction of *AE1*. Michael has a dynamic, computer based stability model of *AE1*; this has been useful to evaluate the impact of damage arising from a grounding.

3.2.2 Hull Plate and Riveted Construction

The specification[5] contains detailed instructions regarding the standard of materials to be used in the construction of the hull. The hull plating was mild steel, measured by its weight per square foot, so thicknesses are approximate. Different weight plate was used depending on the diameter or beam of the hull. At the widest beam, the plating was approximately 12 mm thick, ranging down to 9.5 mm at the narrowest beam sections at the bow and stern. There was an extensive system of internal supporting ribs and backing plates (butt straps) to the longitudinal riveted seams. This arrangement resulted in a strong hull with a maximum operational depth of about 180 ft (55m). BR 3043 advises that the necessity to go deeper during wartime service eventually led to the E class being classified as 200 ft

2 White, Michael W.D, *Australian Submarines A History*, AGPS 1992.

3 Specification for Building The Hull of A Twin-Screw Submersible Boat *(AKA AE1).*

4 BR 3043 is available online at http://www.rnsubs.co.uk/Boats/BR3043/contents.php

5 Specification for Building The Hull of A Twin-Screw Submersible Boat *(AKA AE1).*

boats.[6] The collapse depth is not known, however a depth of 300-400 ft is probably a reasonable extension from this figure.

3.2.3 Fuel Lubricating Oil and Tank Arrangements

3.2.3.1 Fuel Tanks

There were six internal fuel tanks distributed throughout the length of the SM, carrying 42 tons of 'Broxburn fuel', named after the district in Scotland where this shale oil was extracted. This provided a maximum range on the surface of 3,225 nautical miles at 10 Knots.

3.2.3.1.1 Fuel Characteristics

The Australian Naval Representative UK's Report number 52 dated 23rd Jan 1914[7] details the preparations for the delivery voyages including a significant amount of information on the fuel and lubricating oil requirements obtained from the relevant Admiralty experts. The figures used below are quoted from this Report. Supplies for refuelling the submarines with Burmah fuel in lieu of Broxburn shale oil was arranged by the Admiralty as far as Batavia. It is implied that a sample of Australian supplied shale oil had been tested in 1911 and found satisfactory in lieu of Burmah or Broxburn fuel for refuelling in Australia. So, it is likely that *AE1* was carrying similar Australian supplied fuel when lost. The flash point of Broxburn shale oil was given as not less than 150 degrees F and Burmah oil approximately 200 degrees F.

3.2.3.2 Lubricating Oil Tanks.

3.2.3.2.1 Lubricating Oil Characteristics

Vacuum oil No. 2 was to be shipped to the refuelling ports, as it was not available from the trade. In lieu of this, Henry Wells' Oil No. 108 was recommended, alternatively, Vacuum Company's DTE Heavy Oil was widely available, including in Sydney. The latter had the following characteristics:

- Specific gravity at 60 degrees F is 0.9.
- Flash point by Pensky Martin Close Flash Apparatus 395 degrees F.
- Viscosity by Redwood No. 1 Viscometer 613 seconds @ 70 degrees F (a range of further readings is given in the document).

The Naval Secretary's letter to RADM Patey Commanding HM Australian Fleet giving instructions for the passage from Singapore to Sydney advised that there were 6,000 gallons of Vacuum No. 2 oil at Sydney and recommended that HMAS SYDNEY should carry this in lieu of purchasing the oil in Singapore.

6 BR 3043 para 4.12.4.

7 Extract from #52 Report of Naval Representative dated 23rd Jan 14; Navy Office file 14/1398, DB images SDC 15260, 262, 264, 266, 274, 276 and 278.

3.2.3.2.2 Fuel & Lubricating Oil Consumption

The consumption of Broxburn Shale oil at an SOA was given as 4 1/6 gallons per mile and of Burmah Oil at the same speed as 5.5 gallons per mile. The consumption of lubricating oil was approximately 1/10 of the fuel for Broxburn shale oil and 1/8 of fuel consumption for Burmah oil.

3.2.4 Keel Arrangements

AE1 was fitted with a substantial and extremely strong, boxed section keel weighing 52 tons. The centre section of the keel weighing 10 tons could be dropped to lighten the submarine, to assist in surfacing if in extremis whilst dived.[8] This required release of a dog on the forward end of the drop keel by operation of a hand wheel accessed via a small manhole in the bilges; given the difficult access, this would not be a simple or quick operation, particularly if the submarine were experiencing a large bow down/up or list angle.

3.2.5 Ballast Tank Arrangements

3.2.5.1 *AE1* was fitted with eight external ballast tanks, numbered from forward, odd numbers to starboard, even to port, incorporated in the saddle tanks secured to the sides of the pressure hull.

Two main ballast tanks were positioned forward of the broadside (beam) torpedo tube and two aft. Tank capacities measured off the General Arrangement drawings were, #1 – 12.3 tons, #3 – 13.2 tons, #5 – 14.1 tons, and #7 – 15.2 tons. Analysis using the computer based stability model developed from the General Arrangement drawings indicates that flooding two of the large external main ballast tanks (situated in the saddle tanks amidships) on one side would result in a significant list, but would not place the upper conning tower hatch under water or cause the submarine to sink. Unlike the *Oberon* class submarine, these tanks were not open to the sea but were flooded via screw down valves sized according to the capacity of the tank. [9]

3.2.5.2 There were five internal ballast tanks identified by letters A-E. These tanks could be flooded by two means, a connection to the main line, (an internal trimming system) or through Kingston valves fitted in the pressure hull bottom of the tank.[10]

3.2.5.3 The total ballast tank capacity was 141 tons; 110 tons in the external tanks, the balance in the internal tanks.[11] Only the external tanks, i.e. 110 tons could be blown quickly with high-pressure air in the event of a flooding emergency. If the flooding amount exceeds 110 tons the submarine will sink despite having fully blown its external main ballast tanks.

8 BR 3043 para 4.15, para 30.2

9 48 SPECIFICATION FOR BUILDING THE HULL OF A TWIN SCREW SUBMARINE BOAT, para 53.

10 Ibid, para 54.

11 BR 3043 Para 4.17.1

3.2.6 Steering and Hydroplane Arrangements

3.2.6.1 Hydroplanes

AE1 was fitted with forward and after hydroplanes to control the depth. These were operated by hand wheels in the control room, hydroplane motors in the control room then drove rod gearing to mechanically move the hydroplanes. Kinder's diary describes the arrangements well.

3.2.6.2 Rudder

The single rudder was operated by one of three steering wheels; on top of the fin, in the conning tower and in the control room. A similar arrangement of steering motor and mechanical rod gearing was used to move the rudder in response to the movement of the wheel. Michael Rikard-Bell observes that the system would lock up if more than one wheel were engaged.

3.2.6.3 Assessment of the System

Gus Mellon's analysis of the arrangements set out in the drawings[12] notes that the Acme style opposing lead screws on the rudder crosshead, directed through long lengths of rod gearing with numerous bends, knuckle joints and 'worm and worm wheel' gearing and mechanical linkage arrangements for the rudder crosshead make for a complex mechanical system vulnerable to failure. The rudder crosshead itself is very short (due to space constraints where it is located), giving little turning moment compared to the size of the rudder. Any degree of wear, lack of greasing, ingress of grit/dirt/verdigris or initial misalignment when setting the devices in their final positions, will incur side-loading forces, which can lock the opposed lead screw arrangement solid, under high loads. When the rudder is turned hard over the 'feathering' effect across the surface of the rudder will also contribute to make it very difficult to bring the rudder back to centre. The shaft and bearings for the lower rudder are set eccentric (i.e., not in the vertical plane, but canted forward) again due to space constraints. This adds further eccentric loadings onto the upper and lower bearings of the rudder shaft. These bearings also appear to be very small in length to diameter ratio, compared to what one might expect to see in such a circumstance.

3.2.6.4 Handling On The Surface

The submarines may have been difficult to handle at slow speeds on the surface; Henry Kinder's diary of the voyage to Australia notes that special arrangements were arranged for the transit of the Suez Canal:

> *'The speed limit for big boats passing through is five knots but owing to submarines being so hard to steer at slow speed on engine power, the Captain had permission to travel at ten knots.'*

12 Vickers Drwg 2823 — Bridge Strg Gear Arrmnt.jpg, Vickers Drwg 2512 — Arrgt Strg n Hydroplanes.jpg

Alternatively, this may not refer to a steering problem but rather, Kinder may be referring to the difficulty of running the diesels at the slow speed necessary to propel at five knots.

3.2.7 Beam or Broadside Torpedo Tubes

3.2.7.1 Structure of Pressure Hull in Way of Broadside Tubes

The construction of the pressure hull around the beam torpedo tubes is of interest in the beam on grounding scenario, where the outer end of the tube or the pressure hull annulus constructed to accommodate the tubes may be struck. The athwartships bulkhead forming the bulge to accommodate the broadside tube comes out from the pressure hull at frame #54, to the line formed by saddle tank skin, where there is a right angled seam, the bulge then follows the outer line of the saddle tank for 6 frames (6x21"=126" (3.95m) before another seam joins it to the after athwartships bulkhead at frame #48 (frames were numbered from aft). Scantlings and plating appear to be as for pressure hull — as one would expect; it is the pressure hull.

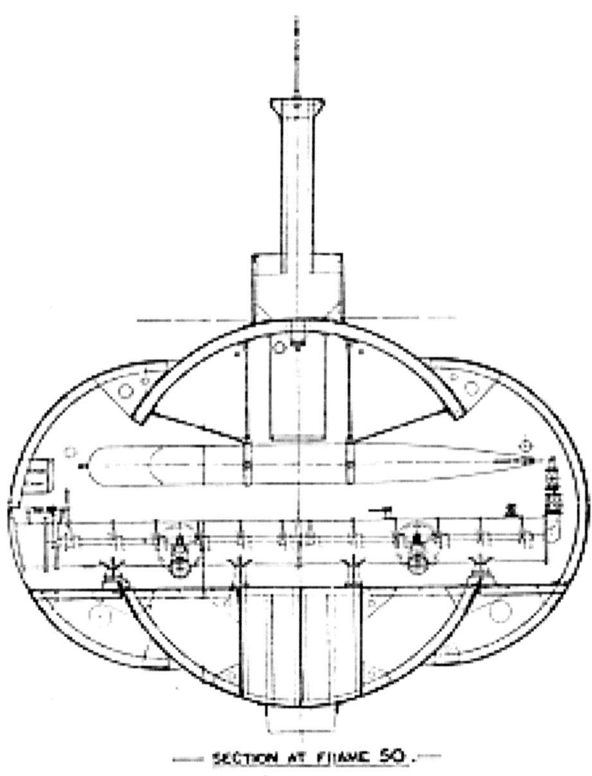

Figure 4 – Cross section at Frame 50.

3.2.7.2 Outer Tube Fabrication

The outer lip ends were steel castings of A quality.[13] Br 3043 para 4.12.2 contains the following information:

> *'In way of the broadside torpedo tubes in the E Class the pressure hull was cut away and the externals built to pressure hull strength. The plating amidships was 19lb reducing to 10lb at the ends, with a 19lb doubler fitted in way of the broadside tubes'.*
>
> *'To accommodate the beam tubes in the E Class the pressure hull in the vicinity of the tubes had to be extended out to the saddle tank plating as shown in Plate 15'.*

3.2.7.3 Tube Arrangements Internal to the Pressure Hull

Inside the pressure hull, the tubes had horizontally divided, hinged halves, BR 3043 advises that '*the top half opened by worm and quadrants operated by two handwheels to each tube*'. The halves were secured together by toggles and wing nuts to allow them to be opened up and reloaded by dropping the torpedo down into the tube. In lieu of a bow cap there was a slide valve inset from the outside of the saddle tanks, the mouth of the tube at the skin of the saddle tank was tapered horizontally in such a manner to avoid the forward speed of the submarine throwing the torpedo off course.[14]

3.2.7.4 Conclusions on Vulnerability

Overall, the broadside tubes would appear to be a source of strength, rigidity and support to the outer plating of the 'saddle tanks', rather than vulnerability. However, the forward corner/seam of the pressure hull annulus built to accommodate the tubes would be vulnerable as its shape could provide a single point to absorb the force of the grounding focusing these forces on a point of the pressure hull, if this were to fail then the pressure hull would be breached.

3.3 Propulsion Arrangements

3.3.1 Main Engines

AE1 was fitted with two 8-cylinder diesel engines. Although these were the best engines then available, they were not trouble free, requiring regular maintenance and frequent repairs whilst underway. The diesels were termed the '***main engines***'. The diesels propelled the submarine on the surface and provided the power to charge the batteries.

3.3.2 Main Motors/Generators

An electric motor was fitted on each shaft, these provided the power to propel the submarine on batteries, the only form of propulsion when dived and could be re-configured

13 Specification, p9, para 16.

14 White, Michael W D, *Australian Submarines – A History,* AGPS, Sydney 2006, Jim Ekin, *Technical Details of The E Class,* p220.

as generators, driven by the main engines to recharge the batteries when on the surface. These motor/generators were called the ***'main motors'***.

3.3.3 Propulsion & Generator Options

The main engines could be used whilst on the surface to propel the submarine ahead and/or charge the batteries via the main motors. The main engines could not run astern, to go astern whilst on the surface the main engines had to be disconnected from the propeller shaft using a clutch (discussed further below) and the main motor used to provide astern power. Changing from ahead propulsion on main engines to astern propulsion on main motors would typically take a couple of minutes to achieve. Where the submarine expected to be manoeuvring, e.g. entering harbour or coming alongside it would stop propelling on the main engines and switch to the main motors prior to commencing the manoeuvre.

3.3.4 Batteries

AE1 had two battery banks, each containing 112 cells; each cell weighed 940 lbs (420 kg). These provided energy to drive the submarine at 10 knots for just over 1 hour or 2.5 knots for 12 hours.[15] The entire battery was in the centre compartment, mostly forward of the broadside tubes, with some cells just aft of the tubes, but still in the centre compartment. The cells were secured in watertight tanks, covered with deck boards for use of the crew moving about, these were then covered with canvas, to keep salt water away from the cell tops.[16] The switchboard was also in the centre compartment, forward of the periscopes, on the port side.[17]

3.3.5 Clutches

The main engines had a claw clutch coupling placed at the flywheel (after) end of the engine, connecting it to the main motor. Arrangements differed between different build standards of the E class. *AE1* had a hand-operated clutch on the flywheel end, followed by a supporting shaft bearing connected to the main motor. This clutch is termed the ***'main engine clutch'***. An intermediate shaft led from the main motor aft to another claw coupling style of clutch, situated beneath the bilge and pumps. This clutch was driven by an electric motor and is termed '***the main motor clutch'***. This clutch was attached to the propeller shaft that led aft to a three bladed propeller.

3.3.6 Propulsion and Generator Options

On the surface, it was possible to use the entire output of each main engine to drive the propeller; with both the main engine and the main motor clutches 'in' and the main motor de-energised. Alternatively, it was possible to divert some of the main engine energy to charging the batteries by configuring the main motor as a generator; this configuration was termed a 'running charge'. Finally, it was possible to open the main motor clutch and use

15 White, Michael W D, *Australian Submarines – A History,* AGPS, 1992, p222.

16 Specification for Building the Hull of a Twin Screw Submarine Boat, paragraph 18

17 Kinder, Henry, *diary,* AWM, PR01466.

all the output of the main engines to charge the batteries; 'termed a 'standing charge'. To change from diesel (main engine) drive to electric drive, (main motor) the main engine would need to be de-clutched using the hand operated main engine clutch. The main motor then needed to be energized to propel either ahead or astern as required, with power drawn from the batteries.

3.4 Aids to Navigation

3.4.1 Equipment

AE1 was fitted with the following navigational equipment:

- Admiralty provided magnetic compass;
- Sperry gyrocompass; and
- Forbes impeller log.

3.4.2 Magnetic Compass

The magnetic compass was mounted in the conning tower, which was a bronze casting to provide an improved magnetic environment. None the less, the presence of the long, steel mass of the pressure hull made magnetic compasses in submarines notoriously unreliable. The compass should have been 'swung' or recalibrated on arrival in Sydney, although no record has been found of this occurring.

3.4.3 Gyro Compass

AE1 was also fitted with a first generation Sperry gyrocompass. Besant reported an accuracy of +/- 3 degrees in his diary of *AE1*'s delivery voyage to Australia. The compasses were reportedly unreliable, with frequent defects recorded in various E boat logs, requiring the attention of specialist representatives from Sperry onboard on some occasions. The compass was fitted with an alarm to alert the navigator that it was wandering. We assess that at the start of WWI, *AE1* and *AE2* were the only vessels in the RAN to be fitted with gyro-compasses.

3.4.4 Impeller Log

The submarine was fitted with a 'Forbes log' driven by a small impeller underneath the submarine to register speed through the water. This could then be converted to distance run for dead reckoning (DR) navigation calculations. This equipment would have required regular calibration, and might achieve an accuracy of +- 10%. The *AE2* diary for the voyage to Australia records difficulties with the Forbes log.[18] There are also numerous entries in other E class ship's logs indicating trouble with the Forbes logs. If the Forbes log failed, then the navigator could resort to rev/speed tables to gauge speed through the water and hence a DR of distance travelled.

18 HMA Submarine *AE2* Diary of events on passage Portsmouth to Sydney, p1, DB Image SDC15118.JPG

3.4.5 Navigational Procedures

The submarine was able to determine (to 'fix') its position by observing bearings of known objects visual from the bridge or either periscope and plotting these on the chart. The low height of eye of approximately 17 ft (5.2 m) from the bridge would limit the visual range to the horizon of approximately five nautical miles to the horizon (the height of the object being observed would increase the range from which it can be observed from the submarine's bridge). Between fixes, the submarine's position would be calculated by DR using the compass and log outputs. Where tidal stream data was available, this could be included to develop an Estimated Position (EP). As indicted above the accumulation of errors in the speed, direction and tidal stream data resulted in an expanding area of uncertainty around the submarine's position, termed the ***'pool of errors'*** in modern day parlance (it is doubtful that this practice was followed in 1914).

3.4.6 Celestial Navigation

When surfaced, the submarine could use a sextant to obtain celestial observations of the sun, moon and stars when visible and the horizon could be sighted, to provide an input to the navigational calculation.

3.5 Defect on the Starboard Propulsion Train

Stoker's account indicates that *AE1*'s starboard shaft was not available on diving and that arrangements had been made for rectification on her return to harbour on the 14th.

3.5.1 Starboard Engine Clutch Jammed In

Whilst the nature of the defect is not explicitly stated, it is most probable that the starboard engine clutch was defective and jammed in. This was a mechanical problem that the *AE1* and *AE2*'s engineering staff would have been well versed in fixing; *AE1* experienced a number of engine clutch failures on the voyage to Australia. A problem on the starboard main motor electrical functions could cause the same result but this seems less likely; depending on the problem, it is likely that fixing a main motor defect at an anchorage would not be a simple matter and would probably need outside specialist assistance. Nor were there any other instances noted of problems with the main motor.

3.5.2 Impact of This Defect

The defect had no impact on *AE1*'s ability to propel ahead on the surface using both main engines. The defect had major implication for power available and redundancy in all other situations:

- Astern power on the surface was reduced to the port shaft only; so a 50% power reduction and no redundancy.
    - o In the event of a delay in disengaging or defect with the port engine clutch, the submarine had no astern power on the surface.
- On diving, the submarine had only the port shaft for ahead or astern power.

- o A delay in disengaging or defect with the port engine clutch would leave the submarine without propulsion power, dived.

- In the event of a control surface failure leading to a large bow down angle/depth excursion, standard operating procedures include the use of full astern power to take the headway off, reducing the effect of the jammed control surfaces, and assisting in correcting the bow down angle.
  - o The submarine's depth is then reliant on trimming or main ballast adjustments.

3.5.3 Had The Defect Been Rectified?

RADM Patey reported that Besant told him in a personal interview on 12th September that *AE1* would be ready for operations on the 14th. However, there is no indication in any of the records that *AE1* had corrected this defect prior to sailing on the 14th; we are reliant on Stoker's account that the defect remained extant.

3.5.4 Contemporary Perspective

Although the rigorous training and procedural methodologies [which were developed from the experience of these early submarine crews] were not available to Besant, from a contemporary submarine operator's perspective, his decision to go to sea with this defect in the face of a possible action with enemy surface ships is inexplicable if not extraordinary.

- x This is particularly so given that *AE2* was available and serviceable to undertake the task.

- x It is difficult to understand why *AE1* did not spend another day at the anchorage to fix the clutch.

- x It is possible that the stores to do this were not available on the morning of 14th September.
  - o SYDNEY's signal log records a signal at 1425 on 14th September, requesting a receipt for the transfer of 'submarine stores' by 2000 (before she sailed that evening).
  - o It is surmised that the 'submarine stores' referred to may have been the toggle bolts required to repair a faulty main engine clutch, responsible for the defect on the starboard power train discussed above.
  - o SYDNEY had been the escort ship for *AE1*'s delivery voyage from Singapore to Sydney and had previously manufactured these bolts to repair a similar defect during the delivery voyage.
  - o SYDNEY's deck log records the transfer of an ERA to UPOLU at 1030 on 13th September, possibly to assist in the repairs (see 5.3 below).
  - o This is supported by Stoker's contention that, arrangements had been made to repair the defect on return to harbour on the evening of the 14th September.

- x Stoker observed in his report on the loss,[19] that:
  - o "This defect would prevent the starboard propeller being used when diving, but beyond limiting the underwater speed, would only slightly affect the handiness of the boat and could not be taken to account for her loss"
- x This appears to be a gross understatement of the impact of the defect and perhaps, an attempt to cover for a lapse of judgment in his lost friend and senior officer.

3.6 Communication Arrangements

3.6.1 Wireless Telegraphy (WT)

3.6.1.1 *AE1* & 2 was fitted with Type 10 tx/rx prior to sailing to Australia; the installation included the casing mounted WT mast (we hold a photograph of *AE1* departing Portsmouth on 2 March 1914 with the WT mast raised). A medium frequency transmitter/ receiver, (tx/rx) is described in OU 5155 – W/T Handbook Type 10 Sets (Submarines), a photocopy of the manual is held in the RAN Seapower Centre. However, since OU 5155 was not issued until well into 1915 (the Admiralty number is G.17325/15) it could NOT have been available to either *AE1* or 2 in 1914 and very doubtfully to *AE2* in April 1915. Nevertheless, an operating document or operator's equipment guide of some kind would have been necessary. The OU page 5 draws attention to The Wireless Telegraphy Manual, Vol 1 (1912) for practical application of wireless telegraphy.

3.6.1.2 John Foster records research revealing that the Fleet WT Officer, Lieutenant FG Cresswell reported to the Secretary by note that the equipment had not been used until arrival in Cairns and had still not been properly installed some weeks after arrival in Australia. *AE1* & 2's crew did not originally include a trained Telegraphist sailor to operate the WT set and Cresswell recommended appointment of a Telegraphist to each boat to operate this new equipment; Besant agreed this in July 1914.[20] Accordingly, Telegraphist Cyril L BAKER joined *AE1* before sailing for PNG. John Foster records that Baker came from Launceston, Tasmania and was the first Australian submariner trained in wireless telegraphy.[21]

19 Stoker Letter dated 16th October 1914.

20 National Archives of Australia_MP 472/1, 5/14/9165 — papers related to delivery voyage of submarines, Besant letter to Naval Board dated 6th July 1914.

21 Foster, John, *Entombed but Not Forgotten*, Australian Military History Publications, Sydney 2006 page 70, 112.

Figure 5 – *AE2* Enroute Australia with WT and Signal Mast raised, no aerials rigged. AWM 01405.

3.6.1.3 The Marconi Type 10 set was pre-valve consisting of primitive components — oscillator, transformers, capacitors, resistors and impedance coils that created an unstable lower Medium Frequency M/F band signal with a range of 30 to 120 miles (depending on atmospheric/ionospheric conditions). Some components were very fragile, such as spark detectors that required constant cleaning or adjusting. The aerial system was vulnerable to 'brushing', or earthing due to brine encrustation, sea matter, loose connections, or broken or frayed wire strands. The handbook indicates decreasing transmission power output may reduce this effect but the process also leads to damping or inaudibility of received signals. Messages were sent by Morse code.

3.6.1.4 Chapter V pages 19/20 of the Handbook describes the "Collapsible Mast" for diving purposes and describes a "two-throw" or "three-throw" 30 foot mast. The submarine had to lower the mast prior to diving. It is assessed that the sets fitted with this style of mast retained a limited range; perhaps to the horizon whilst on the surface with the WT mast stowed. The "W/T Handbook for Type 10 (Submarine) Sets 1915" on page 19 (chapter V) states:

> *"The great advantage of this arrangement (the typical rig approved for submarines) is that boats can signal up to a limited range with the mast collapsed."*

3.6.1.5 *AE1* and 2 WT aerial arrangements fitted on build were quite different to those set out in the handbook. This paragraph describes the original 'as built' installation of a casing mounted WT mast. From the available photographs and drawings, it has been deduced that the following arrangements were made:

Figure 6 – *AE2* & *AE1* alongside at Garden Island with WT and Signal masts rigged in the 'as built' configuration. AWM H11559.

- The WT mast was in one complete length, not telescopic.
- The WT mast was mounted on the casing, immediately aft of the fin.
- In the raised position, the aerial mast was held in place by four wire stays led down forward and aft to eyebolts on the Port and Starboard saddle tanks and to a bracket at the top of the after end of the fin.
    - AWM photo H11559 taken at Garden Island after arrival in Sydney shows the WT mast and wire stays and aerial post on the fore casing.
    - *AE2*'s aerials are not rigged, *AE1* is inboard and her after aerials, including the after spreader are visible (see description below).
- The mast could be removed and stowed, probably under the casing.

- x The aerials consisted of two sets of twin wire spans mounted over each side of a yardarm at the top of the WT mast, thence down to insulators attached to a spreader positioned over the forward and after casing.
  - o The spreaders were attached to a post mounted on the forward and after casing.
  - o Each spreader was fitted with steadying stays led down to the casing.
  - o The WT posts were held in place with wire stays.
- x The aerial was connected to the WT set by a wire run to an aerial post on the fore casing, this aerial post connection led down through the pressure hull to the WT set.
- x It is surmised that the aerial runs would be completely unrigged when the aerial was stowed and hoisted up after the WT mast was raised.
- x Rigging the aerial would have therefore entailed a lengthy operation to remove the WT mast from its stowage, rig the stays and halyards, manhandle the WT mast upright, secure the stays, lay out the aerials, haul up the aerials, rig the aerial posts on the forward and after casings, tension the fore and aft aerial runs and rig the spreader steadying stays. This would have been a major evolution, requiring a well-coordinated team:
  - o Taking perhaps 45-60 minutes?
  - o Limited by sea state or an angle on the submarine.
  - o Requiring a party of 10-12 men.
- x Unlike the installation described in the handbook, *AE1* and 2 would have likely had no WT capability with the aerial mast stowed.

3.6.1.6 Photographs of *AE1* and *AE2* taken after the docking in Fitzroy Dock 3-24th June 1914 and during the PNG deployment indicate that the WT mast arrangements in both submarines were modified, perhaps during the docking:

- x The WT mast was moved to the top of the fin, displacing the signal mast.
- x This allowed the mast to be hinged and lowered along the top of the fin, supported by a bracket on the after casing prior diving, rather than unrigging and stowing it.
- x It was fitted with a yardarm for flag hoists. This function was previously carried out by the signal mast (see para 3.6.2 below).
- x The all-round white light mounted on the signal mast, used as part of the navigation lights and for signalling was relocated to the new mast.
- x The aerial arrangements appear to have been simplified to a single span on each side of the yardarm, hauled up by halyards fitted to the WT mast.
- x The spreaders were led straight to strong points on the forward and after casing, dispensing with the aerial posts on both casings.

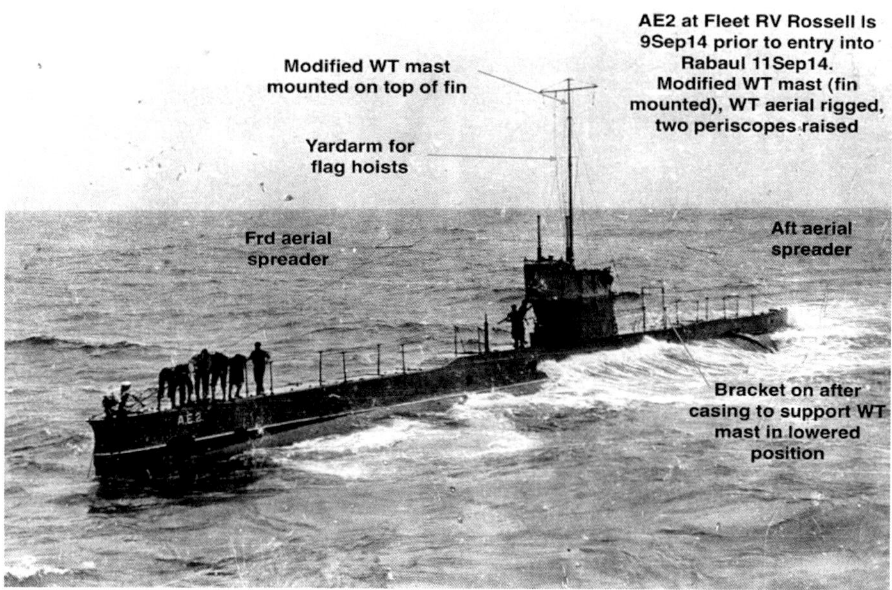

Figure 7 – *AE2* 9th September 1914, on passage to Rabaul, WT mast rigged from top of fin. AWM A01939.

Figure 8 – *AE2* Entering Rabaul Harbour September 1914, WT mast stowed on top of fin and supporting bracket on after casing. AWM A01404.

3.6.1.7 This arrangement is a significant simplification and probably reduced the time taken to rig the WT mast and aerials to 20-30' with 10-12 men. The submarine was still unable to routinely dive with the WT mast raised; to do so would likely cause the destruction of the WT mast as it was dragged through the water. This risk of damage could only be acceptable if a dive was necessary to save the submarine. The arrangement would have had no transmission or reception capability once the mast was lowered — it is assessed that the aerials were removed and stowed prior to diving. Perhaps there was some limited ability to transmit with the mast lowered but there is no evidence about it.

3.6.1.8 After reviewing the Submarine Type 10 WT Handbook with a Weapons Electrical Engineer's eye, Ian Noble concludes that the set would have required careful adjustment to perform satisfactorily and would be unable to change frequency or aerial arrangements easily or without complex adjustments and setting to work.

3.6.2 Flashing Light

3.6.2.1 All Round Light

Flashing light was the only option other than the WT set available to *AE1* for communications over a distance. *AE1* was originally fitted with a hinged signals mast aft of the after periscope, carrying an all-round Morse signalling lantern that also served as an all-round white light as part of the navigation lights, mounted on a platform part way up the mast.[22] As discussed above, it is surmised that the signal mast was displaced by the modified WT mast and that the signalling capability (yardarm for flag hoists and white light for Morse code) was transferred to the modified WT mast.

3.6.2.2 Aldis Light

Alternatively a hand held lantern (generically termed an 'aldis light' after the name of the early manufacturer) could be rigged on the bridge and connected to ship's power supplies. Various sizes existed; it is believed *AE1* was fitted with 6" (150 mm) aldis lamp with a typical maximum daylight working range of 5,000 yards. This equipment was operated by a Signalman; *AE1* & 2 each carried one such sailor.

3.7 Periscopes

3.7.1 *AE1* was fitted with two periscopes, one low power and the other had both low and high SRZHU 7KH\ ZHUH DERXW 23 IW (?P) ORQJ GLDPHWHU RI PDLQ WXEH 5Q (140 PP) UHGXFHG WR 3Q (90 mm) for the top 4 ft (1.2m). They were raised by electric motor and power trained using a ½ hp motor. The periscopes retracted 8 ft (2.4m) but still remained clear of the top of the fin as this photo of *AE2* entering Portsmouth harbour illustrates; the forward periscope is the higher of the two, the after most mast stretching out of view is the signals mast.

22 Source A page 219.

Figure 9 – *AE2* Entering Portsmouth Harbour. AWM P01075.042.

The periscopes were supported by individual periscope standard, heavy, cast tubes bolted to the top of the conning tower. This photo of *E17*'s fin [below] illustrates these, (note there were differences in the layout of the conning tower between *AE1* and *E17*):

Figure 10 – Fin of *E17* at RN Submarine Museum, Gosport.

Note, the two upright tubes on top of the conning tower are the periscope standards; the forward (left hand) standard also houses the arrangements for the upper steering wheel.

Section 4 — Key Personalities

4.1 LCDR Thomas Fleming Besant

David Nicholls has translated the cryptic notes used in Besant's RN service record:

Besant was born in December 1883; he joined the RN in January 1898 aged 15 and was appointed to the Training Ship HMS BRITTANIA (moored in the river Dart). He was awarded his midshipman's certificate (3rd class pass – 675/1000) gaining 4 months seniority on passing out on 15 May 1900. He served as a Midshipman in a number of ships for the next three years.

Figure 11 – LCDR Thomas Besant.

4.1.1 Service Record

During his career Besant:

- Served as a Midshipman in HMS (?), AMPHITRITE, and GLORY, arriving back in England on 8th May 1903 for Seamanship exam on 15th May 1903 and to commence Sub-Lieutenants courses on 26th May 1903.
- He passed his Sub-Lieutenant's courses (not CO Designate. Courses) as follows:
    - Seamanship 1st class pass (904/1000) 15th May 1903
    - Navigation (part 2?) 3rd Class pass (675/1200) September 1903
    - Pilotage 2nd Class pass (820/1000) December 1903
    - Gunnery 3rd Class pass (601/1000) March 1904
    - Torpedo 1st class pass (175/200) April 1904
- Name noted 'to qualify for N (or SM?) duties April 1904.
- Following an appointment to HMS RUSSELL (DUNCAN Class, pre-DREADNOUGHT Battleship) he was awarded his Watchkeeping certificate in February 1905.

- x Appointed to HMS THAMES (SM Depot Ship) for SM Instruction (January 05 – May 06) promoted to Lieutenant during this appointment (31st December 1905).
- x Appointed to HMS THAMES additional for SM command May 1906 – November 1907 [the annotations under Special reports/Service indicate that he was associated with C12, he was 23 years old; there is no report on his professional ability for this period.
- x C12 was laid down at Vickers in November 1906 and commissioned in January 1908 so it might be that he was 'standing by her' for some of the time under construction.]
- x November 1907 – August 1912. Returned to Surface Fleet duties HMS BONAVENTURE, HMS KING EDWARD VII, and HMS HERCULES.
- x August 1912 – June 1913 appointed to HMS VULCAN (actually a Torpedo Boat depot Ship) annotated 'for Submarines – C30 in Command'.
- x June 1913 – September 1913 appointed to HMS DOLPHIN 'additional for S/Ms'.
- x 15th September.1913 (Appointment List 1725) appointed to HMS PRESIDENT for loan to the RAN for Command of S/M *AE1*.
- x 31st December 1913 – promoted to Lieutenant Commander (after the obligatory eight years as a Lieutenant – which every RN Officer completed).
- x Since formal submarine command courses ('Perisher') did not start until 1917, it is assumed that the time in HMS THAMES, at the time of his association with C12, included some form of pre-command /CO Designate course.
- x The comments on his professional ability from August 1910 are almost all 'VGI' (Very Good Indeed).
- x July 1913 comment 'excellent CO of SM & VG Div. Leader; strongly recommended (presumably for promotion or perhaps for further command/overseas duties?)

4.1.2 Social Factors

David has also observed that his father was a Naval Storekeeper; Besant would probably have struggled (socially) against his junior officer peers in the mainstream Royal Navy of the early 1900s. Hence perhaps his early move to volunteer for submarines in April 1904. His 1st class pass in Torpedoes as a Sub Lieutenant would have helped his cause for submarine service. For all the above reasons (and the general exuberance of a young man in command), his enthusiasm for wartime success may have influenced his judgment in relation to the potential operational impact of material defects. All, of course, conjecture.

4.1.3 Contemporary Assessment of Besant's Level of SM Experience

Whilst cited by Stoker as an experienced submarine commanding officer it would appear that other than the period when undertaking submarine training, Besant had little seagoing experience in submarines as a junior officer and about 10 months (August 12-June 13) in command of C30 prior to his posting to *AE1*. From research into C30's activities whilst

Besant was in command it appears that the submarine operated from a depot ship in Dundee or the Tay River and normally had a surface escort whilst underway, relieving C30 of much responsibility for independent navigation. Even allowing for the infancy for the submarine arm and expediency in the run up to war, by contemporary standards this is a very short time so that he had only limited submarine and command experience.

4.2 LEUT The Hon Leopold Francis Scarlett

4.2.1 Scarlett was born in March 1889; he joined the RN in January 1904 aged 14 years 10 months and was appointed to BRITTANIA. He was awarded his midshipman's certificate (granted 3.5 months seniority) on passing out on 15th May 1905. He served as a Midshipman in a number of ships, each evaluated his performance as follows:

Figure 12 – LEUT The Hon Leopold Scarlett.

- HMS GOLIATH (CANOPUS class Battleship) 15th May 1905 – 5th March 1907 (Conduct Very Good Indeed, other Qualities/Attributes Very Good. Intelligent but slow.)
- HMS ROXBURGH (DEVONSHIRE class cruiser) 6th March 1907 – 5th August 1907 — All qualities/Attributes Very good. Languages — French; zealous, very strong.
- HMS SWIFTSURE (lead ship of Battleship class) 6th August 1907 – 15th September 1908. All qualities/attributes now Very Good indeed; zealous, promising, recommended, (*presumably for promotion to Acting Sub Lieutenant?)*

4.2.2 He obtained a 2nd class pass in his Seamanship examination in July 1908 and commenced Sub-Lieutenants courses as an Acting Sub-Lieutenant on 21 September 1908. Scarlett may have been back-classed since he did not finish this course until 17th December 1909 when he was promoted to Sub-Lieutenant, with seniority of 30th July 1908. He passed his Sub-Lieutenant's courses as follows:

- Seamanship (July 1908 2nd class 850/1000)

- x Navigation (September 1908 part 1)
- x Pilotage (February 1909 2nd class 804/1000)
- x Gunnery (December 1908 1st class 850/1000)
- x Torpedo (March 1909 2nd class 159/200)
- x Navigation (December 1909 Part 2: A 2nd class; B 2nd class)

4.2.3 He was noted as a volunteer for submarines in November 1909 with the annotation that "he will be required to serve a period in a seagoing ship before being selected."

4.2.4 He was appointed to HMS HIBERNIAN (KING EDWARD VII class Battleship) 29th January 1910 and on 7th August 1910 and was awarded his Watchkeeping Certificate. All qualities/attributes/skills Very Good Indeed. Thorough knowledge, good judgement.

4.2.5 He was appointed to HMS MERCURY (SM Depot Ship) for SM Instruction 8th August 1910 and re-appointed for service in submarines on promotion to Lieutenant 30th October 1910, followed by an appointment to HMS FORTH for submarines 25th July 1911. This was followed by an appointment to HMS CORMORANT (Gibraltar) for submarines in August 1911. His brief service record completed by Captain Hall, on completion of submarine training:

> "General conduct Very Good Indeed; all other attributes/skills Very Good. Has done very well under training in submarines. Considered promising."

4.2.6 A report on service in submarines (written December 1912) by Lieutenant Lewis (possibly a SM CO) All skills and attributes Very Good Indeed. Thorough Knowledge. Good Judgment. This appears to cover his time served in submarines attached to HMS CORMORANT.

4.2.7 He was invalided via Navy List 7682 September 1912; respiratory infection required him to be sent home (presumably from Gibraltar) when fit to travel due to tuberculosis of the lungs. He left on SS MEDINA on 21st December 1912, arriving home on 23rd December 1912, admitted to RN Hospital HASLAR for 6 weeks on 28th December 12, declared 'unfit' on 4th January 1913 and listed for re-survey at HASLAR on 7th July 1913 (6 months). He was placed on the books of HMS VICTORY for a final period of sick leave from 22nd December 1912 to 3rd July 1913 (194 days) and placed on retired list (unfit - tubercle of lungs) on 13th June 1913.

4.2.8 On 25th September 1914 Scarlett's record notes receipt of a letter from Navy Office Melbourne stating that Lieutenant. Scarlett 'entered temporarily into the RAN for war'. The last notation on his record is:

> 'Lost in Submarine *AE1* [report received 19th September 1914] on or about 19th September 1914'.

4.2.9 His RAN record noted his date of entry (as a Lieutenant) as 10th August 1914 (Gazette No. 74/14) with the same date of entitlement to Submarine pay. His RAN record shows the date of his seniority as a Lieutenant in the RN as 27th December 1911 (his actual date was 30th October 1910).

4.2.10 Contemporary Assessment of Scarlett's Submarine Experience

It is not clear from his service record, which seagoing submarines he served on during the 13 months appointed to CORMORANT. His warm personality was appreciated and remarked on by several commentators (Stoker and Hamilton to name a couple), but he could not be regarded as an experienced seagoing submariner.

4.3 LEUT Charles Lewis Moore

4.3.1 Moore appears to have been a term-mate of Scarlett although Moore graduated six months ahead of Scarlett on completion of their training as Acting Sub-Lieutenants. Notwithstanding, both were appointed for submarine training in August 1910, though in different SM training ships.

4.3.2 Born in Dublin in 1888, Moore joined the RN January 1904 aged 15 (hence a term mate of Scarlett) and was appointed to the Training Ship Britannia (moored in the river Dart). He was awarded his midshipman's certificate (granted 1.5 months seniority) on passing out on 15th May 1905 he served as a Midshipman in HMS LEVIATHAN (DRAKE class cruiser) 15th May 1905 – 26th November 1906; HMS BACCHANTE (CRESSY class cruiser) 27th November 1906 – 17th February 1908 and HMS BULWARK (LONDON class Battleship) 18th February 1908 – 15th September 1908 (Conduct Very Good Indeed, other Qualities/Attributes Very Good. Good Judgement).

4.3.3 Having completed Seamanship examinations in July 1908 (second class pass 882/1000), he commenced Sub-Lieutenant courses as an Acting Sub-Lieutenant on 21st September 1908 and was promoted Sub-Lieutenant on completion with seniority of 30th September 1908. The date of completion of this course is unclear on the records – probably 17th June 1909: He joined HMS BLACK PRINCE on 2nd August 1909 for watch keeping training.

4.3.4 He passed his Sub-Lieutenant's courses as follows:

x Seamanship (Jul 08 2nd class 850/1000)

x Navigation (September 08 part 1 A3, B3)

x Pilotage (December 08 2nd class 799/1000)

x Gunnery (April 09 1st class 509/1000)

x Torpedo (October 08 2nd class 164/200)

x Navigation Part 2 – not noted

4.3.5 He was noted as a volunteer for submarines in April 1909 and again in September 1910.

4.3.6 Moore was appointed to HMS BLACK PRINCE (DUKE OF EDINBURGH class cruiser) 2nd August 1909 – 14th August 1910 and was awarded his Watchkeeping certificate in August 1910. All qualities/attributes/skills Very Good Indeed. Thorough knowledge, good judgement.

4.3.7 Following this he was appointed to HMS ARROGANT (Submarine Depot Ship), for submarine training 15th August 1910, re-appointed for service in submarines on promotion Lieutenant 1st April 1911 and appointed additional for Submarines 11th November 1911 on completion of submarine training.

4.3.8 He was admitted to RN Hospital HASLAR (Scabies) 29th May 1912 for 10 days and again on 25th June 1912 for Tonsillitis for 10 days.

4.3.9 Moore was loaned to RAN for three years Submarine service 14th Oct 1913. His fitness report rendered by Commodore Keyes in August 1912 noted the following:

> *"General conduct, attributes/skills (Submarines) Very Good. Zealous and Attentive."*

By CMDR Palmer January 1914: 2 x very Good Indeed and rest very good. *"Keen and capable."*

Last notation on record; *'Reported missing in Submarine AE1 [report received 19th September 1914] on or about 19th September 1914'*.

4.3.10 Moore was unmarried; his next of kin was his father who had been in the Army (Colonel) and who may have been serving in Ireland when Moore was born (Dublin 23rd August.1888). His family lived in Minehead, Somerset at the time of Moore's entry into the navy.

4.3.11 Contemporary Observations on his Level of Submarine Experience

It is not clear from his service record how much submarine sea time Moore accumulated in the 1 year 11 months between qualifying and being loaned to the RAN, with time out for two bouts of illness warranting hospitalisation. Although the 3rd hand on *AE1* he may have actually had more sea experience than Besant or Scarlett! In any case, his level of experience was fairly brief by today's standards.

4.4 LEUT Henry Hugh Gordon D'acre Stoker

Stoker was born in February 1885 in Dublin; he joined the RN in January 1900 aged 15 and was appointed to BRITTANIA. He was awarded his midshipman's certificate, passing out on 30th May 1901, gaining 3.5 months seniority. He served as a Midshipman in a number of ships for the next three years.

4.4.1 Service Record

- x Served as a Midshipman in HMS IMPLACABLE (FORMIDABLE Class Battleship commanded by Prince Louis of Battenberg), arriving back in England (from the Mediterranean) on 1st August 1904 having completed Seamanship exam on 30th July 1904.
- x He commenced Sub-Lieutenants courses on 4th October 1904.
- x Promoted Sub-Lieutenant 10th July 1904.

Figure 13 – LCDR Hugh D Stoker as a POW in Turkey after the scuttling of *AE2* in 1915. Photo HG Stoker Autobiography S*traws in the Wind.*

- x He passed his Sub-Lieutenant's courses (not CO Designate Courses) as follows:
  - o Seamanship 1st class pass (902/1000) 30th Jul 1904.
  - o Navigation (part ?) 3rd Class pass (No score noted) 29th November 1904.
  - o Pilotage 2nd Class pass (822/1000) March 1905.
  - o Gunnery 2nd Class pass (719/1000) 11th July 1905.
  - o Torpedo 2nd class pass (163/200) 18th August 1905.
- x Following an appointment to HMS JUPITER (MAJESTIC Class Battleship) 12th September 1905 – 15th August 1906 he was awarded his Watchkeeping certificate in December 1906 (Awarded Board of Trade Master's certificate September 1907).
- x Appointed to HMS MERCURY (SM Depot Ship) for SM Instruction (15th August 1906) and re-appointed for service in submarines on promotion Lieutenant (31st December 1906).
- x Appointed in command submarine *A10* 16th January 1909.

x Appointed in command submarine *B5* 1st January 1910.

x Appointed in command submarine *B8*:

   o 25th July 1911 – August 1911 Home Fleet.

   o August 1911 – October 1913 Gibraltar.

   o *B8* Inspected by VADM Brook Oct 1913 'Managed SM very well'.

x Personal report by CMDR Harvey at same time (relinquishing command); all qualities 'VGI' (Very Good Indeed). ''Very clever; good judgement; good SM Officer'.

x Appointed HMS DOLPHIN for *AE2* –October 1913.

x Appointed *AE2* In command 7th November 1913 - May 1915.

x Personal report January 1914, all 'VGI' by CMDR Palmer (promoted LCDR 31st December 1914 and re-appointed in Command).

4.4.2 Various notes are appended to his record in relation to the loss of *AE2* in the Dardanelles, including reference to a report by the American Ambassador (Istanbul?); also reference to his incarceration as a POW, his escape attempts and his strength of character in refusing to give an undertaking to the Turks not to attempt further escapes. A report by VADM Commanding Eastern Mediterranean dated 30th January 1916 notes: '*AE2* was in very efficient condition and reflects the greatest credit on him' (Stoker).

4.4.3 Stoker continued a successful career in the RN:

x Appointed in Command K9 10th February 1919.

x Gazetted for DSO on 22nd April 1919 'DSO awarded in recognition of his gallantry in making the passage of the Dardanelles in Command of HM Australian S/M *AE2* on 25th April 1915'.

x Invested with DSO at Buckingham Palace 12th June 1919.

x Brought to the Notice of the Admiralty – Gazette 17th October 1919.

x Recommended for promotion by CDRE Hall.

x Recommended for promotion by RADM Dent December 1919.

x Promoted Commander 31st December 1919 and re-appointed K9 in command.

x Appointed HMS VICTORY 1st February 1920 for unemployed time (not to exceed six months).

x Placed on half pay 23rd April 1920.

x Placed on retired list (own request) 2nd October 1920.

x 25th January 1922 Commuted £165 for £2150-15-6 (remaining?) leaving £200 per year.

x 10th September 1922 Granted approval to reside abroad.

- x Rejoined RN on outbreak of WWII.
- x Appointed HMS CAROLINE for duty with Chief of Staff Belfast 21st October 1939.
- x Granted Acting Rank of Captain whilst holding this appointment.
- x 23rd January 1940 – Appointed CAROLINE in command.
- x For duty as COS to Flag Officer in Charge, Belfast — in continuation (admitted to Belfast Military Hospital 28th-31st May 1940 for removal of in-growing toenail).
- x 31st July 1940 – Appointed HMS MINOS in command and Naval officer In Charge (NOIC) Lowestoft (Central Depot of the Royal Naval Patrol Service WWII).
- x Two incidents occurred whilst in command, the first (21st November 1941 – grounding of HMS ROWANTREE) resulted in a 3rd Sea Lord's displeasure from the Board of Inquiry outcome.
- x The second (MGB 89 fired upon by MGB 320 on 20th April 1942) Board of Enquiry revealed bad staff work and laxity in operational matters in the office of NOIC Lowestoft.
- x 27th July 1942 – Appointed PRESIDENT (additional) for duty inside the Admiralty as DPD (?) Naval Officer's Section.
- x Reverted to rank of Commander.
- x April 1944 – Requested appointment as War Diarist to Allied Naval Commander, Expeditionary Force (ANCXF).
- x 28th April 1944 — Appointed to HMS ODYSSEY (actually Collingwood Hotel at Ilfracombe) for War Diary Duties on staff of ANCXF.
- x 11th May 1944 – Granted Acting Rank of Captain.
- x 24th October 1944 – Appointed HMS PRESIDENT additional for duties inside Admiralty with Director of Service Conditions. (Granted Acting Rank of Captain WHTA).
- x 1st December 1945 — Dispersed (to be released Class A); 26th January 1946 Released; 27th January 1946 Reverted to Retired List – granted IOS Rank of Captain.

4.4.4 Since the submarine command course 'Perisher' didn't start until 1917, it is assumed that the time in HMS MERCURY included some form of 'pre-command /CO Designate' course, prior to taking command of A10. The comments on his professional ability from August 1906 to the loss of *AE2* are almost all 'VGI' (Very Good Indeed).

4.4.5 Social Factors

His father was a Surgeon in Dublin; they lived in Stephen's Green – a very smart address in Dublin. Early reports as a young officer comment on his zeal, athleticism (good at games), loyalty and reliability. He was clearly highly regarded as a submarine CO.

4.5 LEUT William H F Warren

4.5.1 Role

LEUT William H F Warren RAN was the CO of Parramatta during the time of *AE1*'s loss.

4.5.2 Letter to his Brother

The AWM holds a letter from Warren[23] to his brother recording the outbreak of war and the deployment to Rabaul. David Nicholls read the letter and reports that it records Warren's opinions related to the RAN's preparations for war and broad descriptions of operations en route to New Guinea and whilst on station in the Rabaul area. The letter is quite critical of the execution of maritime preparations for war and of the execution of Rabaul operations. The more remarkable aspect of the letter is that it fails to mention the loss of *AE1* in any regard; even though the period covered by the letter clearly encompassed that loss.

4.5.3 Death

Commander Warren was to die under tragic circumstances at Brindisi. A virulent fever had laid low most of the Australians since their arrival in the Adriatic. Early in April 1918, Warren entered the Naval Hospital at Brindisi for treatment and had recovered when he collapsed whilst taking a walk in the hospital's grounds. When he was found some time later, he was dead. He had drowned in a few inches of water.[24] At the time, he was the Commander of the Australian Destroyer Flotilla, indicating a successful naval career in the interim.[25]

4.6 Other RN/RAN Personnel

4.6.1 CMDR Frederick Campbell DARLEY RN, served in HMAS AUSTRALIA, his diary is held in the AWM (Acc N: 1DRL/0232) and comments on the loss of *AE1*:

> Transcript of 4th and 5th Paragraphs, Letter 10 of CMDR FC Darley RN (HMAS AUSTRALIA) dated 30th October 1914 to "Aunt Marion", (AWM 1DRL/0232)

No one knows what happened to the submarine – some say she was sunk by a small steamer called the "Colonial" or some such name which Jackson found a few days later on a reef and burnt to the water's edge, and on deck was a mounting for a pom-pom and a lot of empty cylinders scattered around; again she may have found a reef or unchartered (sic) rock (New Britain etc, is very imperfectly charted.)

Stoker the Captain of *AE2* does not believe she tried to dive for exercises and never came up, or that there was an explosion. I know this much, there are a lot of trees, quite big ones in the water floating about. I saw two large ones myself. She may have hit one of these and

23 http://trove.nla.gov.au/work/32027997

24 http://www.navyhistory.org.au/hmas-parramatta-first-born-of-the-commonwealth-navy/

25 Navy Office file 1918/89/544/1 letter advising the Governor General of his death dated 19 April 1918.

damaged her horizontal rudders; this might have caused her to dip suddenly, but everything one thinks of seems improbable (sic) as any other theory. The sad disaster cast quite a gloom over the Squadron – none of the work we have had has helped to buck us up much.

Original of letter signed "Erick"

Transcribed by Ian Noble at the AWM, Canberra on 4th May 2011.

4.6.2 LCDR Gerald Ashby Hill

LCDR Gerald Ashley Hill served in HMAS YARRA. His papers are held in the AWM under 1DRL/0351. Hill's diary is expansive; it appears that he writes with his memoirs in mind. In pages 61-65 he indulges in some speculation as to the cause of *AE1*'s loss, but does not add any new information to our understanding:

> "Before closing this chapter I must hark back to submarine *AE1*. Many rumours of course were afloat as to the cause of her disappearance chief among which was that she had been sunk by a small enemy steamer mounting a 3 pdr gun. In support of this theory, a craft of this description ashore on Elizabeth reef not far distant from Rabaul, while a gun was found on the seabed just under her bow.
>
> Nothing of course is ever likely to be known now which would lead us to the truth concerning her end and that of the very gallant men she entombed. But there is very good reason to suppose that she came by that end through an explosion the origin of which is hard to say. I can only add that her loss cast a gloom over the entire fleet a gloom which would not have been as heavy and lasting had we known they had met their deaths as every Soldier or Sailor in his country's service hopes to do when death comes his way."

Transcription from photographs of diary taken by Ian Noble May 2011.

4.6.3 LCDR Cyrill John Percy Hill served in HMAS PARRAMATTA, his diary is held in the AWM (Acc N: 1DRL/0350) and comments on the loss of *AE1*. Ian Noble reviewed the documents in May 2011 and advises that the records are quite legible and readable, and there is nothing unexpected in the diary. In summary relevant entries contain:

x Page 37: September 14th - Monday Last sighting of *AE1* [bottom of page.

x Page 41: 15th-17th September 1914: Search for *AE1* (no detail); "YARRA's" encounter with reef.

x Page 45: 17th-20th September 1914: Friday 18th, "PARRAMATTA", "WARREGO" find "KOLONIALGESELLSCHAFT".

x Page 49: 21st - 24th September 1914: Wed 23rd, " PARRAMATTA" finds MEKLONG at Mioko; 24th September: 40 prisoners from " KOLONIALGESELLSCHAFT ".

x Page 53: 24th September - 1st October: Nil and end of relevant entries.

x Patey's Oporder No 1 dated 7th August 1914: "To attack and destroy German ships in Simpsonhaven and Matupi Harbour and to destroy W/T station at Rabaul". (1 page).

x Patey's Oporder No 3 dated 8th September 1914: "Occupation of Rabaul and

x Herbertshohe, New Britain". (4 pages)

The above pages are the order of presentation and none are missing, despite the page numbering. There was nothing new or unexpected in the diary.

4.6.4 SBLT Henry Hastings McWilliam served in HMAS AUSTRALIA and ENCOUNTER during the period, his diaries are held in the AWM in DRL/0467. Ian Noble reviewed McWilliams's diary, reading in detail pages 54 – 59, the ones that mention *AE1*.

McWilliam transferred to HMAS ENCOUNTER on 15th September 1914 before AUSTRALIA left for Sydney, and re-joined AUSTRALIA on 20th September 1914, when she unexpectedly returned to Rabaul. Judging by his language style, his diary appears to have been written reasonably close to the dates he describes. Overall, this diary does not reveal anything new; excerpts of relevant entries on pages 55-56 (15th September), 57 (16th September) and 59-60 (18th & 19th September) include:

x Page 55: "Still no sign of the submarine. Apparently, in the course of enquiries about the submarine, a noise like firing of guns in the distance appeared to have some bearing on the subject. I remember having distinctly heard it, thinking it was "SYDNEY's" 12 pounder at about 8-15 yesterday evening. Several other people in the ship [ENCOUNTER] heard it, Merewether, Quick and Macdonald.

x "There are all sorts of theories as to what happened but a favourite one is that an armed launch attacked her."

x Other entries on that page about *AE1* refer to the search.

x On page 57, on 16th September, the author mentions that 7 of the crew of 3 officers and 32 ratings are "supernumeraries" (sic).

x On page 59-60, on 18th September, the author refers to the search and finding the steamer aground and on fire, and "WARREGO's investigation and what she found. He then states: This may explain the submarine mystery. Evidently she [KOLONIALGESELLSCHAFT] ran aground and her crew set her on fire and put off to the shore."

x On 19th September, the author mentions the search for KOLONIALGESELLSCHAFT's crew.

4.6.5 Petty Officer Henry James Elly Kinder RAN

Kinder was an ERA in *AE2*, who maintained a regular diary that provides a good insight into the events of the day. His papers are held at the AWM, reference PR01466. His diary adds a couple of points to the record:

x Kinder advises that the last communications between PARRAMATTA and *AE1* was by megaphone.

x Some oil was found in the vicinity of where *AE1* was last seen.

4.6.6 Engineer LEUT Alec Broughton Doyle RAN

On 17th September 1914 Doyle, the Engineer Officer of HMAS PARRAMATTA, wrote an acerbic and highly critical letter to a friend, criticising the RN senior officers in command and Besant's conduct on the 14th. Doyle went on to have a highly successful career in the RAN; principally in repair and ship construction. He was admitted as a Commander of the Order of The BritishEmpire as a Captain in 1937. In 1943 he was promoted Rear Admiral and became the 3rd Naval Member and Chief of Construction. The letter's lack of balance appears studied and deliberate, undoubtedly reflecting Doyle's heartfelt frustration; it is difficult to gauge how much weight to place on it in hindsight, he does restate the German steamer theory for the loss of *AE1*:

> *'Incidentally we have strong reason to suppose a small gunboat to have been lying in D of Y Island observing all our frantic dashing to & fro & probably waited till submarine got quite close & then just biffed off at her & sunk her.'*

4.7 Signalman Aubrey Hodgson

4.7.1 Aubrey Hodgson was an RAN signalman temporarily attached to the NZ passenger liner and supply ship SS AORANGI. In later years, Aubrey Hodgson lived in Sydney. His son advised Gus that he had undergone submarine training and was part of the spare crew for *AE1* and *AE2*. He became the President of the Submarine Society in Sydney and was later admitted as a Member of the British Empire for his life's work. Hodgson's submarine background made him a particularly useful and interested observer of the activities of the submarines and circumstances of *AE1*'s loss. His diary entries are incorrectly dated; placing the loss of *AE1* a week later, possibly the date he made the entries.

4.7.2 Hodgson records in his diary that he had an unsolicited conversation onboard AORANGI in Rabaul harbour with Petty Officer Reuschel, who was one of the German Navy members taken prisoner. Reuschel claimed that he was in charge of the German colonial steamer, the KOLONIALGESELLSCHAFT and boasted that KOLONIALGESELLSCHAFT had sunk *AE1*. Here is Hodgson's diary entry:

In a conversation with a prisoner who,
I understand, is an Engr. Officer of
"German Warship Planet." I gathered the
following, He claimed to have been in
charge of a small yacht named the
"Colonial", and that, when our subm.ne
was "hove to" in St Georges Channel.
on Monday afternoon last, he approached
her, flying a White Ensign, fired at,
and sunk her, and then ran over
her. I assured him, our submarine
wasn't lost, but he wouldnt acept my
argument. He was most callous, and
gloated over the fact, that he caught
them napping so very simply.

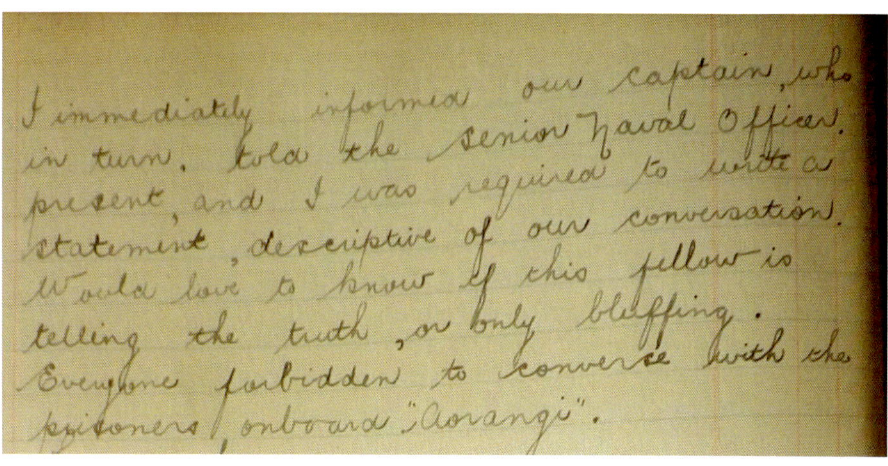
I immediatly informed our captain, who
in turn, told the Senior Naval Officer.
present, and I was required to write a
statement, descriptive of our conversation.
Would love to know if this fellow is
telling the truth, or only bluffing.
Everyone forbidden to converse with the
prisoners, onboard "Aorangi".

Figures 14 & 15 – Aubrey Hodgson's diary entry concerning Reuschel's boast of the sinking of *AE1*. Image: Darren Brown.

The account as relayed by Hodgson is the primary basis for the theory that KOLONIALGESELLSCHAFT was responsible for the loss of *AE1*:

It is an unsolicited exchange and a credible sequence of events to cause the loss of *AE1*. It correctly identifies Monday as the day of the loss.

- x It is difficult to understand why Reuschel would have invented a link to KOLONIALGESELLSCHAFT, an unlikely vessel for a fabricated story and by then, languishing on a reef some 70 miles to the west.
  - o According to other German prisoners KOLONIALGESELLSCHAFT was enroute from Madang to Rabaul and only made it as far as Cape Lambert where she ran aground.
  - o If so, why should Reuschel choose KOLONIALGESELLSCHAFT as the platform for a fabricated story, a ship that in theory did not reach Rabaul?
  - o He also happened to choose a ship that we know had an armed party and 1 pound Nordenfelt gun onboard?
- x Or did Hodgson fill in the gaps to create a good story? If so, he did so in a plausible and verifiable fashion, having allegedly reported his conversation to his CO, etc.
- x Reuschel's account is credible; *AE1* was vulnerable to a weapon such as a 1" Nordenfelt and had few defences except to dive, during this process she would have been very vulnerable to ramming. However we have been unable to find any corroborating evidence that KOLONIALGESELLSCHAFT made it to Duke of York Island or committed the deed.

4.7.3 Inaccuracies in Hodgson's Diary

There are numerous errors in dates and inaccuracies in Hodgson's diary when compared to an account constructed from the ships' deck logs and other official records. It appears to have been written well after the event and based on second hand information, as opposed to the impression given that it is the observations of an alert signalman observing the day's events and writing them up. The extent and nature of these errors cast doubt upon the credibility of the whole. A critique is at Annex D.

4.8 HMAS AUSTRALIA, RADM George Patey and His Staff

4.8.1 In the Australian Centenary History of Defence, volume III, David Stevens records a forward looking, positive remark on the attributes of submarines sparked by the purchase of *AE1* & 2 attributed to RADM Patey [later promoted to VADM]:

> *"With submarines as fists and aeroplanes as eyes, the naval service appears to be at the commencement of a new era".*

4.8.2 RADM Patey did not have a submarine specialist on his staff; indeed the RAN's general failure to prepare for the induction of submarines noted by Michael White[26] meant that Besant was the senior submarine specialist — Patey called on Stoker for advice

26 White, Michael W D, *Australian Submarines – A History*, AGPS 1992, p28.

following *AE1*'s loss. RADM Patey clearly had an interest in submarine operations; despite the pressures of controlling the landings and he personally interviewed Besant on 12th September11 regarding the readiness of *AE1*.

Figure 16 – RADM George Patey National Library. vn3890862.

> *"I personally interviewed Lieutenant Commander Besant on Saturday, 12th September, and questioned him as to the state of his Submarines. He stated that they were both all right, but that he would like Submarine A.E.1 to remain in harbour until Monday, 14th September, to make good minor defects. This I approved of, and he did not go out until the morning of the 14th September."* [27]

4.8.3 There appears to have been no special arrangements made for submarine operations, such as were made during the Allied landings at Gallipoli in April 1915, e.g. a submarine WT guardship. Nor were arrangements made for the rest and recreation of their crews; the nominated depot ship, the UPOLU was manifestly inadequate and inappropriate for its role.

This was belatedly recognised by Patey in his report on the UPOLU rendered to defend the RAN against a damages claim by UPOLU's owners.[28]

> *"SS UPOLU Unsuitability as tender for Submarines*

27 VADM Patey letter NAVY 14/7658 dated 23rd September 1914.
28 Vice Admiral Commanding HM Australian Fleet letter 14/8600 dated 28 October 1914.

Submitted for the information of the Naval Board. I concur in the report of the Court of inquiry contained in enclosure (N; E.191 of 17th October 1914) as to the unsuitability of the S.S. "Upolu" as tender for submarines, or for any other purpose as a Naval Auxiliary."

4.8.4 Patey was clearly concerned about the vulnerability of the submarines; his directions for them to return before dark and personal intervention when *AE2* failed to adhere to his direction on returning from patrol on 13th September demonstrated this:

"The captain's orders were that the boat was to be back in harbour by six pm but we were running a bit late. A signal from the flagship told him to be on time in the future."[29]

Besant would have no doubt learned of this public rebuke for Stoker. He was reminded as he sailed on the next morning; having requested permission to proceed in accordance with previous orders, *AE1* received the following response:

"From Flag, Approved. See that you return before dark. 0703"[30]

Besant would have been highly aware of the need to adhere to this instruction to return by 1750.

4.9 Dr Fred Hamilton-Kenny

4.9.1 Dr Fred Hamilton-Kenny was the medical officer on the UPOLU, the depot ship for *AE1* and *AE2*. He socialised with the officers of *AE1* and *AE2*. From remarks in his diary he apparently had time on his hands and maintained a frank account of events surrounding the disappearance of *AE1*.

4.9.2 In his diary Hamilton-Kenny records that Stoker believed *AE1* had been attacked by a German steamer, (gaps in deciphering the handwritten diary are indicated by question marks):

"Stoker said to me he thought the enemy had got them – two small German boats COMET & PLANET are in these waters – Point Gazelle is where AE1 was last seen & afraid <u>might</u>? have <u>taken</u>? place from a creek or behind a corner & a 3 pound shell pumped into her"[31]

Later entries record rejection of the official line of mishap as the source of *AE1*'s demise:

"Stoker still believes she was spotted by the enemy – he scoffs at any idea of internal explosion or a floating mine or a rock."[32]

4.10 Lieutenant Emil Joseph Lauer

29 Extract from the diary of Henry Kinder, ERA *AE2*.

30 Signal log HMAS AUSTRALIA 14th September 1914, Darren Brown image IMPG 2436.jpg

31 Dr Fred Hamilton-Kenny diary 29th August 1914 – 26th February 1915, MO SS UPOLU, Presented by Fred Hamilton-Kenny to Mitchell Library, State Library of NSW, 1964 (transcribed by Tim Smith on 19th April 2011), p68, Wednesday 16th September 1914.

32 Ibid, p 81 Thursday, 17th September 1914.

4.10.1 This information has been provided by Peter Richardson. Lieutenant Lauer was a German infantry reservist appointed by the German Governor Haber to take charge of a party of 12 armed reservists and ordered to proceed from Madang to Rabaul by the KOLONIALGESELLSCHAFT. There is a slight confusion with his name in the records; with Emil and Ernst in the documentation. In according with the births and deaths registry at Neumagen, it is possible that he was baptised Joseph Ernst but called himself Emil Joseph.

4.10.2 His title was Katasterkontrolleur/Landmesser, Oberleutnant d. Res. He was born on 25th May 1877 at Neumagen in Prussia (Preussen), since 1969, this has been known as Neumagen-Dhron ist eine Ortsgemeinde im Landkreis Bernkastel-Wittlich in Rheinland-Pfalz. He died on 25th September 1915, killed in action at the battle of Ypres. His rank and unit at that time is recorded as Oberleutnant d.R. 3. Oberelsäss. Inf. Rgt. Nr. 172.

4.10.3 His father was a man of standing in the community; Nikolaus Lauer was the Mayor (Bürgermeister) Bürgermeisterei of Neumagen 1876-1902.

4.10.4 It is frustrating at this point that we have been unable to locate Lt. Lauer's report to Governor Haber on his doings on the 'KOLONIALGESELLSCHAFT'. If found it may provide some of the timeline answers that we are searching for, in particular, whether the 'KOLONIALGESELLSCHAFT' was the 'steamer' seen by YARRA on Sunday afternoon, 13th September and whether the 'KOLONIALGESELLSCHAFT' subsequently attacked *AE1*. Although it is not clear given the sequence of events, how such a report would have become available to the German Governor writing his report in Sydney on 30th October 1915 – perhaps Lauer had the opportunity to write it before being deported to Germany, or it may have been cited in anticipation?

4.10.5 Lauer appears to be a man of dedication, zeal, energy and initiative; he managed to avoid internment in Australia, return to Germany, rejoin the German Army and was killed in action on the Western front – all achieved in just over a year from the grounding of KOLONIALGESELLSCHAFT.

4.11 Petty Officer Reuschel

4.11.1 This information has been provided by Peter Richardson, gleaned from Aubrey Hodgson's reference in his dairy, Reuschel's POW record at Liverpool Camp in NSW where Reuschel was registered as an alien on 23rd November 1916 and contact with his niece in Germany. Many years ago after reading Aubrey Hodgson's diary, Peter located Reuschel in the ' SS Murex' shipping list. Interestingly, Reuschel was transported to Sydney with a number of other senior German prisoners and not the rank and file. His name was in fact misspelled; his full name was Wilhelm Gustav Edwin REUSCHEL — Machinist Mate or Petty Officer, on his gravestone O.B. Masch. Mt. = that should translate into: *Chief Machinist Petty Officer* or *Chief Machinist Petty Officer Second Class.*

4.11.2 Peter has been investigating an unconfirmed suggestion that Reuschel was in Rabaul Hospital (Namanula Hill) recovering from typhoid at the time of *AE1*'s loss. How he ended up as a prisoner on the SS AORANGI and where he was taken prisoner in Rabaul is unknown. Reuschel is believed to have been from the German steamer, PLANET (as recorded on his internment records at fig 2 below), Reuschel may have been in Mioko at the time the KOLONIALGESELLSCHAFT pulled in, joined the crew or heard the story of KOLONIALGESELLSCHAFT's action with *AE1* there, he has never been confirmed as being on the KOLONIALGESELLSCHAFT.

4.11.3 John Foster dismisses Reuschel's possible involvement on the basis that he was recuperating from typhoid at the time of the action and would not have been able to assume command from Captain Banzleben, the captain of KOLONIALGESELLSCHAFT in any case.[33] It is not clear how Foster was able to confirm Reuschel's illness. Nor does it explain why Reuschel would invent such a story, or how he managed to come up with such a credible account.

4.11.4 Reuschel died of the Spanish flu in February 1920, he would only have just settled in after he got back from Liverpool POW camp before he died.

4.12 Governor Haber

Aubrey Hodgson commented on the arrival of Governor Haber onboard Aorangi as a prisoner:

> *"The German deposed Governor was brought onboard to await passage to Sydney. He has 3 servants and large amount of luggage.*
>
> *He is a dapper little man, with fat bloated face, large blossom nose, tremendous corporation, wearing a high collar, which I fear, must be a serious menace to his ears. He appears genial natured, and has a "satisfied and self-confident" air with him. He dines in his cabin, and has every comfort that can be extended, and a stalwart Frenchman stands guard over his apartments"*

33 Foster, John, *Entombed But Not Forgotten*, Sydney 2006, p73.

Section 5 — Reconstructing the Sequence of Events

5.1 The Deployment to Rabaul

5.1.1 Level of Operational Work Up In *AE1*

Diaries and records on *AE1* were lost with her, but *AE2* can be looked at instead. According to PO Kinder's diary *AE2* had minimal dived experience:

- The dived trials post build in January 1914 appear to be the only occasion that *AE1* dived prior to deployment to New Guinea.
- These trials were combined with the engine trials and conducted in one day.
- No operational work up was conducted in the UK; the 10 days spent in Portsmouth were employed preparing for the delivery voyage.
- During this period, the gyrocompasses and WT sets were fitted.
- The hydroplanes were removed prior to sailing from Portsmouth for the voyage to Australia to prevent damage in bad weather, so diving was not possible.
- After arriving at Australia on 24th May 1914 *AE2* (and presumably *AE1*) conducted a number of dives alongside to check for leaks and at least one trip outside Sydney Heads, presumably after the docking and refitting of the hydroplanes, where they dived for an hour.

5.1.2 Preparations for Deployment

AE1 and *AE2* completed a docking in Fitzroy Dock, Cockatoo Island 3rd-24th June 1914[34] and were refitting in Sydney when war was declared. The refits were truncated; *AE1* and *AE2* were hastily readied, completing their refits on 8th and 10th August respectively. The requirement for a depot ship was met by chartering the SS UPOLU on 18th August (discussed further below).

5.1.3 The Transit

AE1 sailed for Rabaul on 28th August and *AE2* five days later. PO Kinder in *AE2* records that they made a slow passage northward in company with UPOLU, arriving in Port Moresby on 5th and 6th September for fuel and provisions, sailing on the 7th to rendezvous with the main Fleet at Rossell Island on 9th September, prior to their entry into Rabaul on 11th September. The AWM photograph J03241 of *AE1* at the rendezvous with HMAS AUSTRALIA and HMAS YARRA in the background is one of the first shots of

34 Aubrey Hodgson, diary 22nd September 1914, Australian War Memorial — 3DRL/6032 — Hodgson, Aubrey Wilfred.

the modified, fin mounted WT mast.[35] It is worth noting that there would have been no opportunity to work up and little time for dived operations to induct the new members of the crew; including LEUT Scarlett who had recently joined *AE1* in Sydney as the First Lieutenant.

5.1.4 Support Arrangements in Rabaul

Signal traffic indicates that both submarines were being supported by the engineering staff who had stood by the submarines during building (see para 5.3.2 below). They were embarked in UPOLU.

5.1.5 Trim Dives

The patrol on 14th September was *AE1*'s first period underway after arrival in Rabaul, whilst there is no record of *AE1* embarking fuel or stores on arrival, (this would not have been essential if fuel and provisions had been embarked in Port Moresby on 5/6th September). It is judged to be highly likely that Besant would have conducted a trim dive as soon as convenient after sailing and clearing the anchorage. This may explain why PARRAMATTA lost contact with *AE1* after their exchange of signals early on the morning of 14th September and why *AE1* made ground to the NE (the best course for diving is beam on the prevailing sea).

5.1.6 Operation Orders, Patrol Orders and Correspondence Issued By RADM Patey

Patey's Sailing Order No: 3 covered the deployment of the Fleet to PNG and is extensively quoted in his Report of Proceedings covering this period.[36] The Sailing Order did not include any special arrangements for submarine operations or communications. Ian Noble advises that:

x Patey's report is in AWM E 181 File 1777 and file 1771.

x AWM Personal Record 3DRL/0053 contains RADM Patey's letters in 17 folders.

x Of the 17 folders only Folders 6 and 7 were relevant by time and location, and only General letter No 26 in Folder 6 included anything of relevance to our research.

x The contents of Folder No 5 pre-dated *AE1*'s loss.

x Folder No 7 contained General letters Nos 28, 29 (Oct 1914), 30, 31, 32 (November 1914) and 33 (5th December 1914).

x Patey sent this long series of letters at frequent intervals to the Secretary of the Commonwealth Naval Board of Administration in Melbourne.

35 John Jeremy, former MD of Cockatoo Dockyard advised by Email 160949May11, that the dates are recorded in the original docking books, now held at the National Archives at Chester Hill; there are no details of the work undertaken.

36 White, Michael W D, *Australian Submarines – A History, AGPS 1992*, p31.

- x General Letter No 26 of 20th September 1914 includes ENCOUNTER's Letter of Proceedings as an attachment.
- x Pages XVIII and XIX of Letter No 26 report the loss of *AE1*, and Page XXVI mentions the KOLONIALGESELLESCHAFT.

5.2 Geography and Weather of the Area

5.2.1 Geography

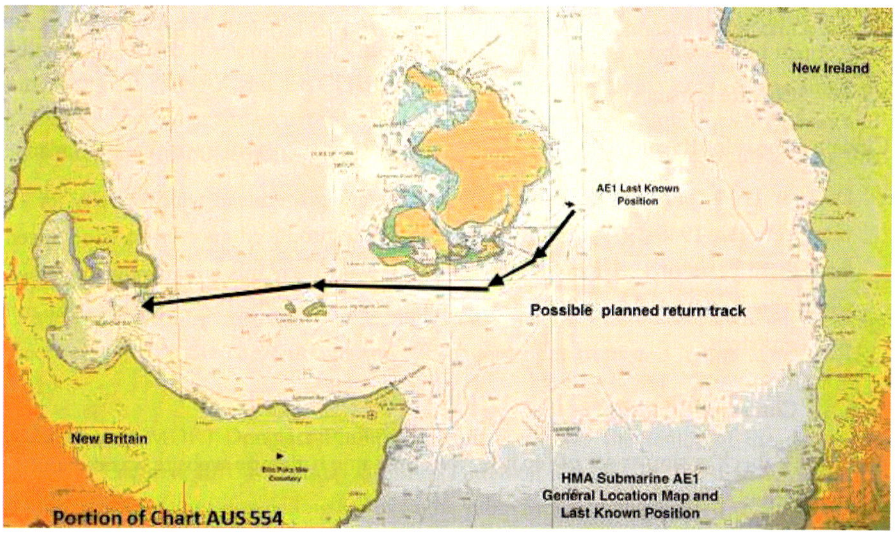

Figure 17 – General Location Chart.

David Nicholls' General Operations Plot reconstruction above, details the geography and relevant environmental data.

5.2.2 PNG Climate

The German Protectorate of New Guinea covered the area bounded by Latitude 1°-8° South and Longitude 141°-156° East. The climate is essentially tropical, it is however equable, with plentiful and regular rainfall. The NW monsoon begins in late November, when the rainy season begins and lasts until March/April, frequent thunderstorms with heavy downpours occur, the weather is hot and oppressive. Towards the end of April the SE monsoon sets in, days are usually bright and clear and the wind although often boisterous, is generally a steady breeze, making conditions more pleasant than the rainy season.[37]

37 Vice Admiral Patey, G, *Report on the Participation by the Australian Seagoing Fleet in the Operation,* p 37. AWM 33, 483047.

5.5 *AE1* & PARRAMATTA Patrol 14th September 1914

5.5.1 Communications between *AE1* and PARRAMATTA

Figure 18 – HMAS PARRAMATTA. AWM 301140.

5.5.1.1 We have been unable to determine if *AE1* had stowed her WT mast prior to sailing on 14th September 1914 in order to be able to dive quickly if required, or to conduct a trim dive. No WT messages from her are recorded in any of the ships' WT logs on the 14th September. Nor have we been able to locate PARRAMATTA's signal or WT logs.

5.5.1.2 Patey's Report of the loss of *AE1* dated 17th September 1914[43] indicates that the aerial was probably rigged and the set working at 1430 when the last message was exchanged with PARRAMATTA:

> *'"PARRAMATTA" and Submarine A.E.1 were in communication by wireless at 2.30 p.m. and when A.E.1 asked "PARRAMATTA" what he considered the visibility was. So that there is no doubt he was all right up to that time.'*

5.5.1.3 Stoker implies in his account that *AE1*'s WT was working:[44]

> *"....Admiral signalling by wireless for information. No reply could be obtained from AE1."*

5.5.1.4 WT contact would explain how PARRAMATTA was able to steam directly to *AE1*'s location having lost visual contact with her earlier that morning. However, it is not

43 Navy file 14/7429, Darren Brown images 373306_0028, 29 and 30.jpg

44 H. G. Stoker DSO, Commander RN, *Straws In The Wind*, Herbert Jenkins, London, p 64.

clear how Patey came by this information, as he indicates in the same report, he had not had the opportunity to talk with the CO of PARRAMATTA:

> *'I had to leave Rabaul at noon on 15th September, so have had no opportunity of seeing the Captain of "PARRAMATTA."'*

5.5.1.5 Nor do the reports from PARRAMATTA confirm this advice that *AE1* and PARRAMATTA were in communication by WT during the afternoon of 14th September. Few, if any records of WT signals being sent from or to *AE1* and *AE2* can be found in the signal logs of the other participants. One of the few was a message from *AE2* to PARRAMATTA was logged in ENCOUNTER's signal log at 1230 on 16th September:

> *"Have wireless mast rigged and will look for you every half hour"*

5.5.1.6 On balance it would appear possible that PARRAMATTA and *AE1* were in WT contact during the course of the patrol on 14th September, but we lack conclusive evidence to confirm this likelihood.

5.5.2 Last Sighted Position

5.5.2.1 LEUT Warren's Report of Proceedings of PARRAMATTA on Monday 14th September 1914 does not actually give a definite position for *AE1*'s last sighting, simply stating that 'At 1430 PARRAMATTA was close to submarine':

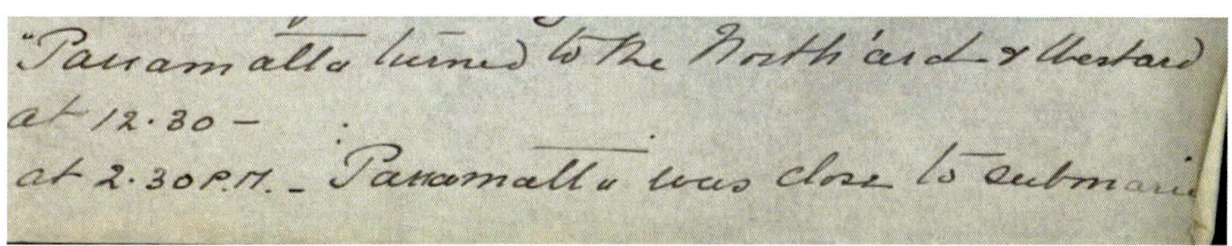
"Parramatta turned to the North'ard & Westard
at 12.30 –
at 2.30 P.M. – Parramatta was close to submari

Figure 19 – LEUT W H F Warren's original manuscript Report of Proceeding of HMAS PARRAMATTA for 14th September 1914. Image: Darren Brown.

The tracing of the chart attached to LEUT Warren's Report of Proceedings of HMAS PARRAMATTA on Monday 14th September 1914 provides the only firsthand record of *AE1*'s 'last sighted' position.

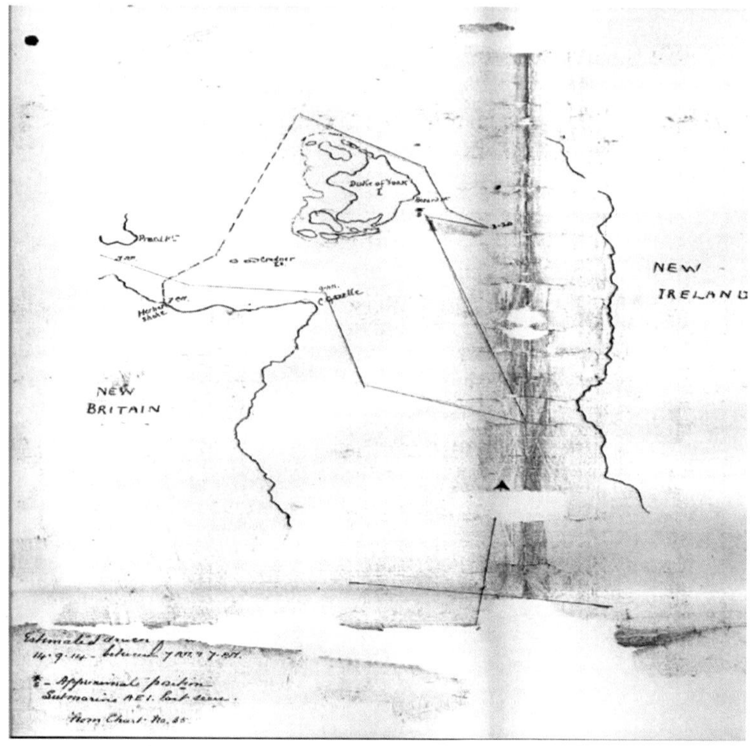

Figure 20 – Sketch attachment to LEUT Warren's Report of Proceedings of HMAS PARRAMATTA on Monday 14th September 1914. Image: Darren Brown.

This is tracing is a reconstruction, rather than a precisely plotted position based on fixing both PARRAMATTA and *AE1* simultaneously.

5.5.2.2 The covering letter to this report dated 21st September at Rabaul advises that it is:

> *'accompanied by tracings shewing estimated courses of PARRAMATTA on that date & approximate position of Submarine A.E.1. when last seen'.*

The asterisk S in the legend at the bottom left hand corner refers to the symbol S on the chart, this is identified as:

> *'Approximate position Submarine AE1. Last seen. From Chart No. 35.'*

5.5.2.3 Page 3 of LEUT Warren's Report of Proceedings of HMAS PARRAMATTA on Monday 14th September 1914 continues, 'At 2.30pm Parramatta was close to submarine...' next paragraph 'At 3.20 submarine was lost sight of...'

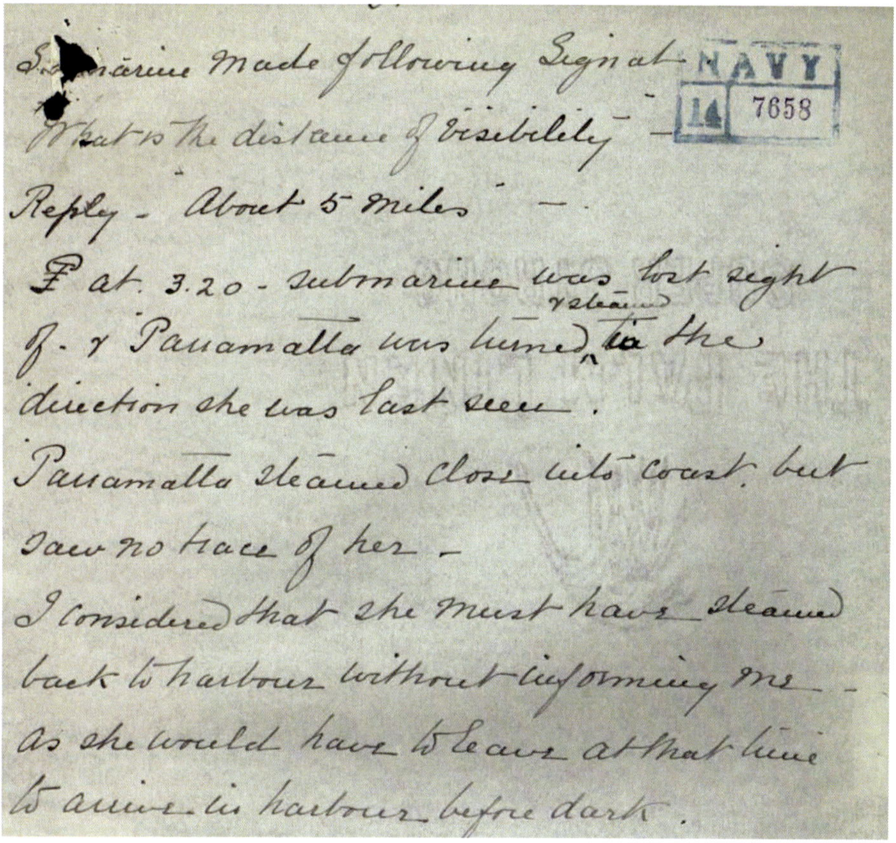

Submarine made following Signal –

NAVY 14 7658

"What is the distance of visibility" –

Reply – "About 5 miles" –

at 3.20 – submarine was lost sight of – & Parramatta was turned & steamed to the direction she was last seen.

Parramatta steamed close into coast, but saw no trace of her –

I considered that she must have steamed back to harbour without informing me – as she would have to leave at that time to arrive in harbour before dark.

Figure 21 – Extract from Page 3 of LEUT Warren's Report of Proceedings of HMAS PARRAMATTA on Monday 141 September 1914, concerning the last sighting of *AE1*.
Image: Darren Brown.

A manuscript letter dated 21st September 1914 covered the Report of Proceedings:

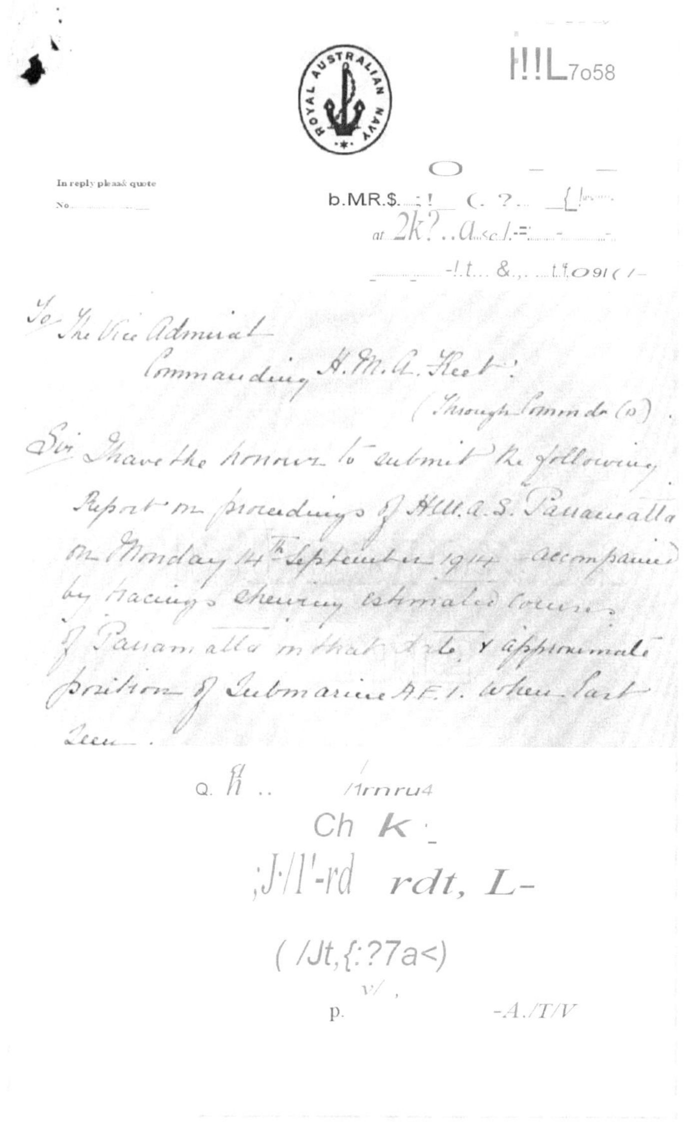
ROYAL AUSTRALIAN NAVY

In reply please quote No.

To The Vice Admiral
Commanding H.M.A. Fleet.
(Through Commodore (S)).

Sir I have the honour to submit the following Report on proceedings of H.M.A.S. Parramatta on Monday 14th September 1914 accompanied by tracings showing estimated course of Parramatta on that date, & approximate position of Submarine AE1. when last seen.

Figure 22 – Photo of the manuscript Covering Letter to LEUT Warren's Report of Proceedings of HMAS PARRAMATTA on Monday 14th September 1914.
Image: Darren Brown.

All records contain the caveat 'approximate' – ergo we are dealing with a reconstruction and should consider the last sighting position as a probability area, rather than a precise position.

5.5.2.4 Likely Navigational Accuracy

PARRAMATTA should have been within visual fixing range of the Duke of York Island, allowing for a compass error of up to 5 degrees, (it is not known what sort of compass PARRAMATTA had, it appears to have been a magnetic compass; Besant's diary of the voyage to Australia reports m*AE1*'s gyro compass had an error of +- 3 degrees[45] this may be typical for the earlier gyro compasses). The position reported by PARRAMATTA should have been within about 1 nm of the reported position after allowing for fixing and plotting errors.

5.5.2.5 Even allowing for the traditions of the 'Silent Service' and 'stiff upper lip stoicism' of the era, Warren's Report is remarkably abbreviated and short of any elaborating detail about the incident, *AE1*'s appearance, movements or state. In the absence of any formal inquiry into the loss, it is the only firsthand record survives today. PARRAMATTA was 'close to submarine' at 2.30 pm. The 'last seen time' is reported in PARRAMATTA's ROP as 3.20 pm; PARRAMATTA then continued in her ROP that she headed back close to the coast and saw no further sign of her.

5.5.3 Subsequent Discrepancies In Last Seen Position

5.5.3.1 At approximately 2140 on 14th September PARRAMATTA advised AUSTRALIA[46] that *AE1* was last seen at 1530, this is marginally different to PARRAMATTA's initial report that records a last sighting at 1520. Nothing much turns on this discrepancy.

5.5.3.2 At 2310 HMAS WARREGO (Commander D) having been ordered by Patey to search for *AE1*, asked AUSTRALIA for the last seen position, after a 2 hour delay AUSTRALIA advised 'St George's Channel' – an area, rather than a position.

5.5.3.3 In response to a query from ENCOUNTER on the last sighted position, at 0820 on 15th September, PARRAMATTA advised, that she had last seen *AE2* at 'Waira Pt., Duke of York Islands, 1530 hrs on 14th September.[47] This appears to be some distance to the north of the position plotted on the tracing accompanying the ROP.

5.5.3.4 Patey's Report of Proceedings of the Fleet Operation to capture PNG continues this air of imprecision, by advising that *AE1* was last seen at about 1530 between Waira and Jaquinot Pt. (the latter is further south and west of PARRAMATTA's reported position on the tracing).[48]

45 Foster, John, *Entombed But Not Forgotten*, Sydney, 2006, p 20.
46 HMAS AUSTRALIA Captain's signal log.
47 HMAS ENCOUNTER Captain's signal log.
48 Darren Brown image IMG2144.

5.5.4 Hypothesis For *AE1*'s Movements 14th September 1914

5.5.4.1 It is difficult to be precise about *AE1*'s behaviour on the 14th — since we have no firsthand accounts to counter any incorrect assertions by us; much of what we are left with is conjecture. We will never know why *AE1* deviated from the instructions issued for patrolling (and followed carefully by Stoker in *AE2* the previous day).

5.5.4.2 One line of supposition is that Besant chose to look for the steamer reported by YARRA on the previous day to the south of Duke of York Island. If so, the southern side of the Duke of York Island was the logical place to investigate:

- x It could be interpreted that Besant chose to view the instructions to PARRAMATTA as not pertaining to him — 'what orders do **you** have' and headed off in search of yesterday's steamer, action, glory and prize money?
- x It is strange that as the senior officer of the two he did not take charge of PARRAMATTA (as Stoker appears to have done the day previously with YARRA). This dissociation with the orders given to PARRAMATTA could explain it.
- x On the other hand, *AE1* could have been wrestling with a defect or series of defects (e.g. a diesel/main motor or gyro) that caused him to part company and not cover much ground at all, only making it to *AE1*'s 1430 position during the course of the day.
- x *AE1* could be expected to conduct a trim dive shortly after 0900, perhaps turning to the north east as the best course for diving (beam on to the sea) and would have lost contact with PARRAMATTA during this evolution.
- x We have been unable to definitively establish how the signals between *AE1* and PARRAMATTA were passed. One possibility was by flashing light or megaphone – this could explain the absence of WT traffic in other ship's logs, perhaps *AE1* had stowed the aerial in order to be able to dive at short notice, this would remove her WT capability.
- x Flashing lights would require them to be reasonably close, say less than 5,000m and possibly explains why there were so few messages between them.
- x The stowed WT aerial would prevent a distress message being sent quickly after an accident.
- x On the other hand, we have Patey's report that *AE1* and PARRAMATTA were exchanging messages by WT on the afternoon of the 14th September 1914. This would also explain how PARRAMATTA was able to relocate *AE1* so readily on the afternoon.

5.6 The Search

5.6.1 The search mounted by the RAN ships was not well coordinated; no instructions were issued regarding a datum or allocating specific areas to the various units.

- x AUSTRALIA was first alerted to *AE1*'s failure to return by a signal from Stoker in *AE2* at 2015.[49]
- x YARRA and PARRAMATTA sailed after 2300 to commence the search; ENCOUNTER joined the search for the period 0525-1045 and WARREGO after 0900 on the 15th.
- x AUSTRALIA and SYDNEY sailed for Sydney pm 15th, leaving ENCOUNTER in charge of the search.
- x Several ships had to request the last known position and status of the search; they seemed to have largely used their own judgement on where to search.
- x Predictably, given this lack of central coordination, ambiguity crept in over the last known position.
- x Nonetheless, the areas searched appear to have covered the areas most likely to contain *AE1*, and any wreckage or debris, albeit the strong currents experienced in the area would disperse these during the hours of darkness.
- x A detailed discussion of the search conduct is contained in Annex C.

5.6.2 It appears from the signal traffic that the direction of the search was largely left to the participants. For example, the decision for YARRA and PARRAMATTA to search 30 nm to the northwest was made by these ships, not RADM Patey. A WT message from PARRAMATTA to the Flag logged at a time of 0442 records:

> *'Submit passed around Duke of York Islands, nothing seen to North with "YARRA" could motor schooner proceed and examine Credner and Duke of York Island and N.E. Coast New Britain at daylight while we search seaward to N.W.'*[50]

RADM Patey's report claims this as his initiative:

> *'On the morning of the 15th September, nothing having been seen, I ordered the "PARRAMATTA" and "YARRA" to make a sweep 30 miles to the N.W. of Duke of York Island. In this, they were joined by "WARREGO", who was returning from an expedition to Kawieng (sic). Nothing was seen.'*

5.6.3 AUSTRALIA made 3 unanswered WT calls to *AE1* on the evening of the 14th as concerns mounted for her safety.

5.6.4 The signal traffic on the morning of 15th September illustrates a level of confusion. For example, ENCOUNTER sailed as ordered at 0525 to look for *AE1* from her position as guardship off the Beehive Rocks in the entrance to Rabaul. By 0720 RADM Patey realised he no longer has a guardship on station and he inquired as to her position and actions. ENCOUNTER responds (to an unlogged signal) — 'I am searching for submarine in

49 HMAS AUSTRALIA signal log 14th September 1914, Darren Brown image IMGP 2450.jpg
50 HMAS AUSTRALIA Captain's signal log 15th September 1914.

accordance with your orders'.[51] This is as pointed as a subordinate can be to a senior officer! The response comes quickly, at 0755 Flag directs ENCOUNTER peremptorily, 'Return to harbour at once'. And the inevitable conclusion to this exchange, relayed by YARRA to ENCOUNTER at 1028, 'Rear Admiral wishes to see Captain on anchoring'.

5.6.5 By 1415 on 15th September, when PARRAMATTA returned to anchor in Simpson Harbour the search is effectively over, apart from motor boats and a motorised schooner.

5.6.6 If RADM Patey or ENCOUNTER had come to a conclusion as to *AE1*'s position when lost they did not record it.

5.7 Events Ashore

5.7.1 The command and control arrangements for what was a joint Army-Navy operation were imprecise by today's standards. Naval forces were controlled by RADM Patey in HMAS AUSTRALIA, Colonel Holmes ('the Brigadier Commanding Australian Forces') remained in HMAS BERRIMA and was in charge of arrangements ashore; Patey steered clear of these arrangements. The single WT circuit operated by the ships provided the real time interface between the two commanders, who also met on a couple of occasions during the engagements ashore. In the event there were some excellent examples of local commanders acting on their own initiative to fill the gaps – with very successful outcomes.

5.7.2 The actions ashore commenced soon after the RAN force arrived off Rabaul and Herbertshohe on the morning of 11th September14. SYDNEY had earlier embarked 50 men from the naval contingent carried in BERRIMA; 25 of these were landed at Herbertshohe, the remaining 25 were transferred to WARREGO and YARRA for landing at Kabakaul (6.5 km east of Herbertshohe). It was believed there were two wireless stations, one operational, sited inland from Kabakaul, and the other under construction, inland from Herbertshohe. The two landing parties were directed to capture their respective WT stations.

5.7.3 One party of 25 under LEUT R G Bowen landed unopposed at 0700 on jetty a little east of the Kabakaul pier. 12 men from WARREGO and YARRA reinforced LEUT Bowen. The party moved inland, soon encountering the German defenders and fighting ensued. WARREGO and YARRA responded to a call for reinforcement by landing an additional 59 men armed with a variety of weapons (cutlasses, pistols and some rifles), under Lieutenant Hill from YARRA. At the same time, further reinforcements were called for and two companies (100 men) from the naval contingent on BERRIMA also landed and reached the firing line at 1300. By 1900, the wireless station was in their hands, with the equipment still intact – *'an affair of continuous good luck, used promptly and to the full by the men concerned'*.[52] The good news finally reached Patey at 0100 on 12th September11. The

51 HMAS AUSTRALIA Captain's signal log 15th September 1914.

52 Jose, Arthur, W, *The Official History of Australia In The War 1914-1918*, Vol IX, Ch 3, Sydney, 19

action is well described in the Official History of Australia's Involvement in the War 1914-1918, Volume IX Chapter 3 and Volume X Chapter 5.

5.7.4 The party of 30 under SBLT C Webber looking for the second WT station under construction landed at Herbertshohe unopposed at 0600 and set out on the road to Toma, 6.4 Km away. Having reached the halfway point without opposition or discovering any signs of a WT station, Webber decided that he had overshot the station or the information was erroneous, since his force was not large enough to maintain contact with the shore party guarding the wharf, he decided to return to Herbertshohe. That afternoon, as concern at the lack of news from Webber mounted, a military detachment of four companies of infantry, a machine gun section and a naval party from SYDNEY with a 12-pounder gun landed at Herbertshohe at 1530 to regain contact with Webber. Webber returned at nightfall and the force garrisoned at Herbertshohe.

5.7.5 The next day, on 12th September BERRIMA re-embarked some of the forces ashore in Herbertshohe and proceeded alongside the Rabaul pier at 1800. A force of infantry and naval reservists was landed and secured Rabaul unopposed. The British flag was hoisted at a ceremony at Rabaul at 1500 13th September 1914.

5.7.6 The ships' signal logs for 13th September are busy with messages concerning the landings and movement of forces ashore. YARRA's sighting of a steamer at 1800 arrived during a period when the shore parties appeared to still be under threat, causing the Admiral to curtly reinforce his orders to the destroyers (WARREGO, YARRA, and PARRAMATTA) not to pursue the steamer and to support the landings at Herbershohe.

5.7.7 In the early hours of 14th September Lt Col Watson, ashore at Herbershohe, was ordered to advance at 0600 on Toma with 4 companies of infantry and a machine gun and field gun landed by ENCOUNTER, in order to arrest Governor Haber. ENCOUNTER advised Watson that captured sketches showed the enemy positions and that ENCOUNTER intended to shell these with 6" 'lydite at 0600 in support of this advance. At 0830 ENCOUNTER advised the Admiral that 48 rounds of 6" had been fired. The signal logs indicate that the day was a busy one providing support to this advance and anxiously waiting for news. At 2143, Lt Col Watson signalled via ENCOUNTER that he had successfully occupied Toma at 1500 and had returned to Herbertshohe at 1830. The Governor had surrendered and arrangements had been made for him to report to Herbertshohe at 1100 the next day, 15th September to negotiate the terms. Watson complimented ENCOUNTER on the accuracy of her shelling; it appears to have had a dramatic impact on the negotiations with the Governor.

5.7.8 This concluded the fighting ashore. Negotiations on the terms of capitulation continued until 17th September and the formal laying down of arms by German forces occurred on 21st September at Herbertshohe. Colonel Holmes managed these operations. In the meantime Admiral Patey had other matters to concern him; the loss of *AE1*, the whereabouts of the German Pacific Squadron and the need to prepare major Fleet units for the escort of the first AIF convoy to the Middle East to name but a few.

5.8 Formal Inquiries & Reports

5.8.1 HMAS ENCOUNTER's Board of Inquiry

Shortly after AUSTRALIA sailed from Rabaul on 16th September Patey directed CAPT C. La P. Lewin, RN, the Commanding Officer of ENCOUNTER, to conduct a Board of Inquiry and to call LEUTs Warren, the CO of PARRAMATTA, and Stoker, CO of *AE2*, as witnesses. AUSTRALIA returned to Rabaul at short notice on 19th September in response to (false) reports that the German Pacific Squadron was enroute New Guinea. This unexpected return may have served to nullify the orders, in the event it does not appear that the Board of Inquiry was held and no records have been found.

5.8.2 RADM Patey's Report of 17th September 1914

5.8.2.1 RADM Patey rendered a three page report to the Naval Board, dated 17th September 1914[53] including the statement that *AE1* had been in contact with HMAS PARRAMATTA by WT at 1430. It is not clear how Patey obtained this information; he advises that he had not had an opportunity to speak directly with LEUT Warren (due to ship movements). If the Patey report is correct (corroboration has not been found), then *AE1* had the WT mast rigged and a working WT set at 1430. A functioning WT capability in *AE1* would have significant implications:

- Since *AE1* was essentially heading for Rabaul, it is judged most unlikely that Besant would have lowered the WT mast for what was intended to be a surfaced passage back to her depot ship, UPOLU.
- If *AE1* was forced to dive to avoid gunfire the WT mast would have had to be left up — in the knowledge that it would probably be carried away (but better to lose the WT mast than the submarine).
- In the event of grounding whilst surfaced enroute Rabaul with the WT mast up one could reasonably expect that *AE1* would have sent a distress call — presuming the mast survived the grounding and someone was listening?
- On the other hand it could argued that if Besant intended to do a check dive, then he would have lowered the WT mast, dived, had a fatal accident of some sort and there would have been no distress call.
- A practice dive at this time of day is considered unlikely by Stoker (and contemporary submarine operators), particularly given the instructions to be back by sunset was reinforced so directly by AUSTRALIA's approval to proceed that morning.

5.8.2.2 RADM Patey concludes that:

> '9. *The weather was fine but hazy, the sea smooth, no enemy in the neighbourhood, so I can only think that she made a practice dive on her way back to harbour, and through*

53 Navy Office file 14/7429 dated 17th September 1914.

some inexplicable accident failed to return to the surface. The water is very deep in the vicinity, i.e., from 200 to 300 fathoms.

This conclusion is heavily qualified:

10. I have interviewed Lieutenant Stoker of Submarine A.E.2, but he can throw no light on what might be the cause. In his opinion, her motive power could not possibly be entirely disabled, nor could any internal explosion have occurred. She cannot have been in collision as there were no craft in the immediate neighbourhood. If she struck on any underwater danger and so foundered, some traces would have been found.'

5.8.3 RADM Patey's General Letter # 26 dated 20th September 1914

5.8.3.1 RADM Patey wrote a series of 'General Letters' to the Secretary of the Navy. AWM Personal Record 3DRL/0053 contains RADM Patey's letters in 17 folders. Of the 17 folders only Folders 6 and 7 were relevant by time and location, and only General letter No 26 in Folder 6 included anything of relevance to our research. The contents of Folder No 5 pre-dated *AE1*'s loss. Folder No 7 contained General letters Nos 28, 29 (Oct 1914), 30, 31, 32 (Nov 1914) and 33 (5th December 1914).

5.8.3.2 Letter # 26 dated 20th September 1914 from Rabaul covers the loss of *AE1*, discovery of KOLONIALGESELLSCHAFT aground on the reef and it forwards a copy of HMAS ENCOUNTER's Report of Proceedings whilst in charge in Rabaul during HMAS AUSTRALIA's absence. The letter contains some new advice on the loss of *AE1* and finding of KOLONIALGESELLSCHAFT and is the first record of HMAS ENCOUNTER's Report that has been found.

5.8.3.3 Page 18 of this Report covers the loss of *AE1*. It includes advice on the loss of *AE1* that is marginally different, or not contained in the earlier Report:

'At 3.30 p.m. "PARRAMATTA" saw Submarine AE1 to the South East of Duke of York Island apparently returning towards harbour. This is what A.E.1 should have been doing.

This is the last definite intelligence of her whereabouts.

I have not had the opportunity yet to interview the Captain of "PARRAMATTA" – he apparently stayed out for a last look around, returned to Herbertshohe, and was relieved by "YARRA" for the night patrol at 7.0 p.m.'

5.8.3.4 We know from PARRAMATTA's Report of Proceedings (see para 5.5.2.1 above) that he lost sight of the submarine at 1520. Further, LEUT WARREN made no comment in his report about *AE1* 'returning to harbour'; he presumed this was what she he had done.

5.8.3.5 It is unfortunate that RADM Patey had still not interviewed the Captain of PARRAMATTA prior to writing this letter. One is left wondering whether fresh information has caused the subtle but significant changes in his account, or the passage of time is blurring his recollection of events or he is adjusting his account to cast his actions in the best possible light!

5.8.3.6 *Letter # 26 continues:*

'At 8.0 p.m. as Submarine A.E.1 had not arrived in harbour, I ordered "PARRAMATTA" and

"YARRA", burning navigation lights and using searchlights as necessary, to proceed to search.'

5.8.3.7 As discussed further below at para 5.8.8 this is incorrect, the orders for the search were not issued until later in the night and the first ship, PARRAMATTA, sailed to undertake the search at 2320.

5.8.3.8 Fresh details on the area searched without result are provided; the statement on the complete absence of oil seems to overlook ENCOUNTER's report of an oil slick, subsequently dismissed as a slick from a passing ship:

'The outlying Islands and their coasts, also the coasts of New Ireland and New Britain and all the neighbouring waters, have been searched for an extent of 30 miles. Not the least trace of the Boat, nor of escaping oil, has been found. I deeply regret to report that there does not seem the least prospect of Submarine A.E.1 being afloat.'

5.8.3.9 It is clear that RADM Patey still expected that a Board of Inquiry would be conducted by Acting Captain Lewin in ENCOUNTER:

'I have directed Acting Captain Lewin of "ENCOUNTER" to hold an enquiry and report the result. I am also furnishing a separate report on this regretful incident.'

Further research in his subsequent letters held in the AWM collection indicates no report of ENCOUNTER's inquiry so it is assumed that none was ever held.

5.8.3.10 Page 26 the letter covers the discovery of the KOLONIALGESELLSCHAFT and also adds some critical new details:

'With reference to the report of the finding of the wreck of KOLONIALGESELLSCHAFT, this craft belongs to the exchequer of the Protectorate of German New Guinea; "SYDNEY" passed this spot at noon on 15th September, the day after the loss of the Submarine and there was no wreck there then. The KOLONIALGESELLSCHAFT must have gone ashore on one of the nights 15th, 16th or 17th September. Subsequent investigation shews that KOLONIALGESELLSCHAFT was from the westward and not the eastward, and therefore it does not appear possible to connect her in any way with the loss of Submarine A.E.1. The wreck was examined on 19th September by Commander (D) and the King's Harbour Master.'

5.8.3.11 What Admiral Patey meant by stating that the KOLONIALGESELLSCHAFT came from the westward, not the eastward, is unclear. She came from Madang, which is to the westward of where she grounded so perhaps he meant that. On the other hand perhaps he meant to indicate her direction of travel at the time of the grounding, although the wreck could also have swung around with the tidal stream before she was discovered. RADM

Patey clearly discounted the possible effect of the tide as he considers it conclusive evidence that she was not involved in the loss of *AE1*.

5.8.4 HMAS ENCOUNTER'S Report of Proceedings by Acting Captain Lewin.

5.8.4.1 RADM Patey's letter # 26 forwarded a copy of Acting Captain Lewin's Report of Proceedings dated 19th September 1914, covering activities during AUSTRALIA's absence from noon on 15th September. The following extract from page 1 of the Lewin Report covers the completion of the search for *AE1* and finding of KOLONIALGESELLSCHAFT aground on the reef:

> *'The PARRAMATTA returned on the afternoon of the 15th from her search for the submarine and reported having seen no trace anywhere; search was made in conjunction with YARRA over a large area 30 miles to the Northward of Duke of York group of islands, the latter group was searched by YARRA'*

It, continues on page two and three:

> *At 7 p.m. on the 17th ENCOUNTER, WARREGO and PARRAMATTA weighed and proceeded at ten knots to the west side of the Gazelle Peninsula,* '
>
> *On returning to Rabaul the Destroyers were sent on ahead with a view to searching ATALIKLIKUN Bay but finding a small steamer ashore near the beacon on the reef on the north west point of the Peninsula, WARREGO sent a boat to examine the wreck and found it was the KOLONIA or KOLONIAL; she had been abandoned and was on fire, apparently by design. In the bow was a pedestal and mounting for a gun, the pivot was quite bright, as it is evident that the ship had not been long on the reef and the gun but recently removed; further a used one pounder cartridge was picked up on board of her and I am strongly of opinion that this steamer is connected in some manner with the mysterious disappearance of A.E.1. I have sent NUSA[54] with Lieutenant Commander Jackson on board, conveyed by WARREGO, to search that part of the coast and to obtain any information he can as to the whereabouts of the crew of KOLONIA; it is possible that they may have taken the crew of A.E.1 with them. The ENCOUNTER and two destroyers returned to Rabaul at 6.30 p.m.'*

5.8.4.2 Lewin's report continues with details of the search for *AE1* on page 3 and 4 and information on the theory of a German steamer involvement in the *AE1*'sloss:

> *'In addition to the search for the submarine A.E.1 by the destroyers, the New Ireland coast was closely searched from Matakin River (Lat 3° 55 S) southward to TAMBAKAR point, also the coast from C.TAVUI to PRAED POINT in the crater peninsula by the Chief Officer of the "Berrima" in the "Nusa" while Lieutenant Commander Jackson made a most minute search of the whole of the Duke of York group. In neither case was any (sic) traces found, but Lieutenant Commander Jackson obtained information from a native that a small steamer had been in there at a previous date and I would suggest that on his return from examining the North west coast he be sent over again in the Duke of York*

54 NUSA was a small German Government vessel commandeered by the ANMEF

group to see if he can obtain any further information concerning this small steamer and anything about her and whether she was carrying a gun at the time.

5.8.5 HMAS WARREGO Deck log and Other Records

Whilst it does not provide a precise position for the wreck WARREGO's fair deck log provides sufficient information on her course and position to reconstruct her track and assess the most likely position of KOLONIALGESELLSCHAFT. The resultant position is consistent with that ascertained from HMAS ENCOUNTER's log. We have not found copies of WARREGO's signal or WT logs and are reliant on ENCOUNTER's records; these are fair versions of these logs.

5.8.5.1 The Lewin Report does not give a date; ENCOUNTER's deck log and Captain's signal log confirms that the sighting took place on 18th September.[55]

5.8.5.2 Reconstruction of the grounding position using both ENCOUNTER and WARREGO's deck logs points to a position on the outer reef of Cape Lambert close to the light (... *near the beacon...*) marked on the modern chart. The reconstruiction under by CMDR David Nicolls RAN Rtd summarises the situation.. Based on this reconstruction it would appear that KOLONIALGESELLSCHAFT grounded on outer edge of the northern extremity of the reefs to the north of Cape Lambert, close to a 13.5 m (42 ft) high beacon marking the extremity of the reef. The grounding is most likely to have occurred at night, as by day it would be very difficult to miss seeing the beacon. This Report is specific that only one used cartridge case was found – contrary to some of the diary accounts of multiple cartridge cases. Nothing turns on the number of fired cartridge cases, as even one shot through the pressure hull would have been sufficient to put the *AE1* at grave risk.

55 HMAS ENCOUNTER fair deck log 18th September14, Darren Brown image IMGO 3571.jpg

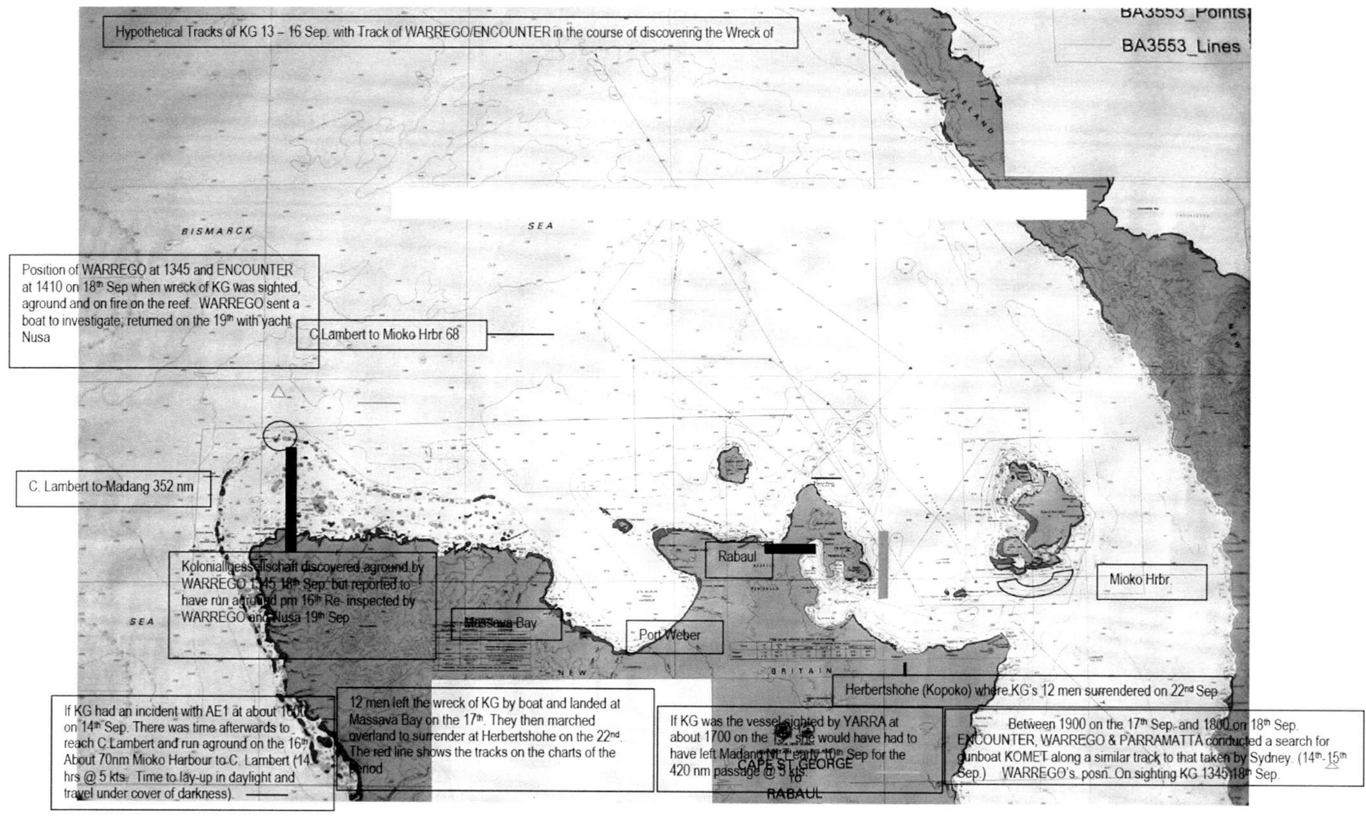

Figure 23 – Hypothetical Track for KOLONIALGESELLSCHAFT, reconstructed from ENCOUNTER & WARREGO's fair deck logs by David Nicholls.

5.8.6 LEUT Stoker's Report

5.8.6.1 Stoker's report rendered from Suva on 16th October 1914 considered four possible causes for the loss of *AE1*:

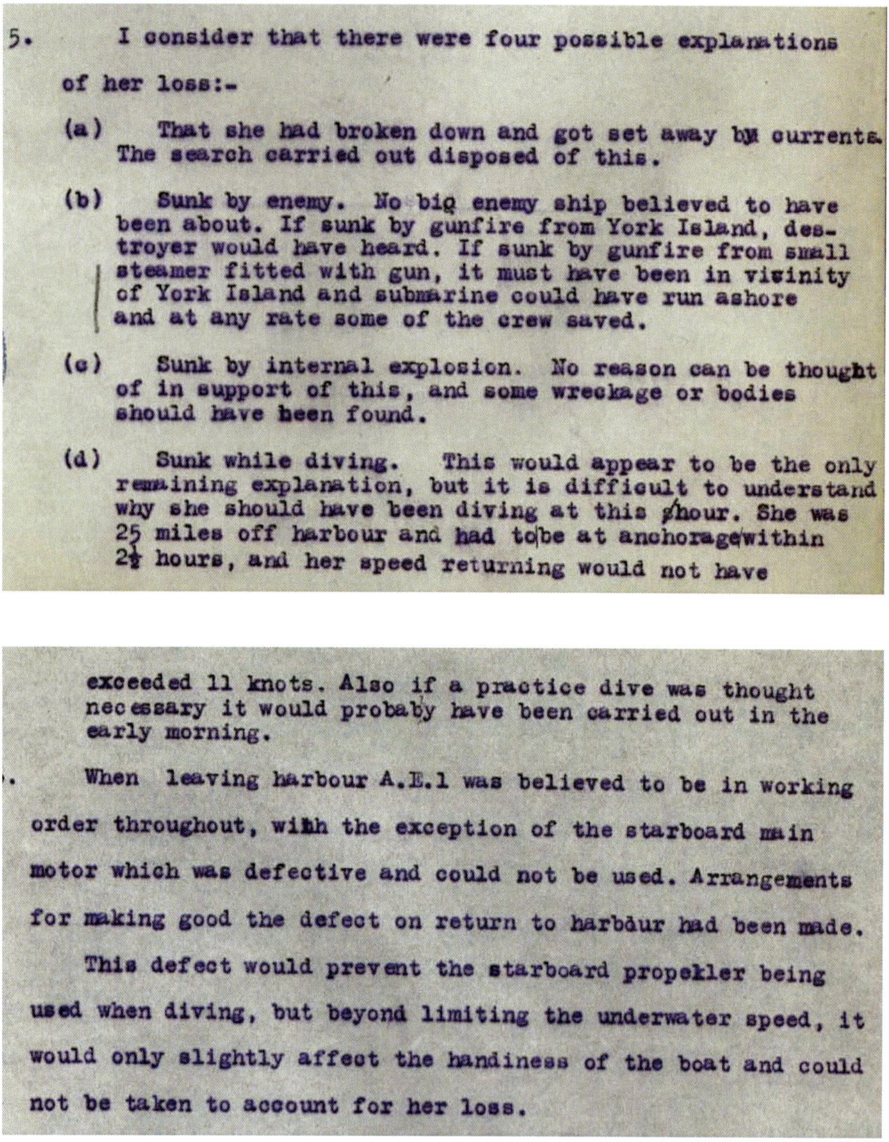

5. I consider that there were four possible explanations of her loss:-

(a) That she had broken down and got set away by currents. The search carried out disposed of this.

(b) Sunk by enemy. No big enemy ship believed to have been about. If sunk by gunfire from York Island, destroyer would have heard. If sunk by gunfire from small steamer fitted with gun, it must have been in vicinity of York Island and submarine could have run ashore and at any rate some of the crew saved.

(c) Sunk by internal explosion. No reason can be thought of in support of this, and some wreckage or bodies should have been found.

(d) Sunk while diving. This would appear to be the only remaining explanation, but it is difficult to understand why she should have been diving at this hour. She was 25 miles off harbour and had to be at anchorage within 2½ hours, and her speed returning would not have exceeded 11 knots. Also if a practice dive was thought necessary it would probaby have been carried out in the early morning.

6. When leaving harbour A.E.1 was believed to be in working order throughout, wihh the exception of the starboard main motor which was defective and could not be used. Arrangements for making good the defect on return to harbour had been made.

This defect would prevent the starboard propeller being used when diving, but beyond limiting the underwater speed, it would only slightly affect the handiness of the boat and could not be taken to account for her loss.

Figure 24 – Extract from LEUT Stoker's Report on the loss of *AE1*. Image: Darren Brown.

5.8.6.2 Stoker's dismissal of an action with a German steamer at para 5(b) above is not agreed – it is possible to construct many credible circumstances where the submarine would be unable to be 'run ashore' or 'some of the crew saved' – see section 7.3 below. His rationalisation of the impact of the defect on the Starboard propulsion train is also questionable; see section 3.5 above for more details on the impact. Further, Stoker quite fails to discuss the possibility that *AE1* was lost due to navigational hazard.

5.8.7 LEUT W H F Warren's Report

5.8.7.1 As discussed above in section 5.5.2 when considering the last seen position,

LEUT Warren submitted an undated, 3 page manuscript Report and covering letter. The letter and report were faithfully retyped, dated 21st September 1914 and submitted under a covering letter from HMAS WARREGO (Captain D) dated 21st September 1914.[56]

5.8.7.2 Warren's report gives no indication of the means of communicating with *AE1*, or how he was able to quickly relocate *AE1* at 1430 in the hazy conditions of reduced visibility then pertaining. We have been unable to locate any of PARRAMATTA' signal, WT or working deck logs. The fair deck logs give no indication of the means of communication with *AE1*. These missing documents would be a high priority target for future research. A search of the AWM, National Archives, RAN Heritage Collection and RAN archives facilitated by the RAN Seapower Centre and Curator of the RAN Heritage Collection has proved fruitless.

5.8.7.3 PARRAMATTA was *AE1*'s escort for the day; no doubt Warren would have been at pains to avoid any blame for failing to execute this task effectively. This could perhaps offer some explanation for the brevity of Warren's Report and official unwillingness to consider any suggestion that *AE1* had been lost in action with a German steamer – something that could have been avoided by a more attentive escort. As discussed at section 5.5.2 above, LEUT Warren's Report seems brief to the point of obfuscation.

5.8.8 Inaccuracies in Patey's Formal Report About the Search

5.8.8.1 Patey's report is inaccurate in the timing of the search; it was not ordered at 2000 and did not begin until several hours later. The following sequence is reconstructed from AUSTRALIA's fair WT logs:

x At 2015 *AE2* alerted HMAS AUSTRALIA to *AE1*'s failure to return:

'From: HMAS *AE2* (to) HMAS Australia, *submit; had HMAS AE1 a Destroyer scouting with her today. She has not yet returned to harbour'*

x At 2025 AUSTRALIA signalled PARRAMATTA inquiring after *AE1*'s whereabouts.

x At 2140 a boat was sent to bring LEUT Stoker, the CO of *AE2*, across to AUSTRALIA to see RADM Patey.

x It was not until sometime later that a search was ordered.

56 Navy Office file 14/7658

- x ENCOUNTER was advised by Flag at 2230 that the destroyers (YARRA and PARRAMATTA) were proceeding to search for *AE1*.
- x PARRAMATTA's log records that she weighed and proceeded in search of *AE1* at 2330.

5.8.8.2 Far from the search beginning about 2000, as Patey's Report implies, the first ships did not start the search until 2330. This could have been up to 7 ½ hours after *AE1* was lost (1600 to 2330). Although he would not be the first senior officer to put a positive spin on a report of a disaster, his inaccuracy raises doubts about the precision of other key sections of his report. Even allowing for the exigencies of the war, it is extraordinary and unusual given the number of unknowns that he did not ensure that a formal inquiry was held.

5.9 Informal Commentaries

5.9.1 The Rumours

The informal commentary in various diaries of participants in Rabaul at the time records the commonly held belief that a German steamer was responsible. This view was also held by CAPT C La P Lewin, RN, the Commanding Officer of HMAS ENCOUNTER who reported this perspective in his ROP submitted to RADM Patey when HMAS AUSTRALIA returned to Rabaul on 19th September. The suggestions do not appear to have been formally addressed in any of the official reports.

5.9.2 Local Observations

5.9.2.1 Gus Mellon advises that there was an oral legend passed down within the people of Mioko Island, which was subsequently related to John Foster after he had been "inducted" into the tribe. Foster refers to it in his book.[57]

5.9.2.2 By the time Foster was taken to the Haus Tambuan and made a member of the tribe; he had had an association with these people for some years. He had arranged for his Rotary Club at Murwillumbah to purchase and assist with the installation of earthen water tanks (berms, for want of a better descriptive term) and the fitting of water tank liners (similar to a plastic, aboveground backyard swimming pool)... The purpose of this was to increase the drought resistance of the DoY islanders, who suffered serious and continuous water shortages during the dryer summers. Foster had also formed a strong friendship with Father Bernie Miller, the local parish priest (now dead), who was also highly regarded by the islanders and who no doubt lobbied on John's behalf.

5.9.2.3 When Gus accompanied John Foster to Rabaul in early 2007, Gus separately discussed these matters with Bruce Alexander, an Australian, and the (then) owner of the Hamamas Hotel, who had lived there for over 25 years and was also a well-known and widely liked local politician for the Rabaul district. Bruce was of the opinion that the Mioko

57 Foster, John, *Entombed But Not Forgotten*, Sydney, 2006 p86-102.

islanders were genuinely grateful to Foster for his assistance with their water problems and that the induction of a 'white fella' into the tribe was no small matter to them, as the induction was widely known locally and could have led to strong criticism by other tribal. As to whether they told Foster something that they thought he might like to hear, in the sure and certain knowledge that they could never be gainsaid.

Bruce Alexander's opinion was that this was quite possible, as the peoples of New Britain and PNG in general are adept in managing complex relationships.

5.9.2.4 As recounted in Foster's book, the Mioko people knew there was a big fight going on between the Germans and the British and were concerned about the effect it might have on them. Early on 14th September 1914 they heard the sounds of HMAS ENCOUNTER's 6" guns off Herbertshohe and, being afraid, had gathered at their traditional place of refuge, a shallow sea cave under a low cliff at the eastern edge of Mioko Island. They told Foster that on the afternoon of that day, they saw the 'devil fish' approach the fringing reef, stop, go backwards, and then disappear. Their oral account was "time stamped" by the fact that went on to say that during that night (of the 14th-15th) they also saw evil spirits flying in the night sky. These were taken by Foster to be the searchlights and star shells/flares fired by the searching ships during the early morning hours, as they scoured the DoY coastline. When questioned by the ANMEF searchers, the local people did not say anything; this is understandable, given the uncertain circumstances of the time.

5.10 The KOLONIALGESELLSCHAFT

5.10.1 Technical Description

5.10.1.1 Design

John Foster's research indicates that the KOLONIALGESELLSCHAFT was built for a German expedition up the Sepik River, led by Dr Behrman of Madang. Once the expedition was completed KOLONIALGESELLSCHAFT was handed over to Dr Gebhardt, the District Officer at Madang for use as a patrol boat. The KOLONIALGESELLSCHAFT's Certificate of Survey[58] issued at Hong Kong on 19th January 12 states that she was single screw steamship built in 1911 in Hong Kong by Ulderup & Schluter for the German Government. She had a single, 180-psi boiler driving a triple expansion engine manufactured by the builders, of 125-horse power. The ship was built from wood, with hardwood frames, teak planking, reinforced by three steel bulkheads, giving a gross tonnage of 73.3 tons. Michael Rikard-Bell estimates that she would have had a loaded displacement of 153 tons (169 tonnes) and a draft of 4' 3" (1.3m).

58 Darren Brown image IMGP 2832.JPG

Figure 25 – KOLONIALGESELLSCHAFT at Karajundo, 20th July 1913 – Exploration of the Sepik River. Source: Peter Richardson from the Bundesarchiv Dr. Thurnwald Photo Collection.

Figure 26 – KOLONIALGESELLSCHAFT, Exploration of the Sepik River, Malu, 20th September 1913. Source: Peter Richardson from the Bundesarchiv Dr. Thurnwald Photo Collection.

5.10.1.2 Fuel and Water

It seems likely that the boiler was wood fired, since coal would not be available on the Sepik River. This assumption is supported by the baulks of timber apparently being loaded onboard in Figure 26. Wood is not as effective as coal as a fuel and this would have reduced her performance. Further, Michael Rikard-Bell observes that the ship was probably not fitted with a condenser, discharging spent steam rather than recycling it and hence requiring to refill with fresh water for boiler feed at regular intervals. This would not be a problem on a freshwater river but would be an issue at sea. Overall it is assessed that KOLONIALGESELLSCHAFT had only limited sea-keeping ability.

5.10.2 John Foster's Research

5.10.2.1 John Foster records the results of his research into KOLONIALGESELLSCHAFT in his book;[59] he cites assistance from:

- Mr Ken Humphreys of Caloundra, a retired PNG officer who had completed much research into the administrative and shipping activities of the German colonies.
- Herr Karl Baumann of Fassburg, Germany, an expert in German colonial history with access to a number of relevant reports.
- A report produced by Herr Fritz Hoyer, postmaster at Frederich Wilhelmshaven (modern day Madang) and a military reservist who took passage in KOLONIALGESELLSCHAFT, under the leadership of Lauer.

5.10.2.2 Based on Hoyer's account, John Foster concludes that the KOLONIALGESELLSCHAFT departed Madang on 9th September 1914 and was delayed on passage by bad weather, only managing to reach as far as Cape Lambert on 16th September 1914, where it ran aground (an overall speed of advance of less than 2 knots). He concludes that it could not have been involved in the loss of *AE1*.

5.10.2.3 Hoyer's account reports that KOLONIALGESELLSCHAFT only carried a crew of two: — a master and a machinist. In this case KOLONIALGESELLSCHAFT was not set up for continuous steaming and probably anchored or went alongside at the end of each day's steaming. Regular stops for wood for fuel and fresh water for the boiler would have also been required (see para 5.10.1.2 above). Allowing for the time lost at the beginning and end of each day a daily distance run of 50 nm, i.e. 10 hrs at 5 knots seems reasonable. In this case KOLONIALGESELLSCHAFT would cover the 350 nm between Madang and Cape Lambert in 7 days, this is consistent with Hoyer's account that they sailed from Madang on the 9th and ran aground on the reefs north of Cape Lambert on the 16th.

5.10.2.4 Alternatively, provided these crewing, fuel and water issues were overcome, our geographical reconstruction at Annex C shows that it was possible that the 'steamer' sighted but not investigated by 'YARRA' on the evening of the 13th September could have

59 Foster, John, *Entombed But Not Forgotten*, Sydney, 2006 p71-78.

been the 'KOLONIALGESELLSCHAFT'. The geographical reconstruction shows that provided KOLONIALGESELLSCHAFT departed Madang no later than 10th September 1914 and proceeded continuously at a speed of advance of 5 knots, there was sufficient time for KOLONIALGESELLSCHAFT to travel from Madang to Duke of York Islands on the evening of 13th September 1914, attack *AE1* on the evening of 14th September and then travel to the vicinity of Cape Lambert where it was recorded as running aground on 16th September 1914. For this to be possible the party of reservists would have had to provide watch keepers and the stokers to run the steamer continuously and sufficient stocks of wood and water carried. This is possible although it seems unlikely for a vessel that was designed as a riverboat.

5.10.2.5 Accurate weather conditions for the passage from Madang to Rabaul for the period 9th-16th September 1914 are not available, the voyage would have been conducted heading into the predominant SE winds which is described as sometimes 'boisterous'. Climate data for Madang and Rabaul indicates that prolonged windy/rough weather would be unusual. Nor do any of the RAN ships' deck logs record high wind speeds, for the period 12th-6th September 1914, the typical wind noted was 4-10 Kn from the SE, with one observation of a maximum wind speed of 17-21 kn on the 16th. See para 5.2 above. This means the sea would have been relatively calm for most of the time.

5.10.2.6 The theory that KOLONIALGESELLSCHAFT steamed to Duke of York Islands in time to be involved with the loss of *AE1* assumes that Herr Hoyer's account that this did not occur is wrong. HMAS WARREGO's investigation of the wreck of KOLONIALGESELLSCHAFT revealed that KOLONIALGESELLSCHAFT had run aground on the 16th. The key distances and timings are:

- The distance from Madang *(Friedrich Wilhelm Harbour)* to Rabaul is 420 nm.
- KOLONIALGESELLSCHAFT (at 5 kts) would have taken just under 4 days for the voyage to Duke of York Islands (DoY).
- YARRA reported sighting a steamer/yacht in the vicinity DoY at around dusk on the 13th – she was ordered not to pursue, by the Flag.
- If Hoyer is correct and KOLONIALGESELLSCHAFT sailed from Madang on the 9th, she had sufficient time to reach the Duke of York islands at dusk on the 13th.

5.10.2.7 Peter Richardson's research into the KOLONIALGESELLSCHAFT has been unable to verify when the vessel left Madang.

5.10.3 KOLONIALGESELLSCHAFT Crew and Passengers

5.10.3.1 Based on Herr Hoyer's account recorded by John Foster, the Captain of the KOLONIALGESELLSCHAFT was Captain Banzleben who was assisted by a 'machinist'. The party of reservists was 13 strong, under the leadership of 'Surveyor' Lauer; all up a party of 15 men.

5.10.3.2 Peter Richardson's research has confirmed the movement by direction of the Governor of German New Guinea of a party of ex infantrymen enlisted as reservists from Wilhelmshaven (modern day Madang) to Gazelle Peninsula on KOLONIALGESELLSCHAFT.

Haber's detailed Report on the War in German New Guinea[60]

I had sent instructions to the District Office in Friedrich Wilhelmshaven via Administrator Täuffert who had left aboard the New Guinea Company's steamer "Siar" on August 27th, and was headed to Dutch New Guinea, to conscript 12 furloughed infantrymen for the armed forces who were skilled in the bush environment — military officers if possible.

They were to be sent to the Gazelle-Peninsula at once, possibly on our Government steamer KOLONIALGESELLSCHAFT.

Late at night on September 20th, I received a message while in Vunadidir, that Lieutenant of the Reserve Lauer had arrived on the KOLONIALGESELLSCHAFT together with 11 white men.

The steamer had run aground at Cape Lambert.

Their detachment was said to be on the march to Taulil.

Since the people could no longer return on the KOLONIALGESELLSCHAFT, I sent instructions to Lieutenant of the Reserve Lauer to betake himself to Rabaul or Herbertshöhe together with his people under the flag of truce, and to surrender to British Military Authorities.

I sent message to the latter and pointed out that the white people who had arrived from Friedrich Wilhelmshaven had not yet been enlisted in the Armed Forces of the Protectorate.

This small group was however armed with 88-guns and carbines, and also carried a machine gun with them.

With reference to that, these people were turned into prisoners of war by the British Military Authorities. A report by Lieutenant of the Reserve Lauer on this expedition is included.'

5.10.3.3.1 Corroboration is provided by Governor Herber's account that it seems that the vessel had the manpower and perhaps the motive to attack the *AE1*. Petty Officer Reuschel may have been one of the patients captured in Rabaul hospital, he is not named in official reports — only four of the eight names that were captured from Rabaul Hospital are known. Dr. Kohl-Larsen's reports have not been found. He treated 8 sailors from the SMS PLANET at Yap Island, where they had contracted the disease, typhoid. Unfortunately, Kohl-Larsen gives no names. Reuschel's involvement is discussed further at para 4.11 above.

60 File Bundes Archive 1001/2613 The War in New Guinea 1914 Vol. 3 see Vol 4, January 15th - July 15th, Includes a Report by Gov. Haber on the War in German New Guinea. A Ill 323/15

5.10.3.3.2 We have been unable to establish that Reuschel was one of the German patients captured at the Rabaul Hospital, or how he could have become aware of KOLONIALGESELLSCHAFT's possible action with *AE1* on 14th September 1914. He could have picked the story up from the reservists ex KOLONIALGESELLSCHAFT; the time difference between Reuschel telling his story to Aubrey Hodgson and *AE1*'s disappearance on the 14th is sufficient for this scenario to be credible. According to Hoyer's account, the reservists disembarked from the KOLONIALGESELLSCHAFT on 17th September 1914, went to Masava Bay (a tidal station) by boat and then overland to Toma on 21st September 1914 where they found the Australians in occupation. They formally laid down their arms at Herbertshohe the following day and so probably arrived onboard AORANGI as detainees on the same day, 22nd September 1914.

5.10.3.3.3 So by the time Reuschel was captured, processed, and sent to the AORANGI the party of reservists from KOLONIALGESELLSCHAFT would probably have also been onboard. Reuschel could have simply repeated the story that he had been told of the KOLONIALGESELLSCHAFT action. Alternatively, but less likely, he may have been a member of the reservists on the KOLONIALGESELLSCHAFT or finally, he may have made up the whole story to upset his captors. Given the inconsistencies with dates in Hodgson's diary (see Annex D – Annotated transcript of Hodgson's Diary), it is difficult to precisely date the diary entry of the exchange between he and Reuschel – the same entry records the departure of the Squadron to take over Madang, this occurred on 22nd September 1914. This is the same day that Lt Lauer and his party of reservist is believed to have surrendered at Herbershohe..

5.10.3.3.4 Reuschel's Assertion

We have not located an official report as such, only a personal reference in the diary of Aubrey Hodgson, RAN signalman on the supply vessel, 'AORANGIi'. He spoke with Reuschel when he was brought onboard. It is believed that Reuschel spoke good English. It appears that Reuschel told Hodgson the story without any prompting, Hodgson responded by saying that *AE1* was not missing. Reuschel insisted that he had sunk her with the KOLONIALGESELLSCHAFT. Reuschel said he saw the submarine 'hove to', ran up the white ensign on the KOLONIALGESELLSCHAFT, approached the *AE1*, fired a shot into her and then rammed her with the KOLONIALGESELLSCHAFT.

5.10.3.3.5 Hodgson says that he told his Commanding Officer of the conversation and that his CO instructed Hodgson to write a report on the matter for submittal to the senior naval officer present and told his crew not to converse with any of the German prisoners. If Hodgson did report it to his CO there does not appear to be any record of the report; the next day Reuschel was transferred to another vessel. We have been unable to corroborate any elements of Hodgson's account. The account is a credible sequence leading to the loss of *AE1*. The weight that can be placed on the account is offset by the numerous factual errors and confused dates in other sections of Hodgson's diary (see Annex D for details of these). As John Foster observes, it is hard to imagine circumstances whereby a German Naval Petty Officer would find himself in command of this coastal steamer.

5.10.3.3.6 An alternative explanation is that Reuschel was captured in Rabaul hospital where he had been one of the German Navy survey ship PLANET's crew members recovering from typhoid and picked up the elements of this story concerning the existence of KOLONIALGESELLSCHAFT from prisoners taken from KOLONIALGESELLSCHAFT, the rest was his imagination.

5.10.3.4 Haber's report is supported by Patey's report to the Naval Board and was quoted by Benjamin Evans AWM:[61]

> *On September 20th a detachment of one officer and eleven reservists reached German headquarters from Port Weber. They had left Madang (Friedrich Wilhelm Harbour) for Herbertshohe in the Government steamer KOLONIALGESELLSCHAFT, in response to the proclamation calling up men liable to serve in the armed forces of the Protectorate; the steamer had stranded on the reefs at Cape Lambert (on the north coast of New Britain), and the contingent had marched along the coast to Port Weber. They had with them a machine-gun. The circumstances were reported by Haber to the officer commanding the garrison at Herbertshohe, and the party was sent in under a flag of truce to surrender.*

5.10.3.5 Use of The White Ensign

The fact that the KOLONIALGESELLSCHAFT allegedly used a white ensign to get close to *AE1* constitutes a legitimate 'ruse de geurre'; provided the German colours were flown prior to engaging *AE1*. Suggestions that this constituted a war crime and hence justified the elaborate cover up implied in erasing KOLONIALGESELLSCHAFT's involvement are not considered justified, given the rules of war then prevailing.

5.10.4 Nordenfelt Quickfiring Gun on the Vessel.

5.10.4.1 These weapons were quite common and widely used from the 1880's through to the end of WWI. An evaluation by the Defence Science and Technology Organisation (DSTO) confirms that at close range when brought to bear in direct fire mode, a 1" (i.e. a 1 pounder gun such as found on KOLONIALGESELLSCHAFT) Nordenfelt gun would have penetrated *AE1*'s pressure hull and cause internal damage, not to mention sweeping the decks clear of men. *AE1* carried small arms, but these weapons would have been no match for a quick firing 1" Nordenfelt gun. Also, the German detachment had other weapons with them.

61 AWM Wartime Issue 16 Summer 2001.

5.10.5 Discovery of the Wreck of KOLONIALGESELLSCHAFT

5.10.5.1 WARREGO sighted the wreck of KOLONIALGESELLSCHAFT aground and on fire near the beacon on the northern extremity of the reef to the North of Cape Lambert at 1345 on 18th September 1914.[62] WARREGO sent a boat and boarding party to examine the steamer. ENCOUNTER recorded what they found in his ROP submitted on the return of Patey on 19th September 1914:

> *"she had been abandoned and was on fire, apparently by design. In the bow was a pedestal and mounting for a gun, the pivot being quite bright, as it is evident that the ship had not been long on the reef and the gun quite recently removed; further a used one pounder cartridge was picked up on board of her and I am strongly of the opinion that this steamer is connected in some manner with the mysterious disappearance of A.E.1."*[63]

5.10.5.2 WARREGO's reports stated that the KOLONIALGESELLSCHAFT had a five barrel 1" Nordenfeldt in the hold (along with barbed wire and native trade goods, including tobacco) and that there were used "one pounder casings" on the deck. They also noted that there was a mount on the deck, but no gun. Patey's Report included advice that on the mounting 'one part had quite a bright pivot' reflecting recent use.[64] Reports vary on how many used cartridges were discovered. Contrary to ENCOUNTER's report quoted above that only one used cartridge case was found, John Foster quotes a second hand report by CMDR F C Darley of HMAS ENCOUNTER that 'a lot of empty cartridge cases'[65] were found. There is also a suggestion that these could have been the result of ammunition 'cooking off' in the fire in a report by Patey, see para 5.10.5.3 below. What ever the number of cartridge cases, there is evidence that the gun had been mounted until recently and possibly fired.

5.10.5.3 Patey reported the finding of the KOLONIALGESELLSCHAFT in his Letter #26[66] to the Secretary of the Navy:

> *"With reference to the report of the finding of the wreck of KOLONIALGESELLSCHAFT, this craft belongs to the Exchequer of the Protectorate of German New Guinea. "SYDNEY" passed this spot at noon on 15th September, the day after the loss of the Submarine and there was no wreck there then. The KOLONIALGESELLSCHAFT must have gone ashore on one of the nights 15th, 16th or 17th September. Subsequent investigation shews that KOLONIALGESELLSCHAFT was from the westward and not from the eastward, and therefore it does not appear*

62 HMAS WARREGO deck log 18th September 1914, DB image IMPG3346.jpg

63 HMAS ENCOUNTER ROP, 19th September 1914, p2, 3, DB images 110713_IMG_2204, 110713_IMG_2205

64 Patey's Report – AWM File 1777 and 3 DRL/0053.

65 CMDR Darley letters, AWM 1DRL/0350

66 VADM Patey letter # 26, HMAS AUSTRALIA at Rabaul, 30th September 1914, DB image 110713_IMG_2187, 2194.

possible to connect her in any way with the loss of Submarine A.E.1. The wreck was examined on 19th September by Commander (D) and the King's Harbour Master."

5.10.5.4 Patey also mentions the finding of KOLONIALGESELLSCHAFT in his ROP titled 'Participation By Australia Seagoing Fleet in The operations.[67] The ROP does not appear to be dated; the final page deals with events occurring on 10th December 14, so it was probably submitted in late 1914 before AUSTRALIA left the Australia station enroute UK. The report adds some fresh details:

"The only find was the wreck of the KOLONIALGESESELLSCHAFT ashore on fire, and abandoned near the beacon on the reef on the north-west point of Gazelle Peninsular. This craft belongs to the Exchequer of the Protectorate of German New Guinea, bound from Papua to Rabaul, ran ashore on the afternoon of 16th September. Her crew and passengers abandoned her on 17th September, landing at Masava. She was set fire to on being abandoned. When examined, tents, barbed wire, and trade tobacco were found onboard her, also 1-pounder cartridge shells evidently exploded by the fire. The dismounted gun was found in her hold."

5.10.5.5 Herr Fritz Hoyer, the Madang postmaster and one of the German Army reservists onboard the KOLONIALGESELLSCHAFT records that she ran aground on 16th September 1914.[68]

5.10.6 NUSA

5.10.6.1 HMAS WARREGO was sent back from Rabaul with NUSA in tow on 19th September 1914 by ENCOUNTER to inspect the wreck and endeavour to locate KOLONIALGESELLSCHAFT's crew.[69] WARREGO'S deck log shows that they spent 50 minutes inspecting the wreck and two hours inspecting the nearby coastline before WARREGO again took NUSA in tow and proceeded at 12 kn for Rabaul. ENCOUNTER's Captain's Signal Log records that WARREGO signalled the results at 1700:

"Investigation shows steamer struck reef accidently, was then fired. The crew landed locally and then proceeded by boat to Toma. Planters interviewed state that she came from New Guinea bound for Rabaul, was ignorant of its doings previously to its striking, so if it had anything to do with Submarine HMAS AE1 they cannot have let anything out about it"

Efforts to locate any more detailed records of this investigation have proved fruitless to date.

5.10.6.2 Ian Noble's research reveals that NUSA was a 60 ton official German yacht captured by HMAS WARREGO in Kavieng on 14th September 1914. She was towed back to Rabaul by WARREGO, armed and pressed into service with a crew from HMAS

67 VADM Patey, Participation By Australia Seagoing Fleet in The operations., p54, 55, DB Images IMGP2140, IMGP2143

68 Foster, John, *Entombed But Not Forgotten,* Loftus, 2006, p75.

69 HMAS ENCOUNTER ROP, 19th September 1914, page 3, DB image 110713_

BERRIMA, under the command of LCDR John Metcalf Jackson. There are no records in the AWM regarding NUSA. "The Official History of Australia in the War of 1914-1918", Vol IX "The Royal Australian Navy" by AW Jose makes one mention of the ship and that is on page on 112. Although AWM photographic records refer to HMAS NUSA, no substantive evidence that NUSA was ever commissioned into the RAN has been found. Colonel Holmes declared that she was to be known as HMAS NUSA when he directed LCDR Jackson to take command and proceed to New Ireland to search for the *SMS KOMET,* possibly to add a more official status to the expedition.[70] There are also 5 files in the NAA, which refer to NUSA, but only in the context of its actual seizure and the subsequent action in Prize Courts.

5.10.6.3 Regarding LCDR Jackson, the only reference is in an AWM file entitled "Official History — Biographical and Research files". This file (AWM43-A416) has biographical information on 12 persons named Jackson, including J M Jackson. It lists him as a LCDR RN (1st Apr 1913), and as a CMDR from 24th Nov 1915. It shows him as posted to WARREGO from AUSTRALIA on 27th Aug 1914, to HMAS UNA on 17th Oct 1914, to PENGUIN on 1st Dec 1916 and as Kings Harbour Master Rabaul from 1st – 10th Oct 1914. It further states: "He was left at Rabaul as KHM and appointed by Col Holmes in command of the NUSA to capture the *SMS KOMET*. It also notes him as in command of UNA from Nov 14 – Nov 16. He died in England between 24th Feb 25 and 1st Mar 26.

5.10.6.4 Since *KOMET* was apparently captured on 10th October 14 some distance from Rabaul, he appears to have been in command of NUSA from about 9th October until he was posted to UNA on 17th October.

5.10.6.5 His Personnel record in the NAA shows that he was temporarily appointed to the RAN Permanent Naval Forces on 27th August 1914 with his RN seniority as LCDR of 1st April 1913, and that he was promoted to A/CMDR on 23rd November 1915 and confirmed on 30th June 1916. He reverted to the RN on 1st July 1917. It also corroborates his postings as above and his appointment as KHM Rabaul, but makes no mention on his appointment to NUSA.

70 Mackenzie, S S, *The Official History of Australia In The War 1914-1918, Volume X – Rabaul,* Sydney, 1941, Ch 8, p130.

Section 6 — Possible Causes for the Loss of AE1

6.1 Introduction

There are a range of possible scenarios that could have led to the loss of *AE1*. In a situation where we do not have conclusive evidence this range of scenarios and the probability attached to each cannot be definitive. None the less they do provide valid input to setting out the search area and attaching priority to those areas. What is fairly certain is that the *AE1* sank on that passage from SE of the DoY Island to Rabaul. If it had been disabled on the surface then the ships searching would have found her.

6.2 Hull Failure/Internal Explosion Leading to Uncontrolled Flooding

6.2.1 Internal Explosion

One possible source of hull damage could be from an internal explosion of some sort.

6.2.2 One of the embarked torpedo warheads could cause this level of damage; but no incidents of these torpedo warheads exploding are known. Each torpedo tube would normally have been loaded and left dry until prepared for firing. There seems to have been little reason to prepare or to launch one of these weapons. The reload torpedoes were stowed adjacent the tubes, the warhead was not fitted but stowed in racks adjacent to the torpedo and only fitted prior to being loaded in the tubes. Overall this seems an unlikely source of an explosion.

6.2.3 There are a number of records of battery explosions in E class submarines caused by a build-up of hydrogen gas. These killed or injured a number of crewmembers, but did not rupture the pressure hull or cause the loss of the submarine. This is therefore assessed as an unlikely cause for the loss.

6.2.4 An explosion of sufficient force to rupture the pressure hull would quite possibly have been heard and noted by the natives on Duke of York Island and possibly other RAN units. It would certainly give rise to a significant debris field and oil slick.

6.2.5 An internal explosion is therefore assessed as an unlikely cause of the loss.

6.3 Sunk in an Action with KOLONIALGESELLSCHAFT or another Armed German Steamer

6.3.1 Cause and Effect

It might be argued that it was theoretically possible that the KOLONIALGESELLSCHAFT came out of Mioko Harbour, fired into and then rammed the *AE1*. The detachment on the German vessel had a usable gun that was capable of holing the *AE1*'s pressure hull. Also the detachment was carrying small arms. However we do not consider this is credible given the KOLONIALGESELLSCHAFT 's low power and insufficient endurance in water, fuel or crew to compete this open ocean transit from Madang, against the prevailing SE monsoon in the time scales required. It is doubtful that a 153 ton displacement, low powered, wooden hulled river/coastal steamer could sink *AE1* by ramming while *AE1* had full buoyancy, notwithstanding that she was heavily built, with teak planking on a hardwood frame and had three internal steel bulkheads.[71] However a ramming whilst *AE1* was in the process of diving to avoid gunfire could initiate a sequence that could have proved fatal:

- x Whilst in the process of diving a SM's stability is much reduced — an impact even from a small wooden steamer could have caused *AE1* to take on a significant angle — say to roll heavily and/or take on a steep bow down angle.
- x If combined with a heavy trim (either bodily heavy, or more significantly, heavy by the bow) then a fatal depth excursion would be the likely result.
- x The impact of a collision on *AE1* whilst diving would have caused it to roll heavily; this would explain why the steamer could have survived the impact without major damage.

  The normal recovery procedure from a steep bow down angle is to apply full power astern to take the way off and reduce the effect of the bow down angle. *AE1* was apparently restricted to the port main motor only whilst dived due to a defect on the starboard power train, possibly the main engine clutch; this would have been a significant limitation in this situation. Also the need to declutch the port main engine from the main motor would have taken at least two minutes; this would have exacerbated the difficulty in regaining control.[72] *AE1* could, therefore, have exceeded its crush depth if rammed while diving.
- x A submarine experiencing a loss of control and depth due to a bow down angle must then catch a stopped trim (neutrally buoyant) whilst it sorts out the control problem that led to the depth excursion, or blow main ballast and surface.
  - o If the SM's trim is bodily heavy then even after stopping by going astern it will continue to sink — either quickly pumping out sufficient water to catch the trim or blowing main ballast are the only remedies in this situation.
- x In extremis, if catching a stopped trim is not possible then blowing main ballast and returning to the surface is the final remedy, this would not be favoured if an armed enemy remained close by.
- x If a bow up angle can be achieved then full power ahead can be used to assist the surfacing process — once again the loss of the starboard main motor in *AE1* would make this option less effective as only the port shaft was available.

71 KOLONIALGESELLSCHAFT Certificate of Registration, Goddard & Douglas, Hong Kong, 19th January 12, Darren Brown image IMGP2832.JPG

72 Foster, John, *Entombed But Not Forgotten*, Sydney, 2006, p69-70 notes that the changeover from ahead propulsion on the main engines to astern on the main motors took two minutes.

- *AE1* had a relatively shallow maximum diving depth (180 ft or so)and apparently a small pumping capacity (noting *AE2*'s difficulty to quickly correct a trim discrepancy on the day of its loss in the Sea of Marmara in 1915).
- In the case of a 'crash dive' at little notice to avoid an attack from a steamer, there would be a short period where *AE1* would not have propulsion available at all until the port main engine clutch was opened and the port main motor energized to propel ahead.
- So it is possible to construct a credible scenario that *AE1* was hit by shellfire, initiated a 'crash dive', was rammed whilst in the process of diving and without propulsion, leading to a loss of control and either hit the bottom at speed if in shallow water or exceeded their crush depth in deep water further offshore.
- If the pressure hull had been holed by gunfire then water flooding in through these holes would quickly add to the loss of buoyancy, overwhelm the crew and cause an uncontrolled descent to the bottom.
- Depending how quickly the flooding equalized pressure the internal and external pressure, the hull and fuel tanks could remain intact, militating against a large debris field or oil slick.
- In these circumstances a stream of bubbles and some oil and diesel fuel would probably be the only external indicators of the submarine's position.

6.3.2 A Possible Sequence of Events

A possible sequence of events in this scenario would have been:

- KOLONIALGESELLSCHAFT sailed from Madang for Rabaul on or before 9th September (John Foster records that Herr Fritz Hoyer, the Madang postmaster and a member of the reservist records that they sailed on 9th September 1914)[73] with the armed party of German reservists onboard under the command of Lieutenant Lauer. Given the urgency of the journey, KOLONIALGESELLSCHAFT carried stocks of firewood and fresh water for the 4 day journey until re-supply was possible at Mioko Harbour.
- After becoming aware of the Allied invasion of Rabaul, KOLONIALGESELLSCHAFT diverted and hid inshore near Mioko Harbour on the Duke of York Island.
- The KOLONIALGESELLSCHAFT may have been the steamer sighted by YARRA on 13th September 1914, but there were other German steamers later discovered in Mioko Harbour.
- On the 14th September the KOLONIALGESELLSCHAFT observed *AE1* patrolling south of Duke of York Island; *AE1* was following up YARRA's sighting the previous afternoon.
- Lieutenant Lauer prepared his team, made up a false white ensign and moved to intercept *AE1* as she was returning to Rabaul on the afternoon of 14th September.

73 Foster, John, *Entombed But Not Forgotten*, Sydney, 2006, p76.

- Approaching with the Duke of York Island (and perhaps the setting sun) behind him, Lauer was able to get close under the flag of deception, before opening fire with the Nordenfelt gun, small arms and machine gun, forcing *AE1* to dive.
- *AE1* had no deck gun or means of defence against this type of attack and was not in company with any of the Navy surface ships at the time.
- The Nordenfelt gunfire pierced *AE1*'s pressure hull and KOLONIALGESELLSCHAFT added to *AE1*'s problems by ramming the submarine as it was in the process of diving.
- *AE1* rolled heavily under the impact, lost control, flooded via the shell hole(s), the hull ruptured by the ramming, or the open conning tower hatch and sank to the bottom.
- KOLONIALGESELLSCHAFT retreated inshore and escaped under cover of darkness, heading back towards Madang, before running aground near Cape Lambert on 16th September.
- Alternatively, perhaps Lauer realized that the maritime battle was lost and decided to join the Governor inland, getting rid of KOLONIALGESELLSCHAFT by grounding in a location consistent with a passage from Madang to Cape Lambert and setting it on fire to destroy any evidence of their involvement.
- When captured Lauer and his party suppressed the story in order to maintain their non-combatant status, constructing an alibi that they had been delayed by bad weather and had only got as far as Cape Lambert, in order to avoid interrogation or being taken as POWs.
- Few others apart from Reuschel, who picked up the story from members of the KOLONIALGESELLSCHAFT crew and relayed it as his own, knew of the incident.

6.3.3 Lieutenant Lauer's Fate

If this was the scenario then Lauer's plan worked. He was not interned as a POW and quickly returned to Germany where he apparently re-enlisted to fight on the Western front as he was killed at the battle of Ypres on 25th September 1915. The story of KOLONIALGESELLSCHAFT's voyage to Rabaul died with him.

6.3.4 The Likelihood of This Scenario

This scenario is mainly circumstantial and runs counter to the weight of evidence presented in the official reports, the Hoyer account and the assessment by John Foster who located material and second hand accounts that we have been unable to access. We have yet to uncover primary source material to substantiate the KOLONIALGESELLSCHAFT scenario. In particular, the search has been unable to find any additional information on:

- The movement of KOLONIALGESELLSCHAFT for September 1914.
- The report prepared by Lauer on his activities whilst onboard (Lauer's report was cited as an attachment to the Governor's report) but it has never come to light.

- x The composition of the party onboard KOLONIALGESELLSCHAFT, along with diaries or other records of their activities.
- x Corroboration of the account of the Madang postmaster, Herr Hoyden.
- x Records of the interrogation and handling post capture for all these German personnel.
- x Weather conditions experienced 9th-16th September 1914 covering the route KOLONIALGESELLSCHAFT would have taken from Madang.
- x The movements of Reuschel and how he came to know of the postulated engagement with *AE1*.

6.3.5 Conclusion – Possible but Improbable

We are at a loss to explain why there has been no subsequent claim made by German authorities or the individuals involved. It was certainly spoken about anecdotally and was judged to be most likely by Stoker if we accept Kenny-Hamilton's diary record of his conversations with Stoker [despite Stoker discounting this possibility in his official report to RADM Patey]. It is also difficult to explain why there were no accounts amongst the natives living near Mioko Harbour of an engagement between a German steamer and a submarine – John Foster established a trusted relationship with the local people and spent some time researching this aspect without success.[74]

There is real doubt that a low powered river steamer with a crew of two could muster the resources — firewood and fresh water for her boiler and crew endurance to make a four day open ocean voyage at five knots to achieve this scenario. Even if the crew was, assisted by the army reserve detachment onboard (some of them may have had the necessary skills) the power, fuel and water limitations would not have been so easily overcome.

6.4 Run Down by HMAS PARRAMATTA

6.4.1 The proposition that HMAS PARRAMATTA inadvertently ran down *AE1*, possibly when she returned towards the last sighted position, or on her track northward was one of the many possibilities floated at the time. This scenario would have required alignment of a number of factors:

- x *AE1* would have had to dive between 1430 when she was in sight and safe and 1520 (when PARRAMATTA reports she lost sight of *AE1*).
    - o o This seems an unlikely occurrence. It is only possible if it occurred when *AE1* was dived and this was unlikely. Apart from other factors PARRAMATTA took a route back to anchorage north around DoY Island and *AE1* likely went south about. Their two routes did cross west of DoY Island but there is no evidence that they actually did cross.
- x PARRAMATTA inadvertently ran over the dived submarine.

74 Foster, John, *Entombed But Not Forgotten*, Sydney, 2006, Ch 11.

  - o Under this scenario the impact did not cause any significant damage to PARRAMATTA but was sufficient to cause *AE1* to lose control and end up flooded or crushed and unable to surface, on the bottom.
  - o It would have required a 'freakish' combination of events to achieve this outcome; PARRAMATTA, at 750 tons was slightly lighter than *AE1* when the latter was dived.
  - o The submarine would have to flood but remain largely intact to explain the lack a persistent oil slick from the sunken submarine.
- x *AE1* failed to avoid the approaching ship – although all ships are obligated to keep a good lookout, the overriding obligation is on the submarine to avoid the ship in this situation.
- x PARRAMATTA's deck log records that she was stopped from 1545-1615 on 14thSeptember 11. Could this have been to investigate the impact? Having noted nothing amiss Warren put the bump down to a collision with a submerged log that were common in the area.
  - o *'I know this much, there are a lot of trees, quite big ones in the water floating about. I saw 2 large ones myself.'*[75]
- x The possibility of a collision between PARRAMATTA and *AE1* was not canvassed in any of the official reports.
- x It seems strange that PARRAMATTA's ship's company did not subsequently air the possibility. However, if the bump had been accepted as a collision with a floating log they would not necessarily make the connection – for example, Alec Doyle's acerbic letter written on 17th September (discussed at para 4.6.6) makes no mention of this possibility.
- x John Foster came across reports relayed third hand of an account said to be from the crew of PARRAMATTA of a collision with something solid at dusk, on 14th September but the position of the impact (near the Beehives Rock off Simpsonhaven) is a further source of doubt and Foster dismisses it as a possibility.[76]
- x A report of PARRAMATTA's next docking following this period showed nothing amiss.
- x PARRAMATTA had a draught of 9 ft (2.74m).[77] *AE1*'s periscope depth was a keel depth of ~ 32-34 ft (10.2+m),[78] this depth places the top of the casing at ~ 14.5 ft (4.5m), the top of the fin at ~ 8-9 ft and the top of the lowered periscopes just beneath the surface, since the periscopes could be retracted 8ft (2.44m)[79] but remained~ 9 ft (2.7m) proud of the top of the fin. In normal circumstances, with *AE1* on an even keel at periscope

75 Darley F C CMDR RN of HMAS AUSTRALIA, *letter to Aunt Marion,* 30th October 1914, AWM 1DRL/0232, transcribed by Ian Noble at AWM, 4th May 2011.

76 Foster, John, *Entombed But Not Forgotten,* Sydney, 2006, p84, 85.

77 http://www.awm.gov.au/units/unit_10632.asp

78 Henry Kinder's diary p4.

79 White, Michael W D, *Australian Submarines – A History,* AGPS, 1992, Appendix I, Technical details of The E Class Submarine by Jim Ekin, p 219.

depth PARRAMATTA would have passed over the casing, without striking the submarine, but would have hit the retracted periscopes/periscope standards and may have just clipped the top of the fin. The periscopes and standards would probably have served to absorb the impact, protecting the upper hatch and would have certainly done great damage to PARRAMATTA. This picture would alter drastically for the worse if *AE1* was shallower than this or had a large angle on the submarine e.g. diving to avoid collision, when the after casing could be significantly closer to the surface for a short period.

6.4.2 Conclusion on Loss Due To a Dived Collision with PARRAMATTA.

Whilst the alignment of factors to result in the loss of *AE1* in such a collision seems improbable, the search area should cover the likely impact area of this eventuality.

6.5 Navigational Incident

6.5.1 Contributing Factors

6.5.1.1 Likelihood of a Navigational Error

An error in navigation resulting in a grounding and sinking is a possible cause of the loss. This patrol was possibly one of *AE1*'s first without an escort or consort. *AE1*'s last sighted position was close to the coast, with adequate fixing marks available to avoid such a problem, but the haze had reduced the visibility. She had about 24 nm to the anchorage in Simpsonhaven – about 2 hours and 10 mins @ 11 kts. Moreover, for the first 6 or 7 nm *AE1* would have an opposing current (reportedly 2 – 3 kts) and thereafter a crossing current. So the speed made good would have been less; allowing for these currents, *AE1* would have needed about 2 hrs and 25 mins to make the passage. She needed to depart the last seen position no later than 1525 in order to be alongside by sunset at 1750. And the Admiral had reminded Besant when he sailed that morning not to be late!

6.5.1.2 Environmental Factors

At this time of the year at 1550, 2 hours before sunset the sun would have been low on the western horizon and *AE1* was headed west.

6.5.1.3 Oceanographic Factors In The Vicinity of Mioko Harbour

The German and British charts used at the time of the invasion in 1914 both showed extensive fringing reefs around the entrance to Mioko Harbour. The reefs were well-formed and visible from close range at that time. Early versions of the British and American Pacific Sailing Directions or Pilots, dating back to the sailing days of the late 18th century also noted the strong current flows of up to 3 knots in St George's Channel. This makes the south eastern corner of Mioko Island forming the western entrance of Mioko Harbour a particularly difficult and challenging spot. The large body of water moving northwest by the current faces a significant obstruction as the depth rapidly decreases near Mioko Harbour and the water strikes the near vertical wall of the fringing coral reefs. The combination would lead to strong, locally variable currents, swirling around to get around the obstructions — navigation in this area required particular care. The water would then split and drive to the north and west around the obstruction represented by the Duke of York Island and its surrounding reefs and minor islands. (See figure 27 below). With a low height of eye (*AE1*'s bridge deck was at 12 ft (3.6m) *AE1*'s lookouts would be looking into the setting sun low on the western horizon, the off lying reefs would be invisible beneath dark reflecting waters. Besant and his officers were an inexperienced command team and unfamiliar with the area. Perhaps they failed to take the precautions necessary when operating in proximity to reefs and were not aware of or failed to appreciate the significance of this confluence of factors.

Gus Mellon has provided this first hand description of the 2007 BENALLA survey off Mioko Harbour, (the plot from this survey is at Figure 29 on page 94).

x *'The last sighted position of AE1 at 1530 is marked at the top right corner of the page and the red, submarine-like blob near the western end of Mioko Island is the contact that was subsequently investigated by YARRA later that same year.*

x *I recall from looking at the 3 D plots which were being generated on BENALLA's charting displays whilst they were plotting that contact, that the slope of the reef face was close to vertical along the detailed area which was surveyed, about 75-80 degrees, with a subsea ledge at about 90m, then nearly vertical again to the bottom in 130m+ water, from memory.*

x *Inspection of the depth soundings on this same chart extract shows that this same sort of nearly vertical reef face profile most likely extends right along the bottom edges of Kerewara and Kabakon Islands, as well.*

x *During BENALLA's plotted survey runs, the current coming up from the southeast at about 3 knots, was hitting this almost vertical wall of island fringing reefs and were "roiling" upwards all around the vessel in a totally confused mass of water which simply did not know which way to go next. Quite obviously, some of it then proceeded north along the eastern side of DoY Island and the rest passed westwards, across the bottom edge of Kerewara and Kabakon islands, before passing in between the Credners and Kabakon and looping around the western DoY's , to join up again to the northwest of the islands.*

x *The best description that I can give for the state of those waters off Mioko island is to look at the state of the huge volume of water issuing into the turbine outlet ponds below some of the Snowy Mountains power stations, or the visual surface effect on the co-joining of two major irrigation canals, in the Shepparton District of Victoria.*

x *Suffice to say that the confused currents were causing BENALLA, with her twin steerable propulsors, to offset 60 degrees from the survey line, in order to keep the required course.'*

This would indeed be a formidable and dangerous spot for *AE1* to venture into — if indeed, that is what she did!

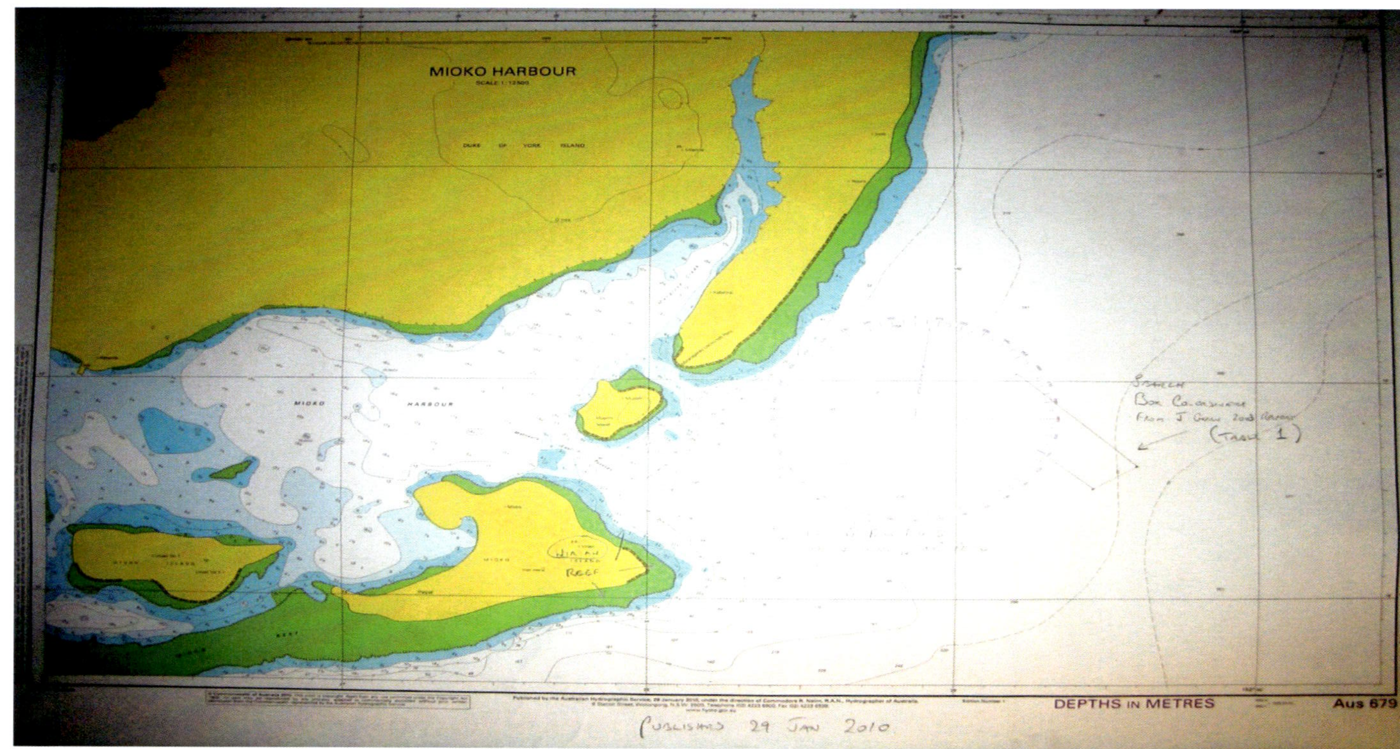

Figure 27 – Modern Chart of The Entrance To Mioko Harbour Showing Wirian Reef off The Eastern End of Mioko Island.
Australian Hydrographic Office Chart.

6.5.1.4 The Pilot notes tidal stream ebb and flow into/out of the entrance to Mioko Harbour of 2 to 3 kts at Springs, with a tidal range of 2.5 ft (0.8m) at Springs and 1.5 ft (0.45m) at neaps. The direction follows the line of the channel (NW / SE). From the US almanac, we know that the moon was a 37% waning crescent (i.e. just over 1/3rd of time from full to new moon (the new moon – 15 days). Neaps would have been on the 12th September 1914, Springs (New Moon) would have been on the 19th September 1914. Hence the tidal range would have been about 1.75 ft (0.53m) and the estimated maximum tidal ebb/flow on the 14th September 1914 about 1 kt. The net set and drift close offshore Mioko Harbour would have been a combination of tidal stream and current.

6.5.1.5 Probability of Steering Failure

Darren Brown has uncovered numerous accounts of steering failures in E class and earlier submarines. Stoker records an occasion of *AE2*'s helm jamming in Lombok Strait during the delivery voyage and 'putting me nearly on a lee shore'. It is assessed that there is a possibility that a steering failure could have played a role in the loss.

6.5.2 The Likely Consequences of a Heavy Grounding

6.5.2.1 Stability Model

Mike Rikard-Bell has developed a computer based stability model from the General Arrangement drawings for *AE1* that enables us to consider the likely consequences of a heavy grounding.

He has considered a number of scenarios; the first involves a bow on grounding onto a gently shelving or a steeply shelving bottom topography. Whilst nothing untoward emerges in these situations, it is worth noting that:

x The forward part of an E boat's pressure hull likely to be impacted in the event of a heavy grounding by the bows is particularly strongly constructed (in anticipation of this scenario), with a strong fore foot at the bow and an enormously strong keel section further aft; the keel does not start for some 21.5 ft (6.5m) aft of the bow and extends aft for 120 ft (36.5m). The arrangements of the fore foot and keel are illustrated in this scale model.

Figure 28 – Scale Model of *AE1*, Port Beam Aspect.

- x The internal tanks that would be exposed should the pressure hull forward of the keel be breached in such a grounding are (from the bow moving aft):
  - o Forward Compensating Tank.
  - o Forward Trim Tank.
  - o Magazine.
- x No 1 Oil Fuel Tank (OFT) starts 26 ft (9.9m) back from the bow and is protected by the start of the keel, although at this stage the keel is fairly small — 18" (458 mm) wide and 7" (178 mm) deep.

6.5.2.2 Heavy Grounding by the Bow

It is difficult to conclude that a heavy grounding by the bow on a steep to obstruction, such as a coral reef, could result in a breach of the pressure hull, because of the strength of the pressure hull and fore foot. In the unlikely event that this occurred, the Forward Compensating & Trim Tanks would offer an inner boundary, as each is a pressure tight tank, tested to 50 pounds per square inch. This boundary could possibly delay flooding whilst the submarine was on the surface. After considering the construction of *AE1* it was concluded that:

- x Such a grounding would not necessarily lead to a major fuel leak from No 1 OFT.
- x It seems likely that in such a scenario the submarine would end up wedged onto the reef.
- x If the submarine subsequently pulled back from the reef (noting that it is believed that only *AE1*'s port shaft was available going astern) and then sank then the damaged bow would be more vulnerable to damage on impact with the bottom, possibly causing a fuel leak from No 1 OFT but this is not a certainty.
- x The volatility of the light lighter diesel fuel would cause a slick to disperse more quickly than heavier oil.

6.5.2.3 A Beam on Grounding Amidships

The consequences of a beam on impact, damaging the amidships ballast tanks situated in the saddle tanks on one side of the pressure hull would cause the submarine to list heavily. Completely flooding two of the ballast tanks on one side would a feasible scenario; since any impact would be likely to slash an opening in the ballast tanks situated in the saddle tank attached to the pressure hull.

6.5.2.4 Implications

Given this 'worst case' scenario of flooding two ballast tanks on one side the submarine would be in a vulnerable position, listing heavily, with reduced stability and reserve of buoyancy and in close proximity to ongoing hazard from the reef. Three resultant scenarios will be considered; a loss of stability resulting in the submarine capsizing by rolling onto its damaged side, an inadvertent or deliberate dive to recover stability, or flooding through the open conning tower hatch.

6.5.2.5 Capsize

In this scenario it is postulated that the submarine under the influence of the rudder or an external force such as the current pinning it against a coral pinnacle was rolled onto its beam ends (i.e. close to a 90 degree list), causing injury and chaos for the crew, spilling battery acid and other liquids, followed by a loss of electric power, rendering normal means for propulsion, control and egress unavailable, inoperable or ineffective. A controlled dive from this situation or release of the drop keel seems improbable given the difficulty of operating equipment in this attitude.

6.5.2.6 Deliberate Dive

Provided the crew remained able to function, with the presence of mind to initiate a dive and there was sufficient water depth to dive and the submarine was ready to dive and was in a reasonable diving trim, then a controlled dive would overcome the list and bring the submarine upright. Considering the need to disengage the port engine clutch before being able to propel ahead or astern on the port main motor, these serial preconditions combine to make this scenario unlikely.

6.5.2.7 Flooding Following A Beam On Grounding

Shutting the upper conning tower hatch would be difficult following such a grounding. Whilst the upper hatch was fitted with a means of closing it from below, it is likely that both bridge and control room personnel would have difficulty maintaining their position and ability to operate the submarine systems due to the list and may not have been able to close the hatch. Under this scenario the submarine is vulnerable to any additional loss of buoyancy, reduction in stability, external force or some combination of these that could force the conning tower hatch under the water, causing the submarine to flood and sink quickly to the bottom.

6.5.2.8 Dived Approach To Simpsonhafen

Given a deliberate dive was successfully achieved this scenario could lead to *AE1* making a dived approach to harbour, perhaps with the intention of beaching the submarine or surfacing in shallow water close to help by releasing the drop keel. Simpson Harbour is suggested as the most likely destination given its sheltered position and presence of support ships. This seems an improbable combination of circumstances.

6.5.2.9 The Most likely Scenario Following a Beam on Grounding

It is considered most likely that following this type of grounding, the list would develop quickly following efforts to manoeuvre clear of the reef and before the crew were able to secure the upper hatch. Any further incident leading to the loss of buoyancy and stability, would allow the submarine to flood via the conning tower. In these circumstances the submarine's descent to the bottom would be more rapid. An oil slick and some debris/

bodies would be likely, if so, it is possible that these were borne away during the night on the strong currents and dispersed by daybreak.

6.5.2.10 Pressure Hull Vulnerability In A Beam On Grounding

It is possible for a portion of the pressure hull between the bottom of the saddle tanks and keel to be damaged in a beam on impact scenario. However this would require a reef of just the right height to hit the pressure hull whilst avoiding the saddle tanks above and with sufficient force to breach the pressure hull that is at its maximum thickness in this amidships section. This alignment of factors seems unlikely. Alternatively, and more likely, if the submarine grounded with headway on then the forward athwartships bulkhead of the broadside torpedo tube annulus could be the single point for arresting the force of the grounding on its leading edge. This would be a major impact and could cause a leak or in worst case, breach the pressure hull, flooding the submarine. The submarine is vulnerable to water entering in this area, particularly with a starboard list (the likely direction), as this could quickly reach the switchboards and main batteries, leading to a loss of power and generation of chlorine gas.

6.5.3 Observations on Analogy with *AE2*'s Groundings

6.5.3.1 *AE2* grounded heavily on Sagandra point on the isle of Mudros at 2145 on 10th March 1915. The submarine was reported as 'hard aground and bumping heavily in short, steep seas'. After three hours of bumping and scraping the weather moderated and the submarine was towed clear. *AE2* was able to make her own way to Malta where 13 hull plates were replaced.[80]

6.5.3.2 *AE2* grounded twice during her famous penetration of the Dardanelles. On the first 'she hit the bottom and slid up on the bank to an actual depth of 10 ft'. On the second occasion, shortly after refloating using full astern power, *AE2* 'slid up the bank to a depth of 8 ft'. As the submarine was facing down the bank towards deep water Stoker came ahead at full power to come off the bank, 'gave a slight bump, gathered way and then bumped heavily. The last bump was calculated to have considerably injured the vessel, and probably impaired her fighting efficiency'. History shows that *AE2* survived both groundings and went on to penetrate the Dardanelles.

6.5.3.3 The 3 groundings tend to confirm the analysis that:

x *AE1* and *AE2* were extremely tough and resiliently constructed vessels.

x They tended to ride up on striking a bank, becoming firmly aground, but without breaching the pressure hull, even though some hull seams might commence leaking.

80 White, Michael W D, *Australian Submarines A History*, *AGPS* 1992, p46.

6.5.4 Internal Bulkheads

Once dived the two internal bulkheads could contain flooding whilst they held. However, the submarine lacked the reserve of buoyancy to remain afloat with a fully flooded compartment:

x The bulkheads were tested to 35-50 Lbs/sq.in and would probably not have withstood the pressure below 200 ft depth of water.

x The submarine would not have sufficient buoyancy to surface or remain on the surface should any internal compartment flood.

x Shutting the bulkhead doors against the angle on the submarine or the inrush of air/water could be difficult or impractical (both doors shut away from the control room) as Kinder attests in his account of the loss of *AE2* following three shell holes in the engine room:

'The watertight door leading into the engine room was closed after a hard struggle owing to the angle of the boat and the engine room was isolated. All the available air was turned on so sufficient pressure could be maintained to get the water out of the tanks as quickly as possible.

The great trouble was the difficulty we had in carrying out our orders. We began to wonder what the results were going to be as no-one knew how fast the water was pouring in through the shell holes.

As AE2 weighed 900 tons, once she began sinking she took a lot of checking and it was not long before we were down to 60 ft, then to 80 ft, then the indicator began to slow down and AE2 was suspended. But would she rise to the surface? Everything had been done and it was just a matter of watch and wait for results. Things were beginning to look serious and it meant a struggle for life or death.

If any of the water pouring into the engine room came in contact with the motors and short circuited them it would be all up. As it was, the motors were working far beyond their safety load and the electricians were standing by with spare fuses in case others blew out. I think it would have been useless as AE2 was just holding her own and a lot depended on whether the water was being blown out of the tanks faster than it was pouring into the engine room. The boat was vibrating so much it seemed as though she would shake to pieces.

At last the gauge indicated that we were rising to the surface but very slowly: would the air pressure last? All the air pipes were frosting so it was being used up fairly fast.'

6.6 Evaluation of the Possible Causes of the Loss of *AE1*

6.6.1 Probability – Not Certainty

We have not located definitive evidence of the cause of the loss and therefore must deal in probabilities. There are a number of clues however:

x Whatever befell *AE1* occurred in a fashion and at such a speed that no effective distress call was made, noting that this may have required the rigging of the WT mast, (if Patey's account is correct, the WT mast was rigged and set working at 1430).

- x There was no persistent oil slick. Whilst the diesel fuel may have dissipated quickly in the tropical temperatures the heavier lubricating oil could have reasonably been expected to provide a persistent oil slick for some time after the sinking. There was no enduring slick found.
- x There was no debris or bodies found.
- x The local people have a story of a submarine approaching the reef from the northeast, stopping off the entrance and moving off to the northeast before disappearing. The story is time and date stamped by a story relating to ENCOUNTER's bombardment on the morning of 14th September 1914 and the searchlights and flares used by the searching ships that night.
- x They have no account of a battle with a German steamer.
- x Apart from YARRA's grounding on a reef, none of the surface ships reported a collision or damage.

6.6.2 *AE1*'s Most Likely Course of Action on 14th September 1914

6.6.2.1 Return on the surface by the Most Direct Route to Rabaul

AE1's most likely course of action after she and PARRAMATTA parted company shortly after 1430 on the afternoon of 14th September was to return on the surface by the most direct route from last sighted position. This is particularly so having been given a direct order by RADM Patey at the time of sailing that morning, (0703 14th September) to be back by dark (sunset was at 1750).

The direct route lies to the south of Duke of York Island, passing close off the entrance to Mioko Harbour and thence heading westerly so as to pass to the north of the Credner Islands – this is not only the shortest but also the safest; leaving the hazardous reefs of the Credner Islands down sun and up tide — thence direct to the anchorage.

6.6.2.2 Distances/Times

The distance from *AE1*'s last seen position on the tracing of the chart submitted with HMAS PARRAMATTA's ROP (see fig 7 above), is about 24 nm to the anchorage in Simpsonhaven – about 2 hours and 10 mins @ 11 kts. However, for the first 6 or 7 nm *AE1* would have an opposing current (reportedly 2 – 3 kts) and thereafter a crossing current. So the speed made good would have been less; allowing for these currents *AE1* would have needed about 2 hrs and 25 mins to make the passage. *AE1* had insufficient time to spare and no obvious rationale for a check dive. The alternative route, north about Duke of York Island was approximately 30% longer and would cause *AE1* to be even later; it also required an unattractive and difficult navigational passage around the north of the Duke of York Island in the dark.

6.6.3 Evaluation of The Clues V Scenarios

6.6.3.1 Clues v Scenario table

Table 1 sets out an evaluation of the clues observed with the various scenarios considered. Clues are assessed on a scale of 0-5; 0 indicates the clue is not applicable to the scenario, 1 that the scenario has a good fit with the clue, ranging to 5 where the clue is contrary to the scenario.

The score represents the degree of the likely consequences that the event fits the clues surrounding the loss of *AE1*, not the probability of the event occurring.

Serial	Clue observed	Scenario 1 Bow On Grounding on a reef whilst surfaced	Scenario 2 Internal explosion, damage sufficient to sink SM	Scenario 3 Grounding on a reef whilst dived, damage sufficient to flood and sink the SM	Scenario 4 Run down by surface ship whilst dived, damage sufficient to flood and sink SM	Scenario 5 Combined Scenario - Glancing Grounding, SM dived to correct list, run down enroute harbour	Scenario 6 Sunk in engagement with German Steamer	Scenario 7 Beam On grounding surfaced, damaging ballast tanks, vulnerable to an additional event leading to sinking
(a)	(b)	(c)	(d)	(e)	(f)	(g)	(h)	(d)
1	Sudden event, no time to rig WT mast and send distress call	4	2	2	1	1	1	1
2	No persistent oil slick	5	5	5	3	3	2	2
3	No debris or bodies (Note currents would have dispersed any debris + shortfalls in search mitigate the significance of this clue)	4	5	3	1	1	1	1
4	No observation by local natives = no story handed down	4	3	2	1	1	5	1
								This scenario is consistent with the story that has been handed down.
5	No surface ships report any damage or collision	0	0	0	4	4	0	0
6	Totals (the lower the score the better the scenario fits the clues noted)	17	15	12	10	10	9	5

Table 1 - Evaluation of Clues v Scenarios

Let us now consider each scenario against these clues.

6.6.3.2 Scenario 1 – Bow on Grounding. The absence of debris, wreckage or a distress call militates against, but does not totally discount the probability of loss following a bow on grounding (see the discussion of the likely impact of a grounding in section 6.5.3 above). A grounding sufficient to breach the pressure hull is assessed as unlikely, but if this scenario is to result in the loss of the submarine then it had to do so. In which case, an oil slick and some debris could be anticipated. If this grounding took place on the reefs near Mioko Harbour then a local story might have recorded it – there were none of these clues.

6.6.3.3 Scenario 2 – Internal Explosion

This event is not judged likely, nor does the absence of an oil slick, debris/bodies or possibly, a local story fit this scenario.

6.6.3.4 Scenario 3 – Dived Grounding

Given the imperative to be back in harbour by 1750 (sunset), we do not assess it is likely that *AE1* would have chosen to dive on the return passage to harbour. Had she done so (against the odds), a dived grounding of sufficient force to breach the pressure hull is judged unlikely – the most usual result of a dived grounding is a rapid ascent, absorbing much of the impact. Had it occurred it would almost certainly result in an oil slick and probably, a debris field?

6.6.3.5 Scenario 4 – Run Down By A Surface Ship

As noted above, we do not assess it is likely that *AE1* chose to dive on the return passage to harbour. Had she done so (against the odds), a dived collision with a surface ship with sufficient force to breach the pressure hull would almost certainly result in damage to the ship, possibly an oil slick and maybe a debris field. None of these clues were present.

6.6.3.6 Scenario 5 – Beam on Grounding Damaging Main Ballast Tanks Resulting in a Dive and then Run Down by a Surface Ship

This combined scenario requires an extraordinary combination of circumstances. Ultimately, the lack of any unaccounted for damage to the ships rules against this scenario.

6.6.3.7 Scenario 6 – Sunk In An Engagement With A German Steamer

This scenario could fit the clues well, except for the absence of a local story recording an engagement that would have probably happened close by Mioko Harbour. Setting aside Reuschel's boast of an engagement between KOLONIALGESELLSCHAFT and *AE1* we have not been able to place any other suitably armed German steamer at the scene. We do not know the identity of the steamer sighted by YARRA on the evening of 13 September, nor whether it was suitably armed.

6.6.3.8 Scenario 7 – Beam On Grounding Damaging Main Ballast Tanks Leading to The Sinking. This scenario provides the best fit to the clues, including the local story. If the submarine damaged two of the ballast tanks located in the 'saddle tanks' on one side of the pressure hull in a beam on grounding, it would have effectively lost 18-20% of its buoyancy and a significant reduction to its stability as the submarine settled to a new equilibrium position on its damaged beam. This alone would not be sufficient to sink the submarine but the submarine would then be very vulnerable to anything that further reduced its buoyancy or stability. To cite a few examples:

x Breaching the pressure hull at the seam where the athwartships bulkhead of the broadside tube annulus reaches the alignment of the saddle tanks, causing a heavy leak or uncontrolled flooding with consequent damage to the switchboards and/or batteries.

x A leaking or open Kingston valve in one of the undamaged external ballast tanks, allowing water into this tank or, perhaps more likely, a failure to achieve full buoyancy by leaving residual water in the ballast tanks after a check trim dive earlier in the day.

x This water would have a double effect; a reduction in buoyancy and the free surface created would also cause a reduction in stability.

x A jammed helm with full astern power on the port shaft.

x Or some combination of any or all of these otherwise manageable events.

Whatever the source, it would take an additional loss of buoyancy or force to increase. the list so as to place the conning tower upper hatch under water, allowing water to enter the submarine via this hatch. Unless this hatch or the lower conning tower hatch was quickly shut the submarine would flood and sink in an uncontrolled descent to the bottom. It would be difficult to get the hatch shut in these circumstances – given the steep angle of heel and rapidly unfolding situation. Even if this had been achieved against the odds, the failure of power supplies and impossibility of working equipment in the resultant chaos would greatly hamper efforts to generate sufficient buoyancy to remain on the surface. In this situation (with the hatch secured), the descent would be much slower and the submarine may have travelled some distance on the current and possibly, moving along the bottom before settling on the bottom. The direction of this movement is most likely to be to the north given the well-established current flows at this time of the year (this is consistent with the local people's handed down story). However, Mioko Island appears to be at a juncture point for the current with water flowing along the reef edges to the north-north-east and west, so it is possible but less likely that *AE1* moved to the west of the impact rather than to the north east..

The absence of an oil slick could indicate that if the hatch was shut then the submarine probably remained intact, i.e. settling at a shallower depth than its crush depth. If it was flooded (considered the most likely outcome) then this proviso is no longer relevant.

6.6.3.9 Grounding the Most Likely Cause of the Loss

6.6.3.9.1 Bow on Grounding

The argument against a bow on grounding option as a cause for the loss of *AE1* is strength of the submarine hull in this situation, the lack of any survivors, bodies, debris or distress messages from the surfaced submarine during its time on the reef, or an significant and persistent oil slick from the wreck should it have sunk with little notice. The lack of these indicators is not conclusive but tends to militate against a bow on grounding as the cause of the loss.

6.6.3.9.2 Beam on Grounding

A beam on grounding, damaging Main Ballast Tanks and resulting in loss of stability, combining with another event leading to a loss of buoyancy could lead to an uncontrolled descent to the bottom with the pressure hull intact and crew secured or trapped inside the flooded submarine seems the more credible of these scenarios. Given the lack of debris field or oil slick it seems more likely that the submarine bottomed with the conning tower hatch secured and did not exceed its crush depth. It remained disabled and intact on the bottom, either fully flooded through the conning tower hatch or a breach in the pressure hull, or if the crew survived (judged unlikely), unable to achieve sufficient buoyancy to surface.

6.6.3.9.3 Beam on Grounding Reconstruction of the Sequence of Events

A possible sequence of events may have been:

- *AE1* headed for Rabaul on the surface shortly after 1430, (say 1500) from the position reported by PARRAMATTA.
- *AE1* was under pressure to get back before dark and had about 30 minutes in hand to make an ETA of 1750.
- The shortest route to the anchorage passed close by Mioko Harbour and the island of the same name on the southern side of the Duke of York Island.
- *AE1* had earlier deviated from the orders given for the day to patrol the southern approaches to Rabaul, in order to check out a report on 13th September 1914 of a steamer off the Duke of York Island — a final look through the entrance enroute Rabaul would have been very tempting.
- Inexperienced in the local conditions, particularly the precautions necessary when operating in proximity to coral reefs *AE1* misjudged the strength of the current surging NW towards the reefs and through the entrance to Mioko Harbour.
- As a result, *AE1* found herself in a rapidly changing, dangerous situation, close in to the reefs off the entrance, on a lee shore with the SE wind and strong NW current pushing onto this hazard.
- Combined with the low height of eye and poor lighting to observe outlying reefs, defective starboard shaft when running astern and the ever present possibility of a helm or propulsion failure, *AE1* was unwittingly standing into mortal danger.
- Looking up sun combined with the disturbed water arising from current hitting the near vertical faces of the reefs (see Gus Mellon's description of this at para 6.5.1.3 above) the reefs were difficult/impossible to see.

x Whilst still making headway *AE1* was washed beam onto a reef outcrop, opening up numbers 1 and 3 main ballast tanks forward of the broadside tube on the starboard side.

x The force of the grounding was arrested by the athwartships bulkhead on the leading edge of the broadside tubes annulus in the pressure hull (para 3.7.2 refers).

x The current held the submarine there, grinding and pivoting against the bulkhead with the diesels still propelling ahead.

x The crew was thrown from their feet by the impact and working with a developing list took several minutes to stop the diesels and to engage astern power on the port shaft.[81] This exacerbated the damage already experienced.

x With difficulty she extracted herself, using full power astern on the one (port) shaft available and moved astern off the reef.

x The natural tendency of the port shaft running astern to pull the stern towards the reefs (to starboard) was probably offset by the wind – most submarines have a strong tendency to swing into wind when going astern.

x As a result *AE1* moved off and in what direction it went is not certain but may depend on where it grounded. A likely scenario is that it moved to the NE swinging to starboard, i.e. making sternway away from the reefs and to the east, swinging to the south east, at the same time, assisted by the NE running current also moving away from the harbour entrance.

x In the process of moving clear it is possible that she struck a second time, adding to the damage already experienced to her ballast tanks and pressure hull.

x A heavy list quickly developed as water flooded into the damaged ballast tanks, causing difficulty for the crew trying to maintain their stations and regain control the submarine.

x A new factor or combination of factors then intervened, perhaps pressure hull was breached at the broadside tube bulkhead leading to flooding and a loss of power as the control room began to flood, with the starboard list channelling water towards the switchboards and main batteries, perhaps the combined impact of astern power, rudder and delicate state of stability combined to force the submarine onto her beam ends drawing the conning tower hatch underwater, before the crew were able to close it, flooding the submarine. We don't know.

x As it sank it *AE1* probably drifted further on the current before settling on the bottom.

81

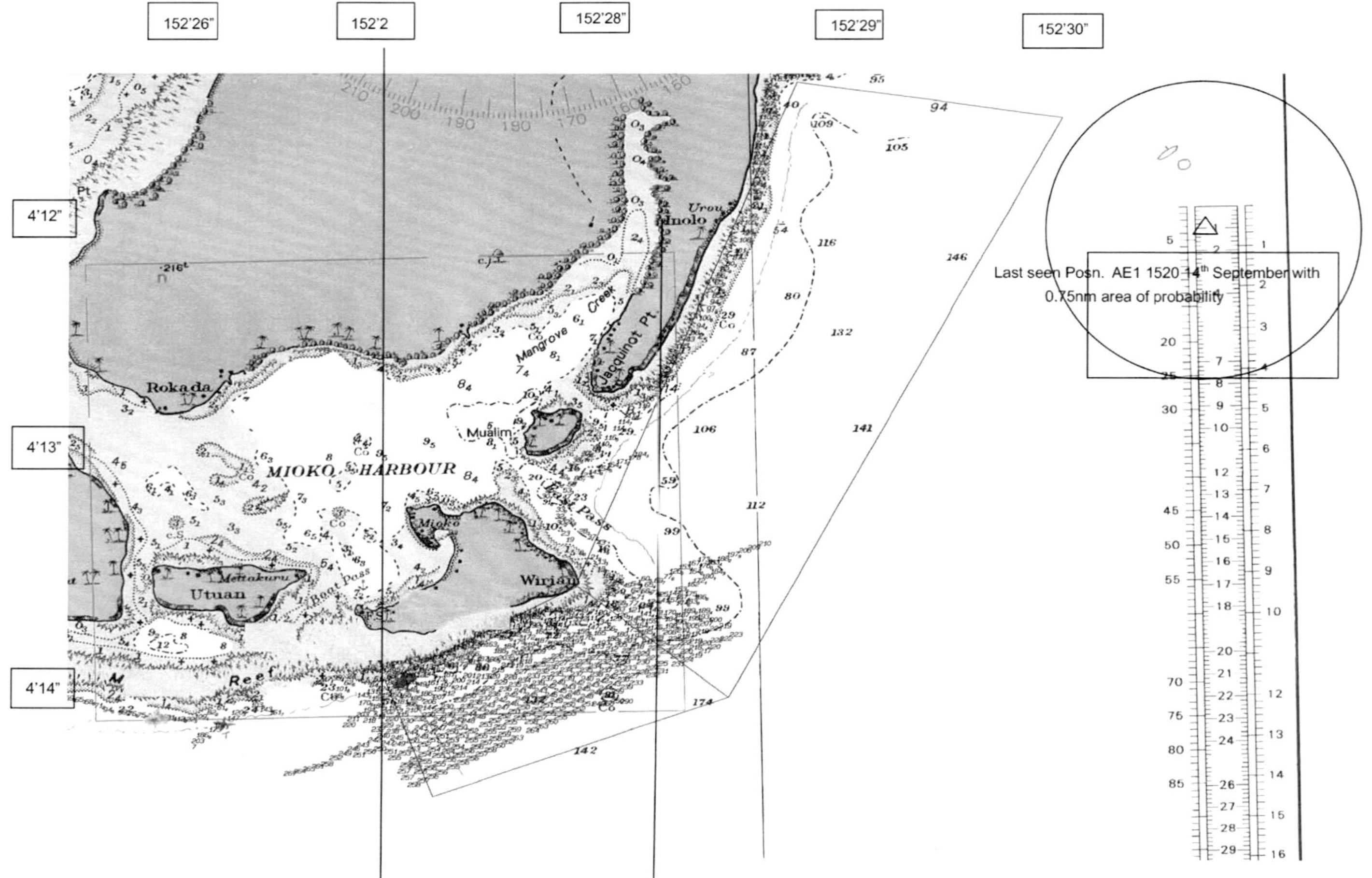

Figure 29 – Extract from Admiralty Chart of Mioko Harbour and Mioko Island With HMAS BENALLA's 2007 Survey Lines and *AE1*'s Last Seen Position Plotted.

Section 7 — Conclusions and Judgements in Selecting the Search Area

7.1 The Balance of Probabilities

It is concluded that on the balance of probabilities *AE1* was damaged in a beam on grounding on the reefs surrounding the southern and eastern end of Mioko Islands rendering it more vulnerable to a further incident, leading to flooding and a loss of stability. Where the submarine was carried after grounding is not certain, but it would likely be to the north and the submarine was probably carried off to the NE on the strong currents and settled on the bottom otherwise intact, some distance from the grounding position. The minor differences, discussed in para 5.5.3 on page 54, as to the last known position of *AE1* and the time of last sighting are not significant in this judgement, on the balance of probabilities, as to *AE1*'s fate or to the recommendation for the search area.

7.2 Selection of the Search Area

7.2.1 Effectiveness of the Search September 1914

7.2.1.1 Impact of Currents On Debris Fields

The effectiveness of the search by the fleet after *AE1*'s loss has been discussed and criticised earlier at section 5.6 above. Nonetheless, the areas searched appear to have covered the most likely areas to contain *AE1* and any wreckage or debris. Gus Mellon has reported on the currents in the St George's Channel area, based on the MARLIN database (CSIRO Hobart) and the SOPAC database. Of all the marine geophysical surveys conducted in the area of interest, only two held any useful information — the cruises made by the Research Vessel FRANKLIN in 1985 and 1986. During these cruises, FRANKLIN laid and then recovered six months later a set of three current meters in the St George's Channel just off Waiara Point on the north east coast of Duke of York Island. They also made a number of runs across the strait between DoY and New Ireland, plotting depths. The unrefined current data is available on the MARLIN website but despite approaches to CSIRO no knowledge of what happened to the depth profile info could be obtained. Basically, the FRANKLIN survey found that the sea floor in this area is like a deep vee formation. The current meter readings for September 1985 showed about 3 knots of surface current, diminishing to about 1 knot at 900 meters (based on a rough interpolation from the unresolved current vectors 'U' and 'V', as plotted). David Nicholls has used the data provided by Gus to estimate the likely drift of any pattern of debris that might have existed and plotted the same to estimate if any of the tracks of the search vessels might have coincided with the set and drift of any pattern of debris. Given that the set and drift would have occurred in darkness, overnight on the 14th-15th September and is likely to have dispersed over an increasingly widening area, thus reducing the probability that it would be seen (if any debris existed).

7.2.1.2 Oil and Bubbles Sighted

There are anecdotal reports in Hodgson and Hamilton's diaries and HMAS ENCOUNTER's ROP of a patch of oil and bubbles being found. Hodgson records that ENCOUNTER located these in deep water:

"At 1 p.m. "Encounter" discovered oil and bubbles in large quantities in St George's Channel. It was too deep, however, to locate the boat, and at dusk the search was abandoned, all ships returning to Rabaul."[82]

This report cannot be correct; ENCOUNTER's deck log records that she anchored in Simpsonhaven at 1045 on 15th September 1914 and remained there for the remainder of the day. The deck log contains no record of sighting oil or bubbles during the search conducted that morning.

At 1700 on 15th September ENCOUNTER reported to AUSTRALIA (now enroute Sydney) that:

'The patch of oil reported has dispersed. A careful search has been made this afternoon on the source area and traces of oil are apparent but no more than might be expected with big ships cruising in the vicinity. Jackson is now proceeding to carry out search with Motor Boat. Prize Steam Yacht is now searching as arranged York Island & New Ireland coast also Coast of North York Island.'[83]

We have been unable to locate the original report of an oil patch referred to in this signal or the source of the advice that it had now dispersed – presumably one of the motor boats or the so called 'prize steam yacht' (presumably the NUSA?), involved in the search. NUSA was fitted with a WT set (and armed) and this could explain how the advice was transmitted back to ENCOUNTER at anchor.

No record can be found of an accurate position for these oil and bubble sightings, this information could be a valuable clue to the location of *AE1*.

7.2.1.3 Board of Inquiry

RADM Patey and the Fleet were still in the process of taking over German New Guinea and had other priorities demanding their attention. The Flagship, HMAS AUSTRALIA weighed anchor and sailed at 1245 on 15th September. Sometime after 1700 on that day AUSTRALIA ordered HMAS ENCOUNTER to conduct a Board of Inquiry and nominated Stoker and Warren as witnesses to be called. The Flagship returned to Rabaul on 19th September and this could possibly be interpreted as effectively over ruling the instruction, i.e. if a Board of Inquiry were to be conducted then RADM Patey should have convened it himself. However, in his Letter #26 to the Secretary of the Navy Board RADM Patey indicates that he is still anticipating a Board of Inquiry to be conducted by Acting Captain Lewin in ENCOUNTER. In the event no formal Board of Inquiry appears to have

82 Aubrey Hodgson, diary 22nd September 1914, Australian War Memorial – 3DRL/6032 – Hodgson, Aubrey Wilfred

83 HMAS ENCOUNTER Captain's signal log.

been conducted. Despite the exigencies of the war this seems an extraordinary outcome, given the number of uncertainties and unknowns. If an Inquiry had been held then its records could provide invaluable information on the loss of *AE1*.

7.2.2 Contemporary Searches

7.2.2.1 Timeline of Searches for *AE1* since 1914

Gus Mellon has provided the basis for this summary of the post-loss day searches for *AE1*:

x 1976 — John Foster first became aware of the *AE1* story whilst serving as the Assistant Defence Attaché in Port Moresby. He commenced researching the history of *AE1* in the Australian Archives and determined an initial search area.

x 1976 — Foster obtained permission from Navy to conduct one side scan search, taking advantage of the presence of the RAN Hydrographic Survey Ship HMAS FLINDERS, which was heading to New Ireland to carry out survey work. One unresolved contact was made in the vicinity of the Credner (Pigeon) Islands, but overall the mission was unsuccessful, due mainly to inadequate scope of the side scan sonar available.

x 1978 — FLINDERS conducted an ad-hoc search for the submarine during an opportunity visit to the Rabaul area.

x 1980-1989 — Foster continued his research and included a preliminary visit to Rabaul to elicit intelligence and talk to local people, in conjunction with his Australian Rotary Club's aid projects to the Duke of York Islanders (helping to provide improved water storage capabilities for the islands). Foster made several trips to Rabaul during this time period, all under the auspices of the Murwillumbah Rotary Club.

x 1990 — Jacques Cousteau (*Calypso*) agreed to conduct an ad hoc search in the vicinity of the Credner Island group on his way to New Ireland. Unfortunately his submersible went unserviceable as it was about to be deployed onto the FLINDERS' (1976) contact. Cousteau was able to conduct a magnetometer search in the area, however this was also unsuccessful.

x 2002 — John Foster established liaison with West Australian Maritime Museum [WAMM][84] seeking advice and support for his search for *AE1*. WAMM sought political support, leading to the former Leader of the Opposition, the Hon Kim Beazley urging the Minister Assisting the Minister for Defence, the Hon Danna Vale to provide assistance to Foster's search. WAMM formally provided support, advice, and archaeological expertise; remote sensing technology and equipment were offered. This support continues.

x 2002 — Foster obtained financial assistance from Baypond Productions and conducted a private search off Wirian Reef (Mioko Island) using local divers. This was based on intelligence gained from the parish priest at Milmila Mission (Fr Bernie Miller – now

84 1995 WAMM decided to create an Australian submarine museum to focus on *AE1*, *AE2*, the 'J' and the 'O' boats as well as the 'Z' force boats in its future exhibits and research activities.

deceased) on Duke of York Island. The local parish's financial assistant and his brother claimed to have sighted a submarine some years earlier whilst diving for trochus in the area. A tower of large sharks over a possible site prevented a full investigation by the divers.

x 2003 — Foster conducted another search at his own expense recruiting two local divers and using the Rabaul Hotel's utility boat as the search platform. The search was again harassed by sharks, but there was no contact of any wreck.

x 2003 — With financial assistance from the Australian Broadcasting Corporation, Foster chartered a local game fishing boat (MV *J Michelan*). In conjunction with Professor Jeremy Green from the WAMM, Richard Smith, the ABC's Film Director (brother of Tim Smith of the NSW Heritage Office) and Peter West of NUMA, they searched the very close littoral area of southern Mioko Island and two adjacent islands along the most probable return track for *AE1*.

x 2007 — Project *AE1* secured Ministerial support (Departments of Defence and Veteran's Affairs) that tasked the RAN to conduct a search. HMAS BENALLA (Hydrographic Survey Ship) with Foster as ship-rider/adviser and Mellon as shore support, located what seemed to be a man-made object close to Wirian Reef, off Mioko Island. This location fitted in with local intelligence about *AE1*'s disappearance but a positive determination was not made at the time.

x 2007 — Later in the same year, the RAN dispatched HMAS YARRA (Minehunter), again with Foster onboard, to conduct a search using Variable Depth Sonar and a controlled Mine Disposal Vehicle with sonar and video to check the BENALLA contact. RAN Clearance Divers were also used but were unable to descend deep enough to reach the wreck site. Whilst the dimensions of the contact (as plotted by the BENALLA's sonars) closely resembled a submarine conning tower and mid pressure hull section, it was later classified as a rock formation following shore analysis of the gathered data by the RAN Seapower Centre and DSTO.

x 2009 — Whilst planning another expedition, Foster had several conversations with former Rabaul salvage diver George Tyers, who claimed he saw a submarine in Simpson Harbour in 1971 off the shore of Vulcan Island to the harbour's west and later realized that it might be *AE1* from photos he saw in 1974. Foster believed the matter should now be followed up. This was despite the Navy's rejection of Tyers' 'find' earlier on.

x 2009 — With the assistance of private donations and the Seven Television Network, a search by Foster was conducted in May using the local dive charter vessel MV *Barbarian*. In the team were Major Tom Hall (*AE1* Descendants Researcher and Project *AE1* member), wreck diver Dr Mark Spencer (of the *AE2* search team) and another well-known wreck diver Mr Samir Alhafith of Sydney. Mike Munro of Channel 7 filmed the event. Whilst the general location of Tyers' marker wreck (KEIFUKU MARU, a WWII Japanese freighter) was found, there was no trace of the submarine nearby. The footage from the mission was aired on Seven's "Sunday Night "program involved some of the descendent relatives and gained favourable publicity.

- x 2009 — Project *AE1* decided to utilize the remaining donation funds left and conducted another search in the Tyers contact area, this time again recruiting the assistance of Dr Jeremy Green of the WAMM and his proton magnetometer, with diving support by diver John Riley (of the *AE2* search team) and ground support by Major Tom Hall. A magnetometer search was conducted, clearly locating Tyers' marker wreck (KEIFUKU MARU). Unfortunately, there were many magnetic anomalies in the area due to the close proximity of the volcano Vulcan. Further, it was discovered that the Japanese marker wreck was now buried under 30 metres of pyroclastic matter, due to the 1994 volcanic eruptions. No submarine wreck was found to seaward of the KEIFUKU MARU location.
- x 2011 – HMNZS RESOLUTION (survey ship) and HMAS GASCOYNE (mine hunter) during Operation RENDER SAFE 2011 found a hitherto unknown Japanese Midget Submarine in Simpson Harbour.
- x 2011 – HMNZS RESOLUTION conducted a brief Multi Beam Echo Sounder Survey of the close in to land portion of the high probability search area for *AE1*. Nothing found.

7.2.2.2 Entombed But Not Forgotten

John Foster provides a more detailed account of the searches conducted up to November 2003 in his book, Entombed But Not Forgotten.[85]

7.2.3 Selecting a Future Search Area

7.2.3.1 Broad Definition

The search area should be broadly confined to an area centred on the last sighted position and a return track by the most direct route, south of Duke of York Islands, north of the Credner islands and thence to UPOLU at the anchorage off Rabaul. John Foster reached a similar conclusion following a number of unsuccessful inshore searches based on local sightings of wreck like objects.[86] However, he incorrectly assumed that *AE1* was heading for Kokopo rather than to Simpson Harbour.

7.2.3.2 Impact of the Most Likely Scenario

The possibility of loss following a beam on grounding off Mioko Island and consequent either slow or rapid descent to the bottom should determine the primary search area. The secondary area should include the last seen position, the most likely area for a dived collision with PARRAMATTA. Finally the tertiary area should be extended to cover a dived collision in the approaches to Simpson Harbour.

85 Foster, John,*Entombed But Not Forgotten*, Sydney, 2006, p86-102.
86 Ibid.

7.2.3.3 Recommended Search Area

The primary search area can be set out, say 3 nm to the north east and west from the possible site of a beam on grounding to allow for drift in either direction depending on which arm of the current predominated, prior to settling on the bottom. Given the geometry and the handed down native account, the north east is the most likely direction of drift. The area should be bounded by the reef edge and extend to seaward to allow for the possibility that the submarine may have moved down any steep slopes on the bottom within this area. Note that this area includes the last known position of *AE1*. The primary area is about 5 Sq. NM of which 15-20% is deeper than 300 metres.

The secondary search area should comprise a five mile circle around the last seen position (it is bounded to the West by Duke of York Islands). The tertiary area can be set out as 3 nm up tide (i.e. to the SE of the track) and 5 miles down tide (i.e. NW of the track) either side of the route back to the anchorage, excluding areas encompassed in the primary and secondary search areas. Three miles is nominated to allow for navigational errors, drift, etc. The NW extremity of this demarcation line will be constrained by the reef fringe of Duke of York Island. The secondary area is approximately 62 Sq NM of which about 87% is deeper than 300m.[87]

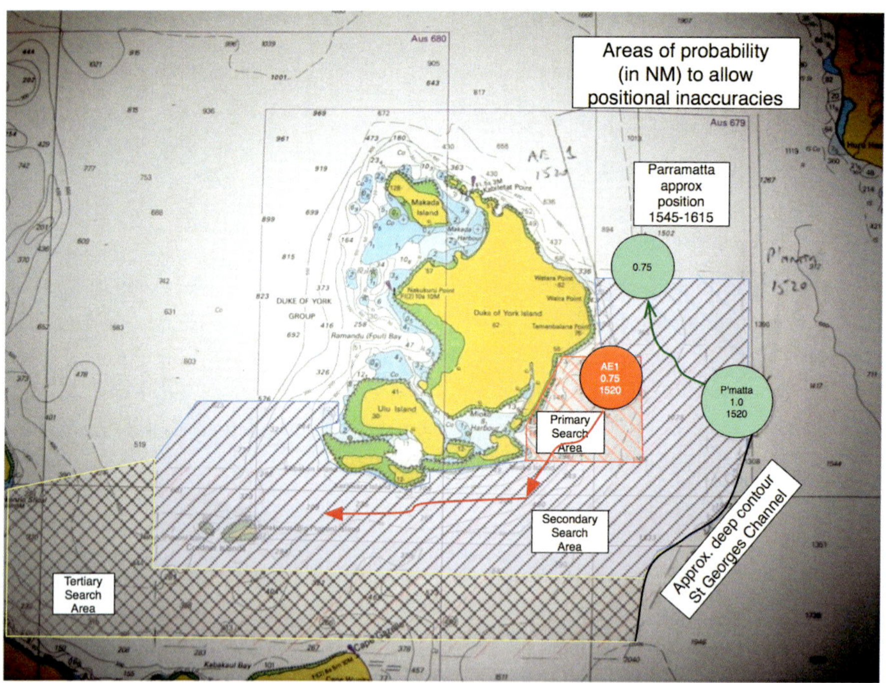

Figure 30 – Recommended Search Areas.

87 Green, J, *The Search for The AE1: Magnetometer and Side Scan Sonar Survey Duke of York islands, East New Britain, 22-28 November 2003,* WA Maritime Museum, Fremantle, p7.

As defined above, the tertiary search area should encompass the approaches to Simpson Harbour along the track of the most direct route back to harbour. The tertiary area is approximately 40 Sq NM of which about 78% is deeper than 300m.

As mentioned above, irrespective of whether the loss of *AE1* was due to a navigational error as we conclude, or by enemy action – sunk by the KOLONIALGESELLSCHAFT, as we discount, there would be considerable overlap of the likely location of the loss, which adds weight to the recommended search areas.

7.2.3.4 Impact of Earlier Searches

It is considered that none of the earlier searches should be considered comprehensive; any areas already searched in the primary and secondary search areas set out above should be searched afresh.

P D Briggs AO CSC
RADM RAN Rtd
Principal Author

Terence Roach AM
CDRE RAN Rtd
Editor and Chairman
AE1 Search Area Committee

Annexes:

A. Contributing Authors and Researchers

B. Geographical Reconstruction

C. General Arrangement drawings of *AE1*

D. Annotated Transcript of Hodgson's Diary

Annex A — Contributing Authors and Researchers

Richard Arundel joined the Royal Australian Naval College in 1947. He specialized in signal-communications and served as the Deputy Director of Joint Service Communications and as the Director of Naval Signals. He retired in 1986 as the Defence Attaché Paris and Berne and lives in his home-state Queensland. His interests include military research.

Rear Admiral Peter D Briggs AO CSC RAN Rtd. Peter retired from the RAN in 2001 after a 40 year naval career. He specialized as a submarine operator, including two submarine command tours. He spent ten years as a senior Defence executive and is the Chairman of the AE 2 Commemorative Foundation Ltd.

Darren Brown of Melbourne, born in the 1960s has spent the last 30 years working for major airlines in Australia in the maintenance environment. He became interested in WWI British Submarines via stories his grand mother would tell about her father. This interest has turned into a full time passion covering the years of 1901 to 1930 & including the Royal Australian Navy. In 2008 he embarked on solving the mysterious loss of his great grandfather's submarine HMS E18 in 1916 in the Baltic Sea. This intense research, using only primary sources from the British, German & Russian Archives led to E18 being found in October 2009. His work in this field continues, heavily focused on discovering who the early submariners actually were as there is no official list. From the years of 1901 to 1930 this research has now discovered 6,400 RN & RAN men & the total grows daily; the focus is to also search through every Submarine log book & patrol report to compile individual histories of all submarines over this period.

Gus Mellon served for 24 years in the RAN, as a marine engineering sailor, NCO and officer, spending 18 of those years in the submarine force. On leaving the navy he worked briefly for the Australian Maritime Safety Authority before entering the subsea engineering and construction side of the offshore oil industry. A chartered marine engineer and also a chartered mechanical engineer, he now works as a consulting engineer in owner's project teams building ultra deep water drilling rigs for the offshore oil and gas industry. Married to Christine, with four children and several grandchildren, his interests include travel, food, wine and beer, reading and naval history, particularly that of submarines.

David Nicholls (Commander, RAN Rtd) spent 34 years as a Naval Officer and the past 10 years as a consultant to Defence Industry. He began his naval career in 1967 at Britannia, Royal Naval College in the Royal Navy and transferred to the RAN in 1977: he is a 'Perisher' (Command Qualified) submarine graduate and a 'Dagger' navigator: he commanded two RAN submarines. He currently works part-time as the Executive Manager of the Submarine Institute of Australia

Ian Noble *(Captain, RAN Rtd)* retired from the RAN in 1996 after a lengthy career as a weapons and electrical engineer, during which he served in submarines and had major roles in two large submarine capability development projects. Since 2005, he has been a voluntary guide at the Australian War Memorial, where he is able to highlight the service of both of Australia's submarines in the First World War, and to research their records.

Peter Richardson Arrived in Rabaul in PNG via Sunderland Flying Boat in September 1953 as a babe in arms.

x Lived at Kerevat LAES (Lowlands Agricultural Experimental Station) until 1960.

x Peter's father John retired from the Australian Govt. and then set about developing a 400 acre cocoa plantation in the Upper Warangoi Valley under the Ex Servicemen's Scheme.

x Began Scuba diving in Rabaul in 1974. By 1980 he was a qualified commercial diver & working in the offshore oil fields of South East Asia & Australia.

x He now manages offshore diving projects for a number of clients in the Malaysian Oil & Gas Industry.

x Peter's interest in the *AE1* began in Rabaul in 1975. Since 1988, Peter has been actively researching & seeking as much information on *AE1* as possible.

x The web site — http://www.ae1submarine.com/ — is Peter's attempt to share his research with the general public.

Terence Roach (Commodore, AM, RAN Rtd) with his wife presently runs beef cattle on a farm near Canberra. He commanded two Australian submarines; was a long-term planner in Defence before retiring as the Naval Attaché in Washington, USA after 41-year career. He is a Director of the *AE2* Commemorative Foundation and a consultant to Defence Industry.

Tim Smith is the Deputy Director of the NSW State Government's Heritage Branch, Office of Environment and Heritage (Sydney, Australia). As NSW State Government Maritime Archaeologist, Tim has been working in the field both nationally and internationally for over 25 years, including participation in archaeological projects in the Middle East, Greece, Italy and Turkey. A member of the initial Project *AE2* expedition that first documented the *AE2* submarine wreck site, Tim is Director — Maritime Archaeology of the ongoing *AE2* Commemorative Foundation's archaeological expedition. Tim is also the Director of the separate Project Beneath Gallipoli expedition that continues to map the 1915 underwater cultural battlefield landscape around the Dardanelles Peninsula. An expert in the heritage management of submarine sites, Tim manages the M24 Japanese midget submarine wreck site (1942) off Sydney. He won a prestigious 'Award of Distinction' from UNESCO for setting a global benchmark in the management of the fragile underwater heritage site. Tim is past Vice President and Secretary of the Australasian Institute for Maritime Archaeology (AIMA), and currently is State Council.

Annex B — Geographic Reconstruction by David Nichols

Possible tracks of Parramatta and Yarra 2320 14th – 1400 15th Sep.

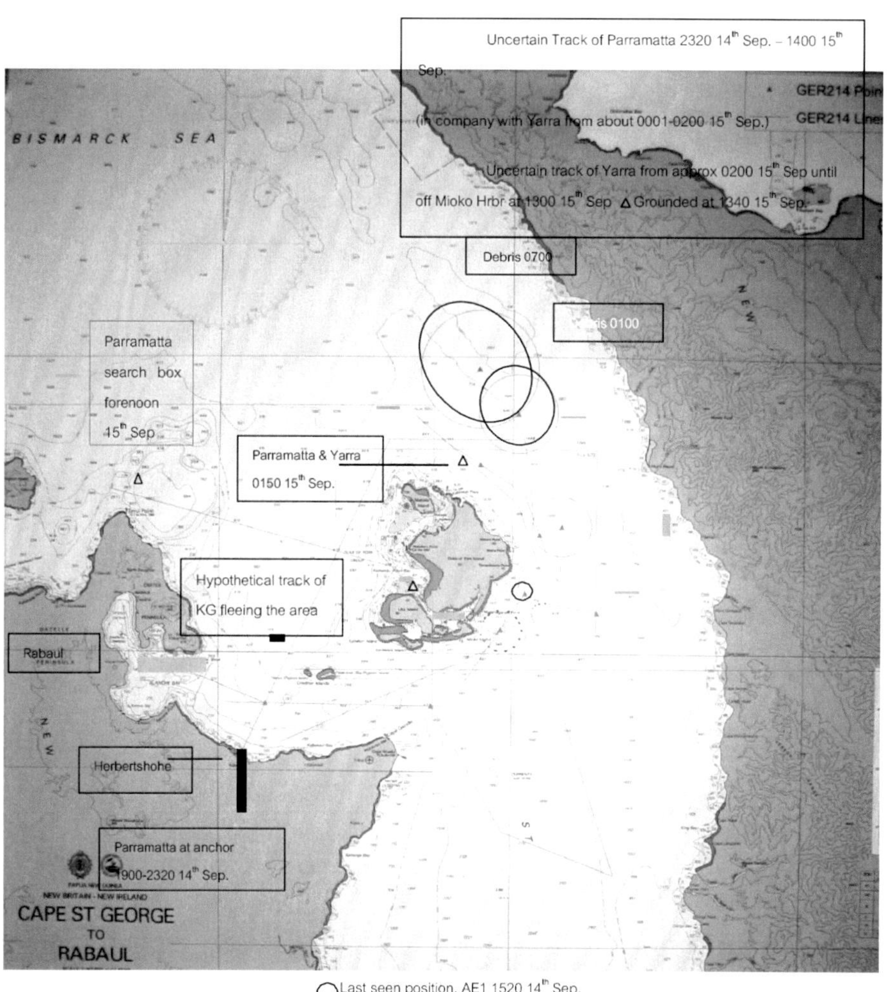

Annex C— General Arrangement Drawing AE Class

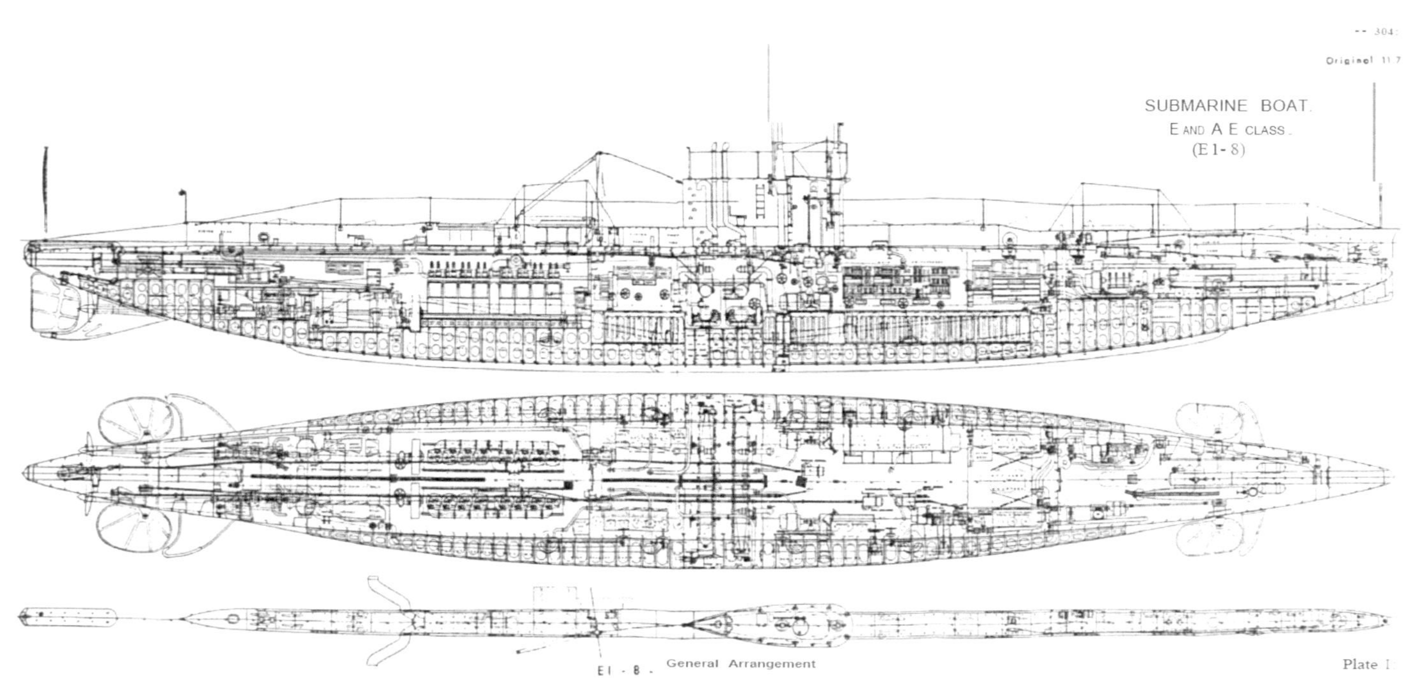

Annex D — Annotated Transcript of Aubrey Hodgson's Diary

A Critique of Aubrey Hodgson's Journal Tue 21 Sep – Sun 27 Sep 1914

The Diary Transcription has been Compiled By Ian Noble, annotations are by Peter Briggs

Monday 21st (Sep)

Rec'd W./T. "Yarra aground in St George's channel. Sumatra sent out and towed her off the Reef, suffered no serious damage beyond a bent shaft, she was placed on the slip, and hauled up for repairs.

> *YARRA ran aground at 1340 on Tuesday 15Sep14 after exiting the northern entrance to Mioko Harbour whilst searching for AE1. Her port and centre propellers were damaged. The ship did not stick on the reef and was not towed back, she returned to Simpson Haven under own power.*
>
> *She was not slipped, divers removed the centre and port propellers and replaced the centre with a spare, the port shaft was too bent to use. YARRA deck log refers.*

At 4p.m. French cruiser "Montcalm" came in, and Admiral sent for our Captain who returned with a guard of French bluejackets and at 5.30p.m. The German deposed Governor was brought onboard to await passage to Sydney. He has 3 servants and large amount of luggage.

> *HMAS ENCOUNTER's deck log records that FS MONTCALM arrived at 1530 on 15 Sep14, providing an accurate date for this diary event.*

He is a dapper little man, with fat bloated face, large blossom nose, tremendous corporation, wearing a high collar, which I fear, must be a serious menace to his ears. He appears genial natured, and has a "satisfied and self confident" air with him. He dines in his cabin, and has every comfort that can be extended, and a stalwart Frenchman stands guard over his apartments. He terms the Australian soldiers as brigands, rumour says, they made very short work of his wine cellar when the Governor's residence was captured. At 10p.m. all Germans were transferred from steamer "Murex" to the "Aorangi" Hope our guests will behave themselves. Guard of 10 men sent with prisoners They were located in 2nd class accommodation quarters. Very motley throng some soldiers, some sailors shop assistants, farmers and well-to-do gents. Hope they don't stay here too long as they take up too much room.

"Sydney" entered at midnight, having captured small steamer with 200 tons of coal in her holds, which couldn't be accounted for

> *No record of SYDNEY capturing a small steamer has been found. The Official History of Australia's Involvement in the War 1914-1918 Vol IX – RAN, Appendix 9 list all ships captured in PNG, none by SYDNEY!*

"Sydney sent a boat over to "Aorangi", and sailed immediately.

Tuesday 22nd (Sep)

The visual signal station at "Potsdorf" captured last night. Three Naval signalmen brought in as prisoners.

At daybreak, Destroyers were sent to sea, to search for "Submarine A.E.I.", which vessel, should have come in last night.

> *The destroyers sailed at 2320 on 14 Sep 14 to search for AE1, not daybreak on 15th (when ENCOUNTER sailed).*
>
> *Wrong, AE1 was due back by 1800.*
>
> *Wrong, PARRAMATTA was with AE1 and last saw her between 1430 and 1520 on the 14 Sep 14*

It seems that she was on patrol duty at the entrance to the harbour, from noon until midnight, but when "Parramatta" went out yesterday at 3.30pm the submarine couldn't be found. Generally a submarine has a parent ship on duty with her, but for some reason, "Yarra" was

> *Wrong. YARRA was not with AE1.*

obliged to leave her,

and it appears on this occasion that the submarine was out of the sight of all ships. It is generally believed that the submarine has sighted an enemy, and gone in pursuit of him.

> *No other accounts giving this explanation were found.*

She was, of course, unable to use her W./T. Apparatus on account of the mast being dismantled preparatory to diving, in case of emergency. No news having been received of the missing submarine by 11 a.m., fears were entertained for her safety.

> *Wrong. The alarm was raised at 2015 by AE2 and a search order at ~ 2230 on 14 Sep 14.*

So all ships were ordered to sea to drag for her.

> *Wrong. Only HMAS PARRAMATTA and YARRA searched overnight on 14 Sep 14, HMAS ENCOUNTER from 0545 until 1045 on 15 Sep 14. HMAS WARREGO (0630-1000) and SYDNEY also searched on 15Sep14 as they undertook other missions. Several boats and schooners were used on 15 Sep 14, but no other HMA ships were involved.*

At 1 p.m. "Encounter" discovered oil and bubbles in large quantities in St George's Channel.

> *HMAS ENCOUNTER anchored at 1045 on 15 Sep 14 and hence could not have sighted bubbles at 1300. HMAS ENCOUNTER was in charge from midday on 15th, HMAS AUSTRALIA having sailed for Sydney. HMAS ENCOUNTER signalled a report to AUSTRALIA at 1700 on 15 Sep14 regarding the finding of a patch of oil that had now dispersed and was dismissed as unrelated to AE1's disappearance.*

It was too deep, however, to locate the boat, and at dusk the search was abandoned, all ships returning to Rabaul.

Two motor boats were despatched at about 8 p.m. under orders of "Yarra", they are to make a thorough search of the many lagoons in the Island group, for German sloops "Condor", "Planet", and "Komet", who are, it is believed, hidden under of Palm trees, along the coast.

Terrific thunderstorm passed over us tonight. The air is now lovely and clear.

Wednesday 23rd (Sep)

> *Presumably this is the morning of 15 Sep 14, not the 23rd?*

No news of the submarine this morning, several theorys (sic) have been suggested as to the probable cause of her disappearance. It is probable that, during the destroyers (sic) absence, she may have been fired at from some small fort, or boat, or she may have been exercising "diving", and, being in deep water, failed to release her 10-ton keel-bar in time to prevent her submerging too deep, and thus the pressure of the water became too great, and so, the boat was forced to the bottom. It is to be hoped some light will be thrown on the mystery very soon. Some of her crew underwent naval training in England with me. "Warrego" arrived about lunch time with a German steamer "Makelong"(sic) in tow.

> *Wrong. According to her deck log HMAS PARRAMATTA captured the NDL Metlong at 1100 on 23 Sep 14 in Mioko Harbour and weighed and proceeded in company with her at 1410 enroute Rabaul.*

She is laden with arms, supplies, coal, etc. for German warships. She has palm tree branches on top of her funnel, and masts. This is quite an ingenious method playing" Hide and seek". The crew are Naval men.

3p.m. "Newcastle" arrived with a yacht in tow. This is the "Nusa" the late Governor's official yacht, and a splendid model.

> *There is no record of HMS NEWCASTLE arriving in Rabaul in any of the ship's deck logs. Nusa was captured by HMAS WARREGO at Kavieng on 14 Sep 14, sailed back by a prize crew with WARREGO and presumably brought into Rabaul on 15Sep11, (WARREGO arrived at 1005).*

Crew sent to "Aorangi", and, Naval men, under a Lieut of "Newcastle" in charge took her over. She is being fitted with W./T. 3 x 12 pounder guns, and 2 maxims.

> *Wrong about the crew and inaccurate about the armament. HMAS ENCOUNTER's ROP rendered on 19 Sep 14 on the return of HMAS AUSTRALIA states that NUSA was fitted with WT, armed with 1x3pdr gun and a maxim gun both from ENCOUNTER and crewed from BERRIMA under the command of LCDR Jackson.*

No doubt our "chief guest" will be pleased when he hears his yacht is now in the "Role" of a "British Man-o'-war". "The Nusa" would look quite at home conveying picnic parties about "Our harbour".

"Steamer Madang" came up from Herbertshohe, with native prisoners and many boxes of money and valuables, which had been taken from the late residents homes.

> *Improbable. The proclamation issued at Rabaul on 12 Sep 14 and the terms of capitulation signed on 17 Sep 14 made it clear that private property was to be protected, the law of the land and many officials administering it were also left in place subject to the latter signing an oath of neutrality. Further, the terms of capitulation negotiated between Haber and Holmes were documented in a series of letters. None of these record a protest about the theft of valuables from local residents. I suspect the valuables referred to were the remains of the German treasury that had been handed over as part of the surrender.*
>
> *The first such signal was sent by HMAS AUSTRALIA WT AT 1610 on 15 Sep 14 (the ship was then at sea, enroute Sydney.)*

The Vice Admiral informed the fleet that He very much regretted to report that the "Submarine A.E.I." had been lost with all hands. Details of the catastrophe would be signalled later.

At 9 p.m. "Newcastle" sailed for unknown destination taking collier "Seaham" with her. "Nusa" sent out to try her guns and torpedoes, also tune her. W./T. Gear.

Thursday 24th (Sep)

News was received during the night, that two large cruisers passed Apia. Samoa, steering Nor'West 15 knots p.h. A Nor'Westerly course would bring them here, or perhaps the Marshalls, but their course may alter dozens of times, soon as they get clear of the land. However, it's nice to know they are still in the Pacific "looking for our ships". This news has caused much excitement in the fleet.

> *This may refer to the reported return of the German cruisers that caused HMAS AUSTRALIA to reverse course on 18 Sep 14 and return to Rabaul, arriving 19 Sep 14?*

Received news that "Newcastle" acting with a Japanese squadron, had occupied the Marshall Isds. "Australia", "Sydney" and "Montcalm" sailed 5p.m., Patrol coast during the night.

> *HMAS AUSTRALIA, FS MONTCALM , HMAS ENCOUNTER and HMAS BERRIMA sailed for Madang on 22 Sep 14, see German timeline. This may assist in correctly dating the conversation with Reuschel?*

"Fantome" arrived bringing mails from "Sydney" The first we have had. In a conversation with a prisoner who, I understand, is an Engr. Officer of "German Warship Planet" I gathered the following, He claimed to have been in charge of a small yacht named the "Colonial" (sic), and that , when our submne. (sic) Was "hove to" in St Georges channel on Monday afternoon last, he approached her, flying a White Ensign, fired at, and sunk her, and then ran over her. I assured him, our submarine wasn't lost, but he wouldn't accept my argument. He was most callous, and gloated over the fact, that he caught them napping so very simply.

I immediately informed our captain, who, in turn, told the Senior Naval Officer present, and I was required to write a statement, descriptive of our conversation. Would love to know if this fellow is telling the truth, or only bluffing. Everyone forbidden to converse with the prisoners onboard "Aorangi".

Friday 26th (Sep)

Friday was the 25th!

Squadron returned to harbour 6 am. "Warrego" sent to sea 8 am.

Saturday, 26 Sep 14 is probably the correct date for HMAS AUSTRALIA squadron's return to Rabaul, they sailed from Madang 24 Sep 14.

memorial service was conducted in "Australia" this forenoon, colours were half-masted as a token of respect to those who lost their lives in "AE1." Flagship made general signal this afternoon describing the position of the Allies in the Western Theatre and things appear very favourable. Think our old friend "Kaiser Bill", was a little out in his references to "Sir John French's" "miserable little Army." being contemptable (sic). Admiral made a signal warning both Officers and men, that correspondence would be confined to "post cards only" should any further case of communicating the doings of the military and naval Forces occur. It must be borne in mind by everyone, that the CinC will give all possible information to the public. Censorship is a most necessary evil. A large guard of soldiers came onboard after tea, and all German prisoners were transferred from "Aorangi" to collier "Whangape" for passage to Sydney. Everyone in "Aorangi" glad to get rid of prisoners.

Following received by W./T.

Heartiest congratulations to Vice Admiral Patey, and all under his command for Naval success in Pacific (signed) Munro Ferguson. Gov. Genl. Australia.

[Unrelated text continues]

Sunday 27th (Sep)

[Second para] Went onboard Submarine A.E.II. in the evening. Was shown over the boat by

2nd coxswain Bray. The "E class" submarines are "one series of wonderful inventions". The periscope can be worked from 3 different positions. She has 4 tubes 21 inch, each torpedo having speed of 45 knots for 6000 yards., she is propelled by "Diesel Engines" has a speed of 19 knots and action radius of 4,000 miles also fitted with Wireless Telegraphy. Complement 35 Officers and Men. We took a sight of the steamer "Oonah" which was approaching, and it is simply wonderful how simple it is, to keep the sights on, and get the exact range of the vessel aimed at.

Arthur Gwynne a member of the crew of A.E.I. came on board and had dinner with me. Gwynne was ill when his boat went out, and Caulbold [Corbould] of no II went out in his stead. Both Gwynne and Cauldbold [Corbould] went to England with us in 1910.

[Unrelated text continues]

Thursday Oct. 1 at 1915

[Fourth para] This afternoon, "Warrego" came in and she has a tripod, with a 5 barrelled Nordenfeldt gun attached onboard. Her report stated that while cruising off Cape Gazelle a motor yacht was found ashore burnt out. Whaler was sent to examine her and the crew had abandoned her. petrol was found on the decks below, also a tripod. A diver was afterwards sent

down, and he brought up the gun which contained 5 shells, one of which had been fired. The gun evidently had only been quite recently submerged. This is most interesting, and bears out the Officers statement, which I submitted to our captain. I feel confident that this is the vessel that sank the submarine.

> *HMAS WARREGO secured alongside SS AORANGI at 1735 on 18 Sep14, having first sighted KG at 1245 that day and sent a boarding party across by boat. Hodgson's is the only account that mentions the removal of the gun and tripod. Other reports including HMAS ENCOUNTER's (the senior officer with WARREGO on the day), tell of finding a used cartridge case on the deck, not in the gun.*

[Unrelated text continues]

[All ships sailed from Rabaul on Sunday 4 October; "Aorangi" sailed in company for Vila late in the afternoon.]

SELECT REFERENCES AND SOURCES

BOOKS AND ARTICLES

Basarin, V & H, *Beneath the Dardanelles: The Australian Submarine at Gallipoli*, Allen & Unwin, Sydney, 2008. (includes first English-language publication of Captain Ali Riza's account of capturing *AE2*).

Bean C. E. W., *The Story of Anzac: The First Phase (The Official History of Australia in the War of 1914-18, vol. 1)*, Angus & Roberston, Sydney, 1921.

Brenchley F & E. *Stoker's Submarine*, HarperCollins, Sydney, 2001.

Cairns, L., *Secret Fleets: Fremantle's World War II Submarine Base*, Western Australian Museum, Fremantle, 2011.

Davison, Jon and Tom Allibone. *Beneath southern seas: the silent service.* Crawley, W.A. University of Western Australia Press, 2005.

Erga, Henry and Menezes, Flavio. "The Economics of Buying Complex Weapons." *Agenda, Volume 11, Number 3, 2004, pages 247-264* . Accessed 27 September 2011, *epress.anu.edu.au/agenda/011/03/11-3-A-5.pdf*

Fewster, K, Basarin H & Basarin, V, *Gallipoli: The Turkish Story*, Allen & Unwin, Sydney, 2003 (originally published 1985).

Foster, J., *AE1: Entombed But Not Forgotten,* Australian Military History Publications, Loftus, 2006.

Foster, J.D. 'Tom Besant where are you?' The Mystery of HMA Submarine *AE'. Defence Force Journal,* No. 5, July/August 1977, pp. 19-23.

Frame, T & Swinden, G., *First In, Last Out: The Navy at Gallipoli,* Kangaroo Press, Kenthurst, 1990.

Frame, T., *The Shores of Gallipoli,* Hale & Iremonger, Sydney, 2000.

Fraser, Ian *Frogman V.C.,* Angus & Robertson, Sydney 1957.

Freeleagus, L G (Sandy Hi Rob), *AAROOOGAH!: Australian Submarine Squadron Reunion 23 September 1988,* L G Freeleagus, Everton Park Qld., 1988.

Grant, David Renwick: *A Submarine at War — the brief life of HMS Trooper,* Periscope Publishing, 2006.

Hutchinson, R., *Submarines, War Beneath The Waves, From 1776 To The Present Day,* Collins, 2002.

Jones, Peter. 'A Period of Change and Uncertainty.' In Stevens, David. *The Royal Australian Navy. The Australian Centenary History of Defence,* Oxford University Press, South Melbourne, 2001.

Jose, A. W., *The Royal Australian Navy (The Official History of Australia in the War of 1914-18,* vol. 9), Angus & Robertson, Sydney, 1928.

Kelton, Maryanne. "New Depths in Australia-US Relations: The *Collins* Class Submarine Project." School of Political and International Studies, The Flinders University of South Australia, March 2004 Accessed 27 September 2011, *www.sapo.org.au/binary/binary622/New.pdf*

Mack, Stephen (2007) 'The US Navy and Royal Australian Naval Relationship. A partnership to educate'. Undersea Warfare (Washington, DC: Chief of Naval Operations Submarine Warfare Division) 9 (4).

http://www.navy.mil/navydata/cno/n87/usw/summer_07/summer_07/royal.html accessed 14 September 2011.

Meade, K., 'Steel Tomb on the Ocean Floor', *Weekend Australian* March 10-11, 2007.

Preston, A., *The Royal Navy Submarine Service: A Centennial History,* Conway Maritime Press, London, 2001.

Robertson, J., *Anzac and Empire: The Tragedy and Glory of Gallipoli,* Hamlyn Australia, Port Melbourne, 1990.

Ryan, Mark. 'Australian defence procurement: Have the lessons from Collins sunk without a trace?' *Dialogue,* (2005) 3:3. *www.polsis.uq.edu.au/dialogue/vol3-3-3.pdf Accessed 27 September 2011.*

Seal, G., 'Traditions of 'The Trade': The Folklore of Australian Submariners', *Australian Folklore* 24, November 2009.

Seal, Graham 'Australian Submarines at Peace: the J-Boats', *Journal of Australian Naval History* vol. 6 no. 2, 2009.

Seal, Graham. 'Money and Morale: A Tale of HMA Submarines Oxley and Otway.' *Journal of Australian Naval History* vol.7 no. 1, 2010.

Seal, Graham 'Finding the Lost Submarine: The Mystery of AE1', *Journal of Australian Naval History*, vol. 5 No 1, 2008.

Smith, T., *Project AE2: Investigation of the HMA AE2 Submarine Wreck Site, Turkey, October 1988,* NSW Heritage Office.

Stoker, Henry, *Straws in the Wind,* Herbert Jenkins, London, 1925.

Straczek, Jozef, 'The Great Amphibious Invasion: D-Day, June', *Australian Maritime Issues 2005,* Sea Power Centre – Australia Annual.

Warren, C.E.T. and Benson, James *Above Us the Waves, The Story of Midget Submarines and Human Torpedoes,* George G. Harrap & Co., London, 1953.

White, Michael., *Australian Submarines: A History*, AGPS, Canberra, 1992.

Wingate, John, *The Fighting Tenth: The 10th Submarine Flotilla and the Seige of Malta*, Periscope Publishing, Penzance, 1991.

Yule, Peter & Woolner, Derek. *The Collins Class Submarine Story – Steel, Spies and Spin*. Cambridge: Cambridge University Press, 2008.

PERIODICALS

Australian Defence Magazine

Dialogue

Navy Engineering Bulletin

Daily Telegraph

Western Mail

The School Paper

Mercury (Hobart)

The Oxley Outlook

Argus (Melbourne)

The Australian Women's Weekly

The Trade

Navy News

Sydney Morning Herald

The Australian

INTERVIEWS

Interviews with Ken Briggs for Australians at War film project DVA 1019 and subsequently on behalf of SIA by Rob and Olya Willis, Brisbane, 2009, National Library of Australia 4699923.

Interviews by Rob and Olya Willis for SIA Australian Submarine Centennial History Project with Peter Horobin, Lloyd Blake, Kim Pitt, Roger Cooper, Nikki King Smith, Rod Peters and Audrey Hudspeth, all available through the National Library of Australia.

ABC TV 'Foreign Correspondent' segment 'The Hunt for the AE1' March 27, 2007.

Piper, Hugh *Submariners* [videorecording], Film Finance Corporation Australia in association with Screenwest Inc. & Lotterywest 2005.

The author also had many informal conversations with Australian submariners, 2005-2013.

DIARIES, LETTERS, MEMOIRS

Brown, Herbert A, Diary 1914-1918, Mitchell Library: ML MSS 5.

Doyle, Alec B Engineer-Lieutenant RAN, personal letter from written aboard *Parramatta* on Sept 17, 1914 at http://www.ae1submarine.com/authors_notes.html, accessed March 2007.

G R 'Contact! HMAS Rushcutter and Australia's Submarine Hunters 1939-1946, Anti-Submarine Officers' Association, Sydney, 1995.

Jones, T., *Watchdogs of the Deep: Life in a Submarine During the Great War,* Angus & Robertson, Sydney, 1935.

Knaggs, A., Diary, Dec 23 1914, Submarine Historical Collection, Spectacle Island. AWM PR85/096).

Lushington, R., *Prisoner With the Turks, 1915-1918*, London, 1923.

Marsland, J., Diary, extracts reproduced in *Naval Historical Review*, December 1974.

Nichols, A C diary 1915-1918, typescript copy, Spectacle Island.

Owen, W L. 'Quiet Achievers: The Story of Australia's Oberonn Class Submarine Force', unpub typescript, 1988.

Person, Harry LTO, diary of *J3* experiences.

Riza, Captain & Dulger, B., *How I Sank the AE2 Submarine in Marmara Sea*, unknown publisher, Istanbul, 1947 (trans. Dr G Izmir), quoted in Brenchley F & E. *Stoker's Submarine*, HarperCollins, Sydney, 2001. (See Basarin H & V)

Shean, M., *Corvette and Submarine*, Fremantle, (1992) 1994.

Shaw, N., 'Recollections of Commander N H Shaw at http://upperiscope.com.au/indepth.html accessed Jan 08.

Suckling, C., Diary, p. 4 AWM 3DRL6226.

Wheat, J., typescript Diary AWM PRM F0026+3DRL/2965

OFFICIAL DOCUMENTS AND REPORTS, ETC

Australian Archives MP472/1, 3/14/8389, 1914-1914.

Director of Navy Accounts to Director Australian War Memorial, Feb 22 1927, (AA: 6411).

AA: MP 124/6 File No. 507/201/237 Defence (Navy) Series 1923-1938).

DVA—Annual Reports 2003-2004 — Annual Report of the Department of Veterans' Affairs Output 3.

War Graves at http://www.dva.gov.au/media/aboutus/annrep04/ar_dva/outcomes/outcome03_02.htm

Foster J, Report by to Commodore RJ Griggs RAN Deputy Fleet Commander Maritime Headquarters, March 8, 2007.

Stoker, H official report of October 16, 1914 at AA: Dept of Navy MP472/1 File No 16/14/8314 General Correspondence 1910-1921.

'Memorandum Concerning the Treatment of British Prisoners of War in Turkey by American Consul Nathan', Prime Minister's Department, Correspondence File SC series (first system): 'Prisoners of War, Agreement with Turkey', 1915-17, Commonwealth Archives Office CP 447/1, item SC 311.

Secret SC1937/2/15 Submarines *Oxley* and *Otway* CAO, now National Archives of Australia, quoted in White, M., *Australian Submarines: A History*, Australian Government Publishing Service, Canberra, 1992, p. 160.

Service Record Brian Mahoney MacFarlane NAA Barcode5 225653 Series number A6769, Series accession number 2002/05135599.

Service Record William Jack Marsden 436 201 350 NAA Series number A6769.

ADF Health Vol 3 September 2002

www.defence.gov.au/health/infocentre/journals/ADFHJ_sep02/ADFHealth_3_2_86-88.pdf. Accessed July 12 2009.

NAA Series number A6769 Series accession number 2002/05135599.

Taylor, C E, Submission to Joint Standing Committee on Foreign Affairs and Trade, Feb 4 1998. minister.defence.gov.au/sydneyii/Parliamentary%20Submissions/PINQ/SUBS/009/PINQ.SUBS.009.0041.pdf accessed June 12 2009.

Navy, "Navy's Response to Submarine Workforce Sustainability Review Part 1 (unclassified), Workforce Sustainability Review http://www.navy.gov.au/Publication:Submarine accessed 5 October, 2011.

Navy, "Navy's Response to Submarine Workforce Sustainability Review Part 2 (unclassified), Workforce Sustainability Review http://www.navy.gov.au/Publication:Submarine accessed 5 October, 2011).

Department of Defence. "Defending Australia in the Asia Pacific century: force 2030," http://apo.org.au/research/defending-australia-asia-pacific-century-force-2030, accessed 5 October 2011

Department of Defence White Paper, *Defending Australia in the Asia Pacific Century: Force 2030*, Commonwealth of Australia, Canberra, 2009.

TECHNICAL REPORTS

Eken, J., 'Technical Detail of the E Class Submarine', Appendix 1 of White, p. 222.

Green, J., *The search for the AE1: magnetometer and side scan sonar survey Duke of York Islands, East New Britain, 22–28 November 2003*, Report No. 174 Department of Maritime Archaeology, Western Australian Maritime Museum, 2003.

Smith, Peter research notes on *AE1*'s trimming and inclining experiments in December 1913, drawn from Submarine Sketch Book No 4 by Mitchell, O J., Shipdraughtsman, Submarine Design Office, Admiralty, London, dated to 1918, Submarine Historical Collection, Spectacle Island.

Upsher, J *et al*, *Micobiological Conditions on Oberon Submarines*, DSTO Aeronautical and Maritime Research Laboratory, Commonwealth of Australia, 1994.

OTHER SOURCES

AE2 The Silent Anzac www.ae2.org.au

Barrow-in-Furness Branch of the (UK) Submariners Association website http://submariners.co.uk/index.php accessed February 2008.

Peter Richardson Besant family history at http://www.ae1submarine.com/authors_notes.html, accessed March 2007.

http://home.st.net.au/~dunn/navy/xe-craft.htm 3 May 2009, http://www.ww2australia.gov.au/farflung/cuttingcables.html 3 May 2009, http://www.museum.wa.gov.au/collections/maritime/submarine/xcraft.asp,

http://eheritage.statelibrary.tas.gov.au/resources/

www.unithistories.com/officers/RANVR_officers.html#S accessed June 15 2009.

http://www.upperiscope.com.au/bios/biowilson.html accessed July 27 2009

http://home.cogeco.ca/~gchalcraft/sm/page26.html accessed June 11 2009.

May, S. 'The Multi-Genre Materials and Rituals of Submariner Associations in Western Australia', Western Australian Folklore Archive 1997.

GRAHAM SEAL AM
AUTHOR

Graham Seal is Professor of Folklore at Curtin University in Western Australia teaching within the Australian Studies program. Professor Seal is the Director of the Australia-Asia-Pacific-Institute (AAPI), Director of the Australian Folklore Research Unit (AFRU) and Deputy Director of the Australian Regional Research Unit. He is founder and convenor of the Australian Folklore Network. He serves on the editorial board of the *Journal of Australian Studies, Australian Folklore, Journal of Australian Naval History* and *Perfect Beat.* His key research interests relate to folk tradition and mythology, cultural history, and representations of national, ethnic, regional and local identities. His publications include the seminal work on the academic study of folklore in Australia.

LLOYD BLAKE
EXECUTIVE EDITOR

Lloyd Blake was a Teacher of marine sciences and navigation. He is a former State Director Yachting Australia and journalist with *News Limited.* Lloyd's work was published in media across Australia; syndicated and distributed to *News Limited* outlets in North America and Europe. Prior to retirement he was a senior executive in tertiary education export management. A Senior Sailor in the Royal Australian Navy Lloyd Blake served ten years in the First Australian Submarine Squadron. He is founding Vice President, Submarine Institute Australia Inc.(1999). Lloyd is a member of the international Historic Naval Ships Association, member and former State President, Submarines Association Australia.